# THE UNSAID ANNA KARENINA

*Also by Judith M. Armstrong*

THE NOVEL OF ADULTERY
ESSAYS TO HONOUR NINA CHRISTESEN (*editor with Rae Slonek*)
IN THE LAND OF KANGAROOS AND GOLD-MINES, by Oscar Comettant (*translator*)

# The Unsaid
# Anna Karenina

Judith M. Armstrong
*Senior Lecturer in Russian and Language Studies*
*University of Melbourne*

St. Martin's Press     New York

First published in the United States of America in 1988

Printed in Hong Kong

ISBN 0–312–01676–X

Library of Congress Cataloging-in-Publication Data
Armstrong, Judith M., 1935–
The unsaid Anna Karenina/by Judith M. Armstrong.
p.      cm.
Bibliography: p.
Includes index.
ISBN 0–312–01676–X: $40.00 (est.)
1. Tolstoy, Leo, graf, 1828–1910.   Anna Karenina.   I. Title.
PG3365.A63A75   1988
891.73'3—dc19                                                87–30765
                                                                  CIP

To My Children, Hugo and Piers

# Contents

# Contents

# Foreword

> Between the unconscious mind and the finished poem there supervene the social intention and the formal control of the conscious mind.

In his essay on Freud and literature, from which the above quotation is taken, Lionel Trilling was mildly reproaching his subject, Freud, for apparently making the working of the unconscious mind equivalent to poetry itself:

> Of all mental systems (he writes), the Freudian psychology is one which makes poetry indigenous to the very constitution of the mind. Indeed, the mind, as Freud sees it, is in the greater part of its tendency exactly a poetry-making organ . . .

But in discussing the concept of psychoanalysis as a 'science of tropes, of metaphor and its variants, synechdoche and metonymy', Trilling has, *en passant* and out of the corner of his eye, left us with a perfect and concise model for a comprehensive approach to the finished poem – or novel. Other terms might of course be substituted for Trilling's: Bernheimer talks more of 'psychopoetics', Eagleton of ideology. But the fact remains that these three large areas – the unconscious mind, the social intention, and the formal control – constitute what must be involved in any but a selective study of a piece of fiction. The fact that each term is a small, neat label dissimulating the complexity, self-contradictoriness and overall vastness of its referent is of course daunting; but the value and fascination of using them in a comparative approach to the study of *one* novel seems self-evident. The novel in question will be Lev Tolstoy's *Anna Karenina*.

# 1

# Tolstoy's Dead Mother

Oedipus-shmoedipus – what does it matter as long as you love
your mother?

Tolstoy's mother died when he was one-and-a-half years old. That
Tolstoy *consciously* considered this an enormous loss is attested to
by a reference he made to her in his last years – and which was
preserved even though it was recorded only on a scrap of loose
paper. It read:

> Felt dull and sad all day. Towards evening this state changed to
> one of deep emotion – a desire for tenderness, or love. I wanted,
> like a child, to cling to some loving, compassionate being, and
> weep with emotion, and be comforted. . . . Become like a little
> boy and cling to my mother, as I imagine her to myself. Yes,
> Mother, whom I never called that, because I could not talk then.
> Yes, her, my highest image of pure love; but not cold, divine
> love – earthly, warm, maternal love. Mother, hold me. All this is
> mad, but it is all true.                               (*SS* 20, p. 235)

Nevertheless, the significant separation from his mother, psychologically speaking, had already taken place even before the hazily
remembered physical loss – and must, moreover, have been a
necessary and positive preliminary step in a maturation process
that would produce not only Lev Tolstoy the adult, but also L. N.
Tolstoy the creative writer. The theory explaining the connection
between the development of identity and creativity has been
mostly visibly put forward by D. W. Winnicott, in his book *Playing
and Reality* (Winnicott, 1971). Concerned with the idea of how an
infant adjusts to the realisation that the mother's breast is not
always and forever available, that longer and longer periods of
separation from the mother must occur, Winnicott suggests that
the infant has access to two sources of consolation. One is his own
thumb, which he has used ever since he was born; the other is the
special object, usually something soft and cuddly, like a teddy-

1

bear, that the mother later offers the child, and indeed expects him to become addicted to. The intermediate period – between the thumb and the teddy-bear – is one characterised by 'transitional' objects and phenomena, for example a corner of a sheet or blanket which is sucked or stroked, or the first babblings which are to lead on to the songs and tunes which an older child will lull itself to sleep with. The infant at this stage does not fully recognise that the transitional objects are part of external reality, just as he has not properly distinguished his mother from himself; thus this period constitutes an intermediate area of overlap between that which is subjectively apprehended and that which is objectively perceived, a blurred border between 'inside' and 'outside'; this is the place or space where the infant's capacity to 'create, think up, devise, originate and produce an object' operates (p. 2). In time the specific transitional object comes to lose its meaning, being replaced by 'the whole intermediate territory between inner psychic reality and the external world as perceived by two persons in common, that is to say, [by] the whole cultural field' (p. 5). '. . . This intermediate area . . . constitutes the greater part of the infant's experience, and throughout life is retained in the intense experiencing that belongs to the arts and to religion and to imaginative living, and to creative scientific work' (p. 14).

Charles Bernheimer, in his book *Flaubert and Kafka: a Psychopoetic Study* (Bernheimer, 1982) sums up one of the ultimate results of the transitional object in an enjoyable sentence. 'Hence', he says, 'in a bemusing genealogy, literature inherits the function of the teddy-bear and the text mediates between subjective meanings, the projections of personal identities, and objective, external realities' (p. 19).

The Winnicottian link between teddy-bear and text becomes one of the chains in Bernheimer's complex and sophisticated argument in which he seeks to establish the links he detects between two opposing but interconnecting poles of psychological and linguistic rhetoric: between Eros and metonymy on the one hand and Thanatos and metaphor on the other. 'Bluntly stated', he writes, 'the textual system of Eros is generated by the absence of the mother's breast' (p. 9). And, according to him, this results in the essentially recuperative structures of the Erotic system, which aim either to recreate the symbiotic relation of infant to nurturing mother, or to compensate for the loss of this relation by the intentional creation of alternative modes of continuity. One such restorative activity is the experience of reading itself, by means of which immersion in the language of the text gives us a marvellous sense of union between subject and object – a union so close, in fact, that it is as comforting and as threatening as maternal closeness itself. Bernheimer is suggesting, in other words, that the baby is to the mother as the reader is to the text, the common elements in both cases being contiguity and nutrition. But contiguity is expressed linguistically by the trope of metonymy, which depends on physical or verbal presence. 'These modes of presence perform an analogous role of metonymic structure to that played by the vital nutritive function of the breast in early infantile development' (p. 12). Bernheimer then quotes Jakobson's association of the predominance of metonymy with realism in literature, which Bernheimer ascribes to the dependence of realism on an external supportive presence that 'functions as a maternal origin'. The realist, he says is 'obsessed by the distance between words and reality because of the intensity of his need to designate each external object with the unique appropriate word linking it to the unifying context. Linking, binding, attaching are generally crucial operations . . .' (p. 16). Bernheimer is however unhappy with the prospect of limiting the metonymic pole of psychopoetic structure to mere realism; he prefers to suggest that the entire symbolic code operates in the direction of the recuperative or feminine orientation of the text, for which he finds support in Norman Holland, in Coleridge and Wordsworth, in Barthes and Paul de Man – despite their very different preoccupations. The differences of approach do not disturb Bernheimer, since each writer in his own way supports Bernheimer's central thesis: that the ego represents the interests of the individual in his totality by insisting upon continuity and integration maintained through a number of binding activities – in particular the process of verbalisation that links internal thought processes with perceptions of the outside world. The argument has thus arrived at a consensus with the Freudian concept of Eros as a principle of binding. 'The aim of Eros', wrote Freud, quoted by Bernheimer, 'is to establish even greater unities and to preserve them thus – in short, to bind together' (p. 22). Summarising his position, Bernheimer states that binding operates in the baby's relation to the mother in metonymy, in Romantic symbolism, transitional phenomena, identity theory, ego psychology, perception and knowledge acquired through verbal representation. 'Each of these structural functions attempts, like the life instincts in

Freud's theory, either to perceive existing vital unities or to constitute, on the basis of these, larger and more organised ones' (p. 23).

Returning to Tolstoy, we remind ourselves that the child's
mother died when he was one-and-a-half years of age, that is
when he was extremely young by comparison with the norm, but
still advanced beyond that other natural absence occasioned by the
gradual separation of infant from mother.

The significance of the latter mother–child relationship is its role
as the source of the space which will one day come to be occupied
by creativity and culture; it will be a necessary component of the
development of individuals and of texts. The mother's death will
also have its effect, but it belongs to a different order of things from
the one we have just been discussing. This second issue has been
profitably studied by Martha Wolfenstein, in three articles published in the journal *The Psychoanalytic Study of the Child*.

In the first, 'How Can They Mourn?' (vol. 21, pp. 92–123),
Wolfenstein argues that the pre-adolescent child is developmentally unprepared for mourning; feelings of protracted grief are
avoided and the finality of loss is denied. The representation of the
lost parent remains intensely cathected, and there are fantasies of
his or her return. However, along with the persistence of these
fantasies, there is also the acknowledgement that the parent has
died. Referring back to this in her second article, 'Loss, Rage and
Repetition' (vol. 24, pp. 432–60), Wolfenstein adds, 'These two
trends, of acknowledgement and denial, coexist without being
mutually confronted, constituting what Freud (1927) called a splitting of the ego.' Such a splitting commonly results in immediate
reactions of rage rather than of grief, which may entail pathological
consequences. However, there are also adaptive reactions to the
loss of a parent in childhood. The first possibility is that in which
there is a parent surrogate available to whom the child is able to
transfer a large part of the positive feelings that were attached to the
lost parent. Wolfenstein remarks that the availability of such a
satisfactory parent substitute is relatively rare 'in our [American]
culture', and adds that in more extended family groups the loss of
a parent may not pose so insuperable a problem. Obviously the
case of the extended Russian family, and in particular the situation
of Lev Tolstoy, is exemplary. When his mother died, he still had a
father, a grandmother, and, above all, an Aunt Toinette, all living
in the family home, to look after him. The last-named was a cousin
of the family whom Tolstoy's father had been attracted to in his

youth, but who had been rejected as a possible wife because of her poverty. She however loved her cousin Nicholas with such devotion that she was able to embrace his rich bride and live gratefully with them both, as an integral and valued member of the extended family. Although after the death of his wife Nicholas did ask Toinette to marry him, she had the dignity to refuse; but that was not quite the end of the story. According to Tolstoy's *Reminiscences* she wrote on a piece of paper which she enclosed in a pearl-embroidered purse: '16 August 1836. Today Nicholas made me a strange proposal: to marry him, be a mother to his children, and never to leave him. I refused the first suggestion, and promised to fulfill the other as long as I live' (*SS* 14, 438).

As for the grandmother, all the Tolstoy children took it in turns to spend the night in her room. Tolstoy recounts again in his *Reminiscences* that this grandmother retained an old blind man whose function it was to tell her stories until she fell asleep. From the bay-window where he sat and ate his supper of left-overs, he would recite tales from Scheherezade or Russian folk-lore. It is tempting to imagine that Tolstoy's story-telling bent was a partial inheritance from the experience of listening to this ritual narration, but it appears he was too young to understand the words and was more fascinated by the sight of grandmother with her white hair, white nightdress, and white sheets, lying high up on her white pillows – or making soap-bubbles between her yellow fingers.

There were also in the Tolstoy household three loved elder brothers (as well as a much loved and petted younger sister); a kindly, indulgent tutor; and at least three servants who were close to the children: the housekeeper, their own maid, and their old nurse. So although the death of the mother was followed by the deaths of both father and grandmother when Tolstoy was nine and ten, he was still in an unusually fortunate situation in regard to adequate parent surrogates. Certainly the evidence of his *Reminiscences* supports the notion not only that he was too young to suffer grief and too well-catered for to exhibit rage at the loss of either parent, but even that he recalled his childhood as one of great happiness, in which he was joyfully aware of being surrounded by good and loving elders.

All this does not however mean that he necessarily came off entirely unscathed. Wolfenstein also discusses a second adaptive reaction to the loss of a parent which is relevant to Tolstoy both as boy and man. In this situation the child incorporates the lost parent into his ego ideal and gains thereby an increased impetus to striving for achievement. We are fortunate in having considerable access to Tolstoy's ego ideals, since from the age of nineteen he kept a diary in which he recorded many of his thoughts and deeds, and in particular his success or lack of it in adhering to his Rules of Life, which he wrote down with a mixture of severity and enthusiasm. The fact that many of these self-admonishments are related to an attempt – nearly always unsuccessful – to repress his sexual appetite, seems to indicate a particular attachment to the ideal of sexual purity, although he also accuses himself of vanity, boasting, conceit, sloth, apathy, affectedness, deceitfulness, instability, indecisiveness, waiting for miracles, a tendency to copy others, cowardice, contrariness, excessive self-confidence, inclination to voluptuousness, and a passion for gambling – all in one month! (March 1851) (*SS* 19, pp. 55–7). However, his struggle to refrain from having intercourse with serf-girls and gypsies is an even more frequent burden of the diaries of this period; I quote one example out of many:

> Could not restrain myself; there was a hint of something pink in the distance which seemed very attractive to me, so I opened the door from behind. She came in. I can't bear her; she is difficult, ugly. I even hate her, since, because of her, I break my rules.
>
> (*Diary*, 18 April 1851)

What is odd about these confessions is not the behaviour itself, which was characteristic enough of a young man of his age and class, but rather the extreme moral sensibility which Tolstoy displays. In a society in which an adolescent boy was typically given a serf-girl from whom to learn the practice of sex, going to the gypsies or following 'something in pink' into a barn was not usually a cause for shame. Nor indeed was Tolstoy ashamed of his behaviour on behalf of his partners, whether they were willing or not. His disgust is directed at his own lack of self-control – his inability to live up to an ideal imposed from within and unrelated either to compassion for his victims or to any outside social ethic.

The moral impulse of his self-generated Rules of Life is in fact not dissimilar to that of the maxims and uplifting meditations on life that were recorded regularly by his mother, some of which have been quoted by his biographer Henri Troyat (Troyat, 1967,

p. 11): 'The generous impulse of youth must become the principle of adulthood . . .'; 'When we are young we seek everything outside ourselves . . . but, gradually, everything sends us back inside . . .'; 'Often we might resist our own passions, but are swept away by those of others . . .'. Whether or not it was this kind of example that influenced Tolstoy to write down his injunctions to himself, it is quite evident that this pious being, either by what she wrote or by what was said of her, became for Tolstoy a lifelong 'ideal of saintliness', as he put it in his diary entry of the 10 January 1908 (when he was 80 years old). His *Reminiscences*, written from 1902 to 1905, also give evidence of an idealised figure:

> Everything that I know about her is quite beautiful, and I think this is not just because everyone who has spoken to me of my mother has tried to speak only good of her, but because there really was in her a very great deal of this goodness.
>
> (*SS* 14, p. 418)

He also remarks that he was glad that he never saw a portrait of his mother, as this enabled him to preserve his 'spiritual' impression of her. In other words, the maternal image that he carried with him forever was a fantasied spiritual ideal that exerted upon him a moral imperative. The attempt at repressive moral attitudes exhibited in his diaries can justifiably be interpreted as based on self-reproach for his failure to incorporate into his own behaviour a saintliness modelled on that of his lost mother.

The third of Wolfenstein's articles on parental loss, 'The Image of the Lost Parent' (vol. 28, pp. 433–56), explores yet another of its effects: the inability of an adult who has lost a parent before adolescence, and hence is unable to grieve in the normal way, to renounce completely his lost parent. Repeating her earlier statement that 'the representation of the lost parent remains intensely cathected' – the result of her work with forty-two children in this situation – Wolfenstein applies her hypothesis to a study of the works of two men, a poet and a painter, each of whom lost his mother in boyhood. In the poetry of A. G. Housman, her first example, she finds the attempt to arrive at an effect of an 'endless alternating of a sense of loss and denial of loss' (p. 439) and '. . . a pervasive sense of transience and of the ever-living past' (p. 444).

Magritte's paintings, her second object of scrutiny, create 'uncertainty about the location of objects in space, the illusion of something far off being very close . . .'. Wolfenstein sums up:

> I have tried to show in the work of a poet and a painter, each of whom lost his mother in boyhood, some derivatives of the persisting image of the lost parent as both dead and alive . . . absent but enduring, far and near. This exemplifies the ability of artists generally to dissolve the inner barriers of the mind, to combine the devices of primary and secondary processes, to subject archaic memory to the highest organising principle. What is otherwise contradiction assumes for the artist the aspect of rich ambiguity. (p. 456)

Wolfenstein's clinical surveys have finally led her to the world of creativity, and perhaps it is high time to emulate her. But before we turn to the fictional writings of Tolstoy, two observations should be made. The first is this: Wolfenstein seems to have given us more than adequate reason to look for a connection between the effects of parental loss, and what or how Tolstoy wrote. This is in part what we are about to explore. But if Bernheimer is also correct in making much broader connective links – for example between the mother's breast, identity, metonymy and the whole psycho-poetic process, through their common source in the binding principle of the Erotic drive – then the two following quotations, one from Tolstoy's letter of 23 April 1876, the other from his diary of 11 June 1851, are also relevant: 'In everything,' he writes in the first, 'in almost everything that I have written, I have been led by the need to gather my ideas, each connected to the next, in order to express myself . . .'. In the second he says, 'Man is made for unity – unity not in material things, but in moral ones.' Thus by his own admission Tolstoy contributes to the notion of the writing process as a binding and stylistically metonymic activity, as elaborated by Bernheimer. Moreover the reader can observe this to be overlaid by a related drive – the strong propensity towards a moral impulse derived from the implicit desire to emulate, and thus in some sense retain, a mother he associated above all with saintliness, and, by extension, with purity.

The second observation is this: Wolfenstein's commentary is brief, but illuminating; yet it should be noted that her account of poet and painter does not attain to Bernheimer's concept of the proper application of psychoanalytic techniques to the study of literature, since he prefers to analyse rhetoric rather than theme. Nor is she attempting the goal of Peter Brooks, whose article 'Freud's Masterplot: a Model For Narrative' (Brooks, 1984, pp. 90–112[1]) argues from a close reading of Freud's essay 'Beyond the Pleasure Principle' (1920) that 'there can be a psychoanalytic criticism of the text itself that does not become – as has usually been the case – a study of the psychogenesis of the text (the author's unconscious), the dynamics of literary response (the reader's unconscious), or the occult motivations of the characters (postulating an 'unconscious' for them)'. Wolfenstein's value, like Winnicott's, lies in the ability to throw a more powerful beam of light upon the hidden forces that partially shape the text. Knowledge of these processes is a necessary beginning to the kind of enterprise that Brooks and Bernheimer are indicating, but it does not of itself constitute such criticism.

What is attempted here is, similarly, neither a portrait of the man that the parent-deprived child who was Lev Tolstoy grew into, as revealed by his writings; nor a study of the kind Ben Karpman has made of Tolstoy's later novella, *The Kreuzer Sonata*, in which the hero is reduced to a manifestation of latent homosexuality and castration complex (Karpman, 1938–39); but rather an examination of the text and structure of *Anna Karenina* in the light of some insights afforded by psychoanalysis (mainly the observations of Bernheimer, and of Meredith Anne Skura in her book *The Literary Use of the Psychoanalytic Process* (Skura, 1981)). The next section, however, consists of two further preliminaries, one a selective study of Tolstoy's first published work, the novella *Childhood* (*SS* 1), which appeared in print in 1852, the other a similar excursion into a slightly later minor work, *The Cossacks* (*SS* 3), published ten years after.

Many years later Tolstoy described *Childhood* and its companions *Boyhood* and *Youth* as an incoherent 'jumble of events' and it was this dissatisfaction that induced him to make a start on a straight memoir. But the *Reminiscences* were never completed, and they are not read with the universal enjoyment accorded to *Childhood*. Yet *Childhood* is a strange mixture of some of the happenings in the lives of the neighbouring family, the Islenevs, with whom the Tolstoy children played, and events from his own family life; similarly the characters are drawn from both families, although it is always accepted that the 'I' of the narration is Tolstoy himself – or at least the amalgam he had become of his present and past self, the remembering and the remembered, the writing and the written about. But the question begs to be asked: *why* did Tolstoy choose to write this mixed-up account of the lives of two families instead of just retelling in the usual style of a memoir or autobiography the history of his own self and family, which is in fact what constitutes the bulk of the book? It is surely not insignificant that while the majority of characters are portraits of the members of his own siblings and household, the two notable exceptions are the mother and father of the fictional family. It would seem that the introduction of the neighbouring Islenevs was simply a pretext enabling him to model his story on a family whose parents were not both dead.

But while the father in *Childhood* appears to be a 'scrupulously transcribed' (Troyat, 1967, p. 94) reproduction of the Islenev father, the mother is more like a reconstruction of Tolstoy's own mother, her demise delayed by about eight years. The child narrator, Nikolai, is not present at the death-bed of this mother but hears a detailed account of it from his mother's greatly loved personal maid of long standing, whose flesh and blood counterpart did indeed live at the family home, Yasnaya Polyana, in the same relationship to her mistress as the Natalia Savishna of the story; the very real and heartrending grief that is expressed at the death-bed is thus that of the real life maid who recounted her emotion to the boy Tolstoy; and it was also from her that Tolstoy gleaned the impressions of a funeral, whose effect he imaginatively reconstructs: 'I kept forgetting that the dead body which lay before me and which I was mindlessly gazing at, as at some object that had nothing to do with my memories, was *she*.' Then follows an observation which embodies the loss and denial-of-loss effect already referred to in the discussion of the Wolfenstein articles. The 22-year-old Tolstoy writes:

> I imagined her now in one, now in another situation: alive, gay, and smiling; then suddenly some feature of the pale face on which my eyes were fixed would strike me and I would remember the dreadful reality, and shudder, but would not stop looking at her. And again visions would replace the reality, and again the consciousness of the reality would shatter the visions.
>
> (SS 1, pp. 110)

(The boy then goes through postures of grief and mourning which he knows to be assumed for the sake of convention – which Wolfenstein would argue to be the only stance available to a child of his age). The story of *Childhood* now appears as a macrocosm of this death-bed scene; the narrative repeats on a lesser scale the swing between acknowledgement and denial that chases through the child's mind. For both the boy, grieving, and the man, writing, the mother is simultaneously there and not there.

It is also interesting that the chapter in *Childhood* actually entitled 'Mama' contains only a vague description of a maternal figure presiding over the samovar, and putting six lumps of sugar on a tray for 'certain especially esteemed servants'. This rather conventional picture of a typical mother in any Russian household contrasts with the chapter entitled 'Childhood' which deals exclusively and compellingly with an intimate scene between a younger child, still in a high-chair, and a Mamma whose presence and personality are strikingly vivid and individualised. Here we have reconstituted for us the fantasy that Tolstoy must have kept before his eyes almost until the day of his death. Sleepy, and with drooping eyelids, he sits in his high-chair drinking warm milk with sugar in it. He hears her sweet warm voice as she talks to someone, and screwing up his eyes, he makes the image of his mother become button-small, no bigger than 'a little boy reflected in the pupil of an eye . . .'. In several years of using this chapter of *Childhood* as a text in the old-fashioned sense for translation and explication, I have always been struck, but mystified, by its potency. Why does this memoir stand out from the others? In what resides the power of the effect? It now seems to me that it is because the passage operates at a number of levels, not all of which are apparent to the casual reader. Even at a first, superficial reading, the visual clarity works both subjectively and objectively – an effect achieved by the ambiguity of the second person singular: 'Having run about to your heart's content, you sit in your high-chair . . .'. We *see* the child in the high-chair; we *are* the child in the high-chair, looking at the mother. We taste the warm, sweet milk, feel our eyelids droop, and are ecstatically gathered up in our own mother's tender love. Clearly the passage enables us as adult readers to remind ourselves of our own childhood and to momentarily drop for a while the system of defences by which we pretend that we no longer yearn for our mother's love expressed in the ways appropriate to when we were children. It succeeds superbly as a device of recall for the willing reader, whose conscious regression to childhood is both achieved and excused by the fictional medium.

However, as Stanley Leavy has pointed out, 'Everyone knows that he has affective ties to his parents or to his memories of them; the Freudian contribution lies in the recognition that the ties are mainly unconscious . . .' (quoted by Skura, p. 58). Tolstoy was certainly conscious of the great loss to himself that was constituted by the death of his mother; but he was naturally almost entirely unaware of the contribution of the effect of this loss to the image which he unconsciously retained. Thus the description of the child screwing up his eyes, so that the mother becomes small enough to be reflected in his own pupil, can be seen as an imaginative physical image of the desire ascribed by Wolfenstein to the parent-less child – the desire to take into himself something of the lost mother. Both by its originality of image and by the poignant strength of the hidden desire for union with the lost parent, the passage reveals a depth which is sensed rather than understood by the ordinary reader. Nor, moreover, does it seem unwarranted to interpret the reference to warm, sweetened milk as a further unconscious regression to, and recapitulation of, the blissful time when the baby nursed at the mother's breast. The ability to recapture the in-reality lost mother and to draw her into himself through his own distorted vision would appear in fact to be also related to an early fantasy of omnipotence which can be explained in the following way.

Winnicott relates (1971, p. 11) that at the very early stage of an infant's life, by an 'almost 100% adaption', the mother 'affords the infant the opportunity for the *illusion* that her breast is part of the infant'. 'It is as it were', he engagingly recounts, 'under the baby's magical control. The same can be said of infant care in general. Omnipotence is nearly a fact of experience.' Wolfenstein, for her part, remarks that 'For immature individuals the loss of a parent is also an intolerable injury to their fantasied omnipotences' (*Psycho-analytic Study of the Child*, vol. 28, p. 539). The juxtaposition of these two suggestions leads to the conclusion that Tolstoy unconsciously wished to regress to that stage when the illusion of omnipotence obtained, both in order to recapture that initial state of unity with his mother when he nursed at her breast, and also to reinforce his attempt to re-create her once she was dead. The impossibility of retaining the captured presence is almost immediately established by his deliberate invocation of reality – the child moves his position and 'the spell is broken'. Try as he might, he cannot revive the magical moment when his mother is caught in his own pupil, just as the real Tolstoy child was unable to regain the lost presence of his really dead mother, yet constantly recreated her in his imagination.

It is in fact striking that although many happy occasions are described in this story, any one of which could have symbolised what Tolstoy refers to as the 'happy, happy, never-to-be-recalled days of childhood', full of memories which 'refresh and elevate the soul', the one which he chooses to designate 'Childhood' is confined to this one specific reincarnation of his mother. He even fondly conjectures that she begs him not to forget her if she were to be no longer there – an imaginary injunction that we have seen him take willingly to heart; he then says his prayers, experiencing in the process the love of her and the love of God mingling into one unified emotion, and finally falls asleep to dreams of pure love and hopes of radiant joy. The chapter ends with lines now spoken in the voice of the adult narrator who contrives to dignify the cherished childhood fantasy – 'Will that . . . craving for love, that power of truth that one possesses in childhood ever return?' – by clothing it in the respected words of Russian poetic tradition. It is impossible not to associate the lines: 'A guardian angel flew down from heaven and with a smile wiped away those tears [of emotion] and wafted away those sweet dreams into the uncorrupted imagination of infancy', with the lines of the Lermontov poem 'An angel flew in the midnight sky',[2] which Tolstoy, like most children of educated parents, would probably have known by heart. Yet it is also the case that the psychoanalytic association appears more productive of overall understanding of the text than the literary source. This extract has in fact verified what could only be hypothesised from the Wolfenstein article: that despite Tolstoy's excellent adaptive reactions to the death of his mother, that event exerted a lasting psychic impact on the one-and-a-half year old child which he deals with in a relatively devious but fascinating way in his story *Childhood*.

There remains one more extract from another early work to be considered before we turn to the main task. The passage in question is to be found in the novella *The Cossacks*, which appeared in 1852, after taking close to ten years in the writing.

Olenin, the hero of *The Cossacks*, is a young man at odds with the authoritarian regime of Nicholas I. Discussion of such protagonists normally has a historical or sociological basis, and can readily be found in the critical literature dealing with the concept of 'the superfluous man'. It seems possible, however, that a psychological account of this phenomenon may be equally valuable, and perhaps less hackneyed. Olenin, and many of his generation like him, are frequently depicted as suffering from what might popularly be called 'identity problems':

> At eighteen he was as free as only a wealthy young Russian of the forties, left without parents at an early age, could be. He could do anything he pleased, lacking nothing and bound by nothing. He had no family, no country, no faith, no needs. He believed in nothing and recognised nothing . . .   (*SS* 3, p. 167)

The young man decides to leave this life behind him and to set out for the Caucasus in an attempt to 'find himself' – an enterprise much parodied by the author: 'Till then [Olenin] had not really tried to live properly, but now, with his departure from Moscow, a new life was beginning, in which there would be no more mistakes, no more remorse, and surely nothing but happiness' (p. 168). The search for happiness in fact produces nothing *but* mistakes and remorse, although Olenin perceives only the fact of this; he has no conception of the cause, and neither, one realises, does Tolstoy: the ramifications of the Caucasian experiences appear to be obscure to both parties – although not quite in the same way.

Olenin's identity fantasies are amusingly sent up by Tolstoy in the early part of the novel when the hero is still making his journey. Basically they consist of a desire to throw off the personality that civilisation, aristocracy, and breeding have moulded on to him, and to become one with the primitive Cossacks, sharing their simple lives, assured that no barriers exist between him and them. This fantasy is partly nourished by his friendship with an old Cossack with whom he strikes up a close friendship and regularly goes hunting. One day the two penetrate deeper into the forest than Olenin has even been before, and this absorption into rampant nature seizes his whole being with awe and ecstasy:

> It was very quiet. The sounds from the settlement could no longer be heard by the huntsmen; there was only the sound of brambles cracking under the dogs' feet, and the occasional

bird-call . . . The forest of elms and plane-trees on either side was so dense and overgrown that nothing could be seen through it. Nearly every tree was covered from top to bottom with wild vines; underneath grew thick blackthorn. Every little glade was overgrown with blackberry bushes, bullrushes, and grey waving reeds. Here and there large hoofprints and small funnel-shaped pheasant-trails led from the path into the thicket. Olenin, who had never seen anything like it, was amazed at the luxuriance of a forest untrammelled by cattle. This forest, the danger, the old man with his mysterious whisperings, Marianka and her virile, graceful figure, and the mountains – all seemed like a dream to him. *(SS* 3, p. 239)

There are two curious features in this passage. One is that the writer makes no distinction in his text between the old man, who is physically present with Olenin, and the Cossack girl Marianka, who is not there at all, having been merely a topic of conversation and a focus for Olenin's lustful thoughts. Yet he introduces her as though she were present, into what Tolstoy labels a dream. Why does Olenin think he is in a dream – or, more accurately, a daydream – when he is patently reacting to a very real geographical and botanical location? Freud's highly relevant essay of 1908 'Creative Writers and Daydreaming' *(PF* 14, pp. 129–42) describes a process by which something in the present reminds the writer or dreamer of a childhood experience, which in turn awakens an old wish; thus both present and past material is involved. More modern commentators, such as Skura, remind us that the daydream's emphasis on motives or wishes made the earliest psychoanalytic studies of literature little more than 'exercises in biological or biographical determinism', but Skura claims that analysts are now more and more appreciative of 'the activities involved when we not only defend ourselves against fantasies but respond to them 'adaptively' (Skura, pp. 60–1). In this particular instance we are dealing with a writer writing and a dreamer daydreaming, and it is more than usually difficult to tell to what degree Olenin is or is not Tolstoy – indeed many critics would think this an improper question. But it would be naive to ignore what we do know: that in general, as with *Childhood*, the experiences of the character were those of the author; indeed here there is even less attempt to pretend otherwise. Tolstoy's biographer Henri Troyat simply assumes that the one is the 'alter ego' of the other; the infinitely more sensitive writer and critic John Bayley (1966) also takes seriously the problems of where Tolstoy leaves off and Olenin begins; and of course the continuing diaries reveal themselves as sources of the characters and events of the novel. That 'Marianka' existed and that Tolstoy conceived a passion for her is fact; that many of Olenin's thoughts and feelings were those of Tolstoy is an assumption generally taken to be a valid one; and it is on this presumption that the following speculation is based.

In the thicket, as we have seen, Olenin has an experience of oneness with nature: he feels plunged into the dense vegetation of a forest which seems to be identified with the whole of nature including the girl Marianka. It is an unexplained situation and one that is interrupted at this point by the demands of the hunt. As if to understand it better, Olenin returns to the thicket alone, next morning, ostensibly to find the horned stag that he and the old man had disturbed the previous day. On the way he shoots many pheasants and exhausts himself retrieving their carcasses, which he strings around his waist. By the time he finds the thicket of yesterday he is covered with mosquitoes, which sting him continuously. Instead of feeling irritated by this, he gives himself up to being devoured – a sensation which becomes 'almost pleasant'. He then crawls into the thicket to rest, stretching out under a bush, in the place where the stag has lain, surrounded by dark foliage, the marks of sweat, and the dry dung of the stag. In this earthy lair where animal and vegetable come together as one, he is so overwhelmed by happiness and universal love that he surprises himself by reverting to a gesture from childhood – he crosses himself, thus initiating the theme of the passage, that happiness and morality are in some way connected. Then he begins to think long and deeply, as he examines his pheasants and wipes the warm blood off his hand and on to his coat. His thoughts begin by verbalising his own isolation and individuality, but only to negate this by recognising that his identity is no greater than that of a mosquito: 'Here am I, Dmitri Olenin, a being quite distinct from all others, now lying all alone heaven knows where in the place where the stag lay [the Russian for stag is *olen*]. . . . One, two, three, four, a hundred, a thousand, a million mosquitoes, all for some reason buzzing around me, and each one of them as distinct and separate a Dmitri Olenin as I am' (p. 243). He continues to invite the gnats to eat him up, feeling that indeed there is no difference between him and a mosquito or a pheasant or his namesake – a stag, and that he will ultimately become part of the earth itself, with 'grass growing over me'.

At this point, while Olenin still lies in the thicket, at one with Nature, we might consider the implications of his state of being. Bernheimer states unequivocally that 'to want to become matter is to want to regress to union with the mother, not incestuously, but narcissistically'. He supports this notion by quoting Michael Balint (1968) in which Balint argues that the objects of primary love are 'first of all, one's mother and, remarkably, for many people most of the four elements which are archaic mother symbols: water, earth, air and, less frequently, fire' (Balint, pp. 68–9; Bernheimer, p. 7). Bernheimer continues: 'These objects are loved because they contain the most primitive cathexis of an environment, the foetal relation to the homogeneous universe of the womb. This relation, in Balint's phrase, institutes a "harmonious interpenetrating mix-up" (p. 66). The mother "is not an object with solid contours and a distinct separateness but rather a gratifying substance that surrounds and holds the infant much as the four elements surround and sustain man"' (p. 70). If Bernheimer can then state that it seems to him that 'Anthony [the hero of Flaubert's novel, *The Temptation of St. Anthony*] wishes matter to function much as the mother does', I think we can say that Olenin/Tolstoy is also doing his best to crawl back as far as he possibly can into a womb-like environment created by the identification of his own mother with Mother Nature.

However, unlike the Flaubertian case, another figure has insinuated itself into Olenin's first retreat into the maternal embrace; this is the person of Marianka, with whom Olenin has not yet had any kind of carnal relationship, but who tempts him whenever she moves into his sight, 'her smock revealing the strong, virginal body of a beautiful girl . . . '. But Marianka is excluded from the second experience in the thicket, as though Tolstoy has repudiated the possibility of any rival feminine presence, particularly one which arouses him sexually. In other words the identification of Nature with Mother is acceptable, indeed necessary, as his way back to maternal union; but while his adult behaviour would tend towards replacing the maternal image with that of a female erotic partner, the hidden self that will not relinquish the mother-image (as in the cases argued by Wolfenstein) re-establishes the maternal/

natural environment. This is achieved by a gesture that operates against the maturation process, at least as this latter is defined by the Winnicott/Balint school.

The elimination of Marianka, therefore, can only superficially be interpreted as a moral rejection on the part of the grown Tolstoy, who wages a constant but losing battle with his shameful sexual appetites. A more insightful understanding would allow that this excessively moral attitude, quite anomalous with the prevailing ethic of his brothers and companions, was a result not only of the implantation of his mother's saintliness in his own ego-ideal, but also of his anxiety that a closer emotional involvement with another female might threaten or betray the ideal union with his mother that he perpetuated all his life.

Something of this sort might perhaps have been guessed at by any reader with a rudimentary knowledge of psychology; but I know of no critic who has alluded to this background as a structural source of Tolstoy's plot-lines. What is perhaps even less apparent is the possibility that here may also lie the revelation of a Thanatotic (or death-related) theme amidst the perpetual but idealised yearnings for union with the maternal life-force. (Here I am not going to attempt to recapitulate Bernheimer's very complex argument for the connection between Thanatos and metaphor; but it is observable that what I have to say does not disagree with his claims.) The psychic as well as physical separation from the mother is as we have said a necessary event in the life of the child; but it may also be catastrophic if the separation is too sudden, or violent, or in any way distressing. Non-adaptive recognition of the otherness of the mother may lead to 'aggressive-destructive impulses', claims Bernheimer:

> These experiences of a non-adaptive separation between self and (m)other are, however, inevitable and constitute the area of what Balint calls 'the basic fault'. He uses the word 'fault' in both the geological sense of an irregularity in structure that normally lies hidden but, under stress, may lead to a break, and in the sense of a felt deficiency in the self that cannot be removed or resolved.                                                              (p. 70)

Olenin, in the thicket, having eliminated Marianka from his thoughts and, by implication, overcome his impure tendencies in her direction, begins to wonder how he can transfer his present happiness to life outside the thicket. A revelation hits him; he is bowled over by its brilliance and simplicity. 'The need for happiness is innate in every human being: therefore it must be right. Attempts to satisfy it selfishly – by pursuing wealth, fame, material comforts or love – might turn out to be thwarted by circumstances so that it is impossible to satisfy such desires. It follows then that it is these desires that are wrong, not the need for happiness. What then are the cravings that can always be satisfied, irrespective of external circumstances? What are they? Love, self-sacrifice . . .' (p. 245). Olenin is so excited that he leaps to his feet and begins wondering to whom he can sacrifice himself . . .

Even before the actual attempt to put this resolution into practice goes disastrously awry (he determines to give his horse away to a Cossack friend – an action so unnatural that it earns him nothing but suspicion and mistrust), he experiences a profound swing of mood: as he emerges from the thicket he finds that nature is no longer warm, sweaty and enveloping, but wild, sombre and menacing. The air has grown cool, the sky is clouded, and he sees nothing but reeds and decaying trees. The wind howls, birds screech, and the tracks are now of those wild beasts. His feelings of dread and fear – the fear of death – are symbolised by the pheasants at his belt. Whereas before he had felt only pleasure as their warm blood dripped on to his hands, now he is terrified to discover that one of them has come adrift from his belt, leaving only the bleeding head and neck. It is as if he himself is torn away from life, nature, warmth – and mother – and is now nothing but a cold and staring head.

The inclusion of the word 'mother' is of course my own gloss, for Tolstoy himself offers no such explanation. Indeed the whole passage is mysterious, at least from the point of view of everyday logic. *Why* does Olenin sustain such a violent swing of mood, from extreme happiness to a 'terrible sense of dread'? The text does not supply any reason other than an unpredictable effect of nature, which has transformed itself from a place of reassurance and comfort to a hostile wilderness. 'Everything – the weather and the forest – has suddenly changed.' But other than the sun having gone down – not even below the horizon but merely beneath the tops of the trees – nothing has really happened; what has changed is Olenin's subjective apprehension of the outside world. And this has come about through the invasion of terror into his ecstatic union with Mother/Nature. Happiness had been briefly achieved through the loss of external identity – 'It was clear to him that he was not a Russian nobleman at all, a member of Moscow society, friend and relation to this person and that' – and submersion of the self in nature. But reason has now intervened with the reminder that this moment cannot be forever – at least on this side of the grave – and the realisation comes to him that he must still live; when he looks to his past life to provide a model for the continuation of being he is overcome by disgust and self-revilement. *Olenin* thinks that the answer therefore is to begin to live a better life, to live unselfishly, for others. Tolstoy knows that this is not the answer, though he allows Olenin to find out by his own experience that it is not. Tolstoy senses that no mere course of projected action, no matter how morally admirable it is, will be powerful enough to console him for the loss of that soothing, healing, secondary union with nature – that sweet substitute for the loss of mother. Loss of identity, re-immersion in Mother/Nature, is inordinately appealing, but it also holds a threat. The idea of substitute implies that nature has entered into a *metaphoric* relation with the mother, has become something that can *replace* her. This thought is intolerable. He allows Nature to punish him for thinking it. He invites Her to become angry, sullen, hostile, totally inimical; she is not the bad mother who generates rage in the child by her failure to supply his wants, but the still good mother who instils terror in the child through her power to punish. Of course she metes out the punishment by temporarily withdrawing her love, but the child knows that in this as in any other case he can regain it by being good. So Olenin, without seeing anything but a change in the weather, endures the feelings that Tolstoy regards as appropriate in this situation – fear (of the mother's wrath); dread (that she might not forgive no matter how good he is); and terror (that he might die before he has had time to show her that he *will* be good). As we have seen, Olenin goes on to try various forms of being good, only to find that they are not the answer. When the hero leaves the Caucasus, and the novel, to make his return to Moscow, he has only found how *not* to live; he has made the unsurprising discovery that a Moscow nobleman cannot in fact turn himself into a noble savage. The reader, somewhat differently, has learnt that Tolstoy's longing for his lost mother construes union with her as *the only* happiness; immersion in nature is a close earthly substitute – a kind of secondary happiness. In other words, between nature and mother the only possible relation must be a metonymic one – or more precisely anaclytic (meaning resting upon, or leaning on), in which the enjoyment of secondary happiness is *dependent upon*, but not *substitutive* for, the primary happiness of union with mother. Olenin goes off to *strive* unsuccessfully, for *renunciation* of self; Tolstoy secretes the knowledge that *loss* of self has now already been achieved and may be recaptured through union with nature, so long as nature does not try to oust the cherished image of the lost mother.

This unravelling of the primacy of Tolstoy's attachment to the lost mother dictates the character and resolution of Olenin's infatuation with Marianka. While he is far from indifferent to the girl's tall, stately figure, her magnificent shoulders and bust, her virginal strength and health – all of which splendour is never anything but thinly disguised beneath her smock – Olenin tames lust into an idealised love by identifying Marianka with Nature. 'Perhaps in her I love Nature, the incarnation of all that is beautiful in Nature; but I have no will of my own: some elemental force loves her through me. The whole of God's universe, the whole of Nature, impresses that love on my heart and says "Love her". . . . in loving her I feel myself to be an integral part of God's joyful world' (p. 294).

Had Olenin's love for Marianka become explicit before the episode in the stag's lair, it may have had more shattering results: who can say what might have ensued if the physically present Marianka had challenged the memory of the dead mother as the significant feminine other in Tolstoy-Olenin's life? As it is, Marianka becomes part of the attraction of secondary happiness only; she takes her place not as a rival, but merely as the living embodiment of a Romantic platitude, the female half of the noble savage phenomenon. No threat at all to Tolstoy, she is only a temporary attraction even to Olenin. Despite a playful toying with the notion of marriage to Olenin, Marianka soon returns to her real love, the Cossack Luka, and Olenin starts back to Moscow with, as we have said, a head full of the negative answers to Tolstoy's eternal questioning of what men do, or should, live by. With a maternal transformational object as yet prohibited, Tolstoy allows Olenin to try out a couple of unsatisfactory ideologies – living-for-others and living-for-Romantic-love – but in circumstances which are in themselves a defeat of these attempts. Olenin's life-in-narrative meets its closure when he is twenty-three; but Tolstoy had to live on for many more years; the recognition of what adulthood demanded of him is one of the strands written into the novel *Anna Karenina*.

# 2
# A Life for Levin

Interpretation lays claim to an approximation of the truth. . . .
the value of this approximation . . . does not lie in analysing the
author, but rather in seeking to discover what underlies the
text's effect on the potential reader . . .

(André Green, 'The Double and the Absent')

The discussion in Chapter 1 began by noting the deep but hitherto
mysterious effect on the reader of two passages from minor works
by Tolstoy, and offered the hypothesis that their extraordinary
impact is produced by their power to recreate in every reader the
memory of a universal experience – separation from the mother –
regardless of whether that separation resulted from the 'natural'
growing that begins at, and continues on from, the moment of
birth, or by the more traumatic event suffered specifically by
Tolstoy, when the loss was caused by the mother's physical death.
It was suggested that it is because all readers respond sharply to
the rehearsal of this deeply embedded experience, and to the
tapping of the emotions surrounding it, that the passages operate
with such potency.

It was also noted that Tolstoy, *qua* author, complained of his
dissatisfaction with the verbal expression of ideas which always
appeared to lose their meaning as soon as they were set down on
paper. Further on in the essay quoted above, Green uses the
example of Tolstoy to adumbrate a striking axiom: 'The function of
the text, reduced to the linearity of written language, is to resusci-
tate all that has been killed by the process of writing' (Green, 1978,
p. 298).

For Green, the text is constituted both by what it says, and by
that about which it is silent: beneath the negation of loss lies loss
itself; and if there is a pleasure in either reading or writing, it is a
substitute, he asserts, for a lost satisfaction. But this loss, it must be
stressed, is not simply a direct expression of the author's loss. 'We
are talking about the *text's* anxiety and loss' [my emphasis] –
'about something which inhabits the text's space and emerges

from it'. The author's unconscious is not uninvolved, but there is, also, the text's unconscious. 'This textual unconscious is present in the text's thematic articulations, its brutal silences, its shifts of tone . . . ' (p. 284) But the reader, who responds for the most part unconsciously to these aspects of the novel he is reading primarily for 'for the plot' (to use Peter Brooks' useful shorthand), as well as the more searching critic, after he has exhausted traditional techniques, must still ask why these articulations, these silences, and the play between them, work their effect upon, 'mean' something more than obvious informational content.

The search to answer that essential question may take us to the *hors-texte* (which is another way of saying, with Derrida, that there is none . . . ), that is to the life of the author, to the communal life in which the work circulates, to the response of the reading audience, in so far as it is recorded; but in whichever sphere or combination of spheres it is conducted, that search *must* attend to absence as well as presence, silence as well as voice, to the hidden sources of the visible images.

This injunction is by now commonplace in contemporary criticism, particularly in the deconstructionists' camp, but we shall see later that it is vital also to the arguments of Marxists such as Macherey, who points to the fissures and flaws which lie beneath the apparently smooth surfaces of the realist novel, and, *par excellence*, to the psychoanalysts. Shoshana Felman, for example, writes in her introduction to the volume *Literature and Psychoanalysis*: 'A theoretical body of thought always is traversed by its own unconscious, its own "unthought", of which it is not aware . . . ' (Felman, 1977, p. 10).

But if the work of psychoanalytic criticism is to study how the text reveals or even draws attention to those elements which cast the surface reading into doubt, it is nevertheless only vulgarly supposed to *resolve* the resulting ambiguities. Felman's views point her in the direction of the deconstructivists' celebration of *aporia* (undecidability); but what must be taken into account here is the selectivity – including the self-selectivity – of many of the texts commonly used to illustrate hermeneutical enigmas. Felman herself admits that Henry James (whose works along with those of Edgar Allan Poe are among the most favoured sites for deconstructive analysis – see the almost ludicrous succession of critical articles on *The Turn of the Screw* and 'The Purloined Letter') was explicitly concerned to avoid a language whose discourse was 'outspoken and forthright; and whose reserves of silence [had] been cut' (p. 107).

Green notes, however, that the opposition between voice and silence is not commonly foregrounded in Russian literature, despite the outstanding exceptions constituted by some works (such as Gogol's 'The Nose' and Dostoevsky's *The Double*). And indeed, Tolstoy does appear to speak with such authorial assertiveness that there would seem to be little place in his writings for reserves of silence; magisterially outspoken and forthright, he has made generations of critics behave as though interpretation were both unnecessary and impertinent. If much Tolstoy criticism reverts to commentary, it is precisely because the works appear to be beyond interpretation. The overall message is to all intents unequivocal; in *Anna Karenina* Levin makes the right choices and so lives and flourishes beyond the back cover of the book; Anna chooses wrongly, and therefore must die even before the last chapter. Nothing could be clearer.

But if the passages from *Childhood* and *The Cossacks* discussed in Chapter 1 can be shown to contain 'more than meets the eye', one would expect the same claim to be made *a fortiori* for a much more complex novel. *Anna Karenina* is hardly a work of mere autobiographical retrieval, despite the fact that there are incorporated in it many instances of factual recall (such as: the death of a brother, the courtship scene in which the wooer writes the initial letter of certain words on a green baize card-table, the attempt to placate an outraged husband, etc.). No matter how marked the similarity between event and account, the relation between the two remains problematical; as Roy Schafer comments, 'The alleged past must be experienced consciously as a mutual interpenetration of past and present' (Schafer, 1981, pp. 25–49). Schafer is here discussing the role of narration in psychoanalytic dialogue, but what he says holds good also for narrative *per se*. 'The time is always present' (p. 49). This obtains for both writer and reader, each of whom must shuttle back and forth over a complexity of time-zones – not simply the past and the present, but a constantly changing present which interacts with various fragments of the past. In other words, a multi-levelled temporality parallels the spatially-conceived images of surface and depth referred to earlier, and it becomes obvious that the tensions required to hold together all these levels produce texts whose apparent vectorial progress, and the inclusion of overtly autobiographical events from 'the past', mask a complex interplay that is not transparent even to the author.

There is also a more obvious reason why Tolstoy's writing appears to admit no silences: all the middle ground between the polarities of the contrasting fates of Anna and Levin is filled in – the main protagonists are far from being the only examples of conjugality in the novel. In *Anna Karenina* there are all sorts of marriages: the neat complementarity of the Anna/Levin opposition is in fact teased out into a large number of strands which combine to give an amazingly total picture of the various forms married life can take. With the Oblonskys, the Lvovs, the older Shcherbatskys, the Sviazhkys, the Tverskoys all offering variations on the same theme, the critic has few gaps to close. Tolstoy has filled the entire canvas. The multifarious quality of his writing, with its effect of saying all that conceivably can be said on a subject, has often been noted and usually celebrated. In particular, Sir Isaiah Berlin, in his famous differentiation between hedgehogs, 'who know one big thing', and foxes, 'who know a vast number of little things', points to Tolstoy's ability to mask a profound want of positive convictions with an enormous appreciation of the variety of life – 'the inner and outer texture and "feel" of a look, a thought, a pang of sentiment, no less than of a specific situation, of an entire period, of the lives of individuals, families, communities, entire nations' (Berlin, 1978, p. 51). Another, John Bayley, reminds us that Tolstoy 'does not forget that most human beings are incapable of feeling one thing for long', and even goes so far as to claim that 'at no point are we asked to accept anything definitive about passion, nor are the numerous contrasting patterns of love required to imply a judgment on the central one . . . ' (Bayley, 1966, pp. 226–7). For him the novel itself has the same quality as Mikhailov's painting *in* the novel: both 'come alive with the inexpressible complexity of everything that lives' (p. 229).

Bayley is right, of course, to draw attention to the many variations that Tolstoy can ring on one theme, but he ignores Berlin's equally important understanding that despite his love for the many-faceted aspects of life, Tolstoy wanted to inhabit a universe governed by one unifying principle, and never relinquished the hope that the desperately sought-for 'real' unity could somehow be achieved. Arguing that 'Tolstoy perceived reality in its multiplicity . . . but . . . believed only in one vast unitary whole' (p. 51),

Berlin persuades us that Tolstoy speaks both with the voice of the would-be hedgehog *and* of the inveterate fox, thus introducing yet another source of contradiction into a narrative that still deceives the reader into believing that all its voices sing in unison. The power of the false impression may be grasped by the fact that even the expert on monologism and dialogism, Mikhail Bakhtin, had trouble in characterising Tolstoy's style. Tsvetan Todorov points out that in the two editions (1929 and 1963) of his book on Dostoevsky, Bakhtin asserts that Tolstoy's writing is monologic; but in the essay on 'The Word in the Novel', written in 1934–35, he remarks, unfortunately without elaboration, that it is characterised by 'clear internal dialogism' (Todorov, 1984, p. 63).

It is interesting to note that just this ambiguity stands defiantly at the very head of his text: it confronts, challengingly, the reader who opens the novel at the very first page, and whose eye falls naturally upon the opening lines:

> All happy families are alike; every unhappy family is unhappy in
> its own way.                                                    (*SS* 8, p. 7)

But this bravado statement is, even in the overt terms of the novel, manifestly untrue. There is as much difference between the ways in which the rather small tally of happily married couples maintain their domestic harmony, as there is between the more numerous examples of conjugal discord. The Sviazhkys are as different from the Shcherbatskys as the Karenins are from the Oblonskys, although the first pair of marriages is 'happy' and the second 'unhappy'.

Moreover, not only is the aphorism untrue, it happens to contravene Tolstoy's stated belief as to how novels should begin – *in medias res* – the way Pushkin famously began his fragment: 'The guests were gathered at the dacha . . . '. (The immediacy of this line so impressed Tolstoy that he was determined to start his novel with an imitative sentence. However, he later moved that episode to Part 2, Chapter 6, which begins, 'Princess Betsy went home without waiting for the end of the last act . . . '.) The next few lines of the opening chapter – 'Everything was upside-down in the Oblonsky household . . .' – do of course fulfil the criterion of immediacy, yet they are made to stand second to a brash and untrue claim which must, one assumes, have some other, underlying, importance.

I would suggest that its significance lies in the fact that it hints at what Tolstoy does not suggest openly – that the unhappy families will in the end prove more compelling, and perhaps more authentic, than the happy ones. For the line in question not only deviates from both common sense and aesthetic principle, it is deceptive in its arithmetical implications. Because of the universalising effect of the word 'all', we are led to assume that the happy families are quite numerous, and that there is a lesser number of individuated, countable, unhappy ones. But this logic is not pragmatically justified by the contents of the novel. The number of happy families, as Sydney Schulze points out (Schulze, 1982, pp. 92–104), is less than the number of fingers on one hand; the number of unhappy marriages is vastly larger. There is a dichotomy between what the opening implies and what is, according to the rest of the novel, the case: the generality of the universal ideal is incompatible with, and hence betrayed by, the repeated weaknesses of innumerable individuals.

The famous first line of Tolstoy's novel is therefore full of holes, and can only be seen at best as a piece of strikingly expressed wishful thinking, or at worst as an attempt to persuade the reader into accepting a particular viewpoint that has profound moral implications, although, deceptively, they are at this point masked. It has less to do with the world about to be uncovered by the rest of the novel than with how the author wanted that world, or perhaps the world he lived in, to be. Ironically, Henry James himself missed the hidden pockets in the skin of Tolstoy's 'large, loose, baggy monsters'; but it is precisely the folds that best re-pay exploration, once their existence has been accepted.

For example: it is conventional in *Anna Karenina* criticism for Levin to represent 'life' (and Anna, 'death'). Surely if matters were as simple as that we ought to be very surprised by Levin's first appearance in the novel, when he has a door shut in his face. But the door after all leads into Oblonsky's office, where affairs of state are conducted; no doubt it is only the dusty world of officialdom that is barred to Levin. And Oblonsky will in a minute invite him into a private room and make arrangements to dine with him later in the day. Thus through his friend and future brother-in-law Levin participates in Petersburg society; but the 'life' he represents is clearly not that of the bureaucracy. The vitality, strength and agility which characterise him emanate from the outdoors and the countryside; they are not appropriate to the musty corridors of government, where officials gaze with disapproval at his feet clattering noisily up the stairs, and remark disparagingly on his excessive energy. They detect and deprecate not simply the boisterousness of the open air, but the erotic tension of Levin's quest; he has come to the city to court Kitty, the youngest princess, having forfeited her two older sisters to earlier and more ardent suitors (one of whom was of course Oblonsky himself, now married to Kitty's older sister Dolly).

In fairy stories it is common for the hero to begin by courting the two 'wrong', older sisters before he correctly gains the hand of the third and youngest daughter. It is also normal for devices of repetition and retardation persistently to stave off the finality of Propp's thirty-first function until at last the appropriate moment is reached when 'the hero is married and ascends the throne' (Propp, 1968, p. 63). End of story, at least according to Propp. In *Anna Karenin* however, the account of Levin's earlier aspirations to the two elder Shcherbatsky girls is both retrospective and over and done with by page 30; it serves not so much as to retard as to charge up the action, making available the unresolved energy of the past to the hero's renewed attempt – the third and final one – to capture the princess.

However, the fairy-tale formula, (which is made quite self-referential when Kitty's nurse recalls Levin's old joke of referring to the little Shcherbatsky girls as 'the three bears'), has another equally important purpose. Incorporated as part of a series, Levin's previous hopes – fancies entertained before the novel really opens – contribute to the establishment of his life as something not limited to what is contained by the covers of this particular book; not only do we *feel* he existed fully before his entry into Stiva's private room, but the clues to this earlier life that are scattered throughout *Anna Karenina* strengthen the postulation that Levin assumes the *persona* who as Nikolai conjured up the lost mother of the nursery and as Olenin recreated her presence in Caucasian Nature. The lines, 'Levin himself could not remember his mother, and his only sister was older than he, so that in the Shcherbatsky household he discovered for the first time the *ambience* of an old, aristocratic, well-educated and honorable family, such as he had been deprived of by the death of his own father and mother. . . . He knew that everything that went on there was beautiful, and he was in love with its mysterious perfection . . . ' (*SS* 8, p. 31) are the prelude to a rite of passage whereby Levin displaces Nikolai and Olenin and positions himself to take the more mature step of replacing the lost mother with her similar. Steeping himself in the *ambience* of the Shcherbatsky household – 'or at least the feminine half of it' – he invests the three girls with the ethereal spirituality that for him is equated with femininity, and that they themselves quite ignore. After the two older daughters have eliminated themselves from the selection process by marrying elsewhere, on Kitty alone falls the mantle of mystery and inevitability: 'Kitty seemed so perfect to him in every respect, a being so transcending everything earthly . . . ' that at the beginning of the winter that inaugurates the action of the novel, her unattainability has had the effect of banishing the bashful would-be suitor into retreat on his country estate.

It is not until he has passed two solitary months that he is activated by a combination of the energy of desperation and the compulsive imperative of the third casket, and resolves to press his suit more assertively; yet even this moment of sexual longing and willed determination reaches back to that state of pre-pubic innocence which is his yardstick for permissible feminine appeal:

> When he thought about her [Kitty], he could vividly picture to himself the entire person, and especially the charm of that *small*, fair-haired head, so *lightly* poised on the sharpely, *girlish* shoulders, and the *childlike* brightness and kindness of her face. In the *childlike* expression of her face, combined with the slim beauty of her figure, lay her special charm which he remembered very well; but what always struck him afresh, almost unexpectedly, was the expression of her eyes – mild, calm, and truthful – and above all her smile, which always carried Levin into a *fairyland*, where he felt softened and filled with tenderness, as he remembered feeling on rare occasions in his *early childhood*. [My emphasis] (*SS* 8, p. 39)

He quickly turns Kitty's invitation to skate into a metaphor for his secret ambitions; conjugal life is seen as a glorious eternal *pas de deux* with this enchanting child forever clutching his arm.

His clumsy ardour, however, only embarrasses the decorous Kitty; and Levin, sensing displeasure, skates away, leaving the old chaperone to state the obvious: 'Tiny Bear has grown up.' Levin's frustration is expressed in the violent execution of inner and outer circles on the ice, though his natural naivety prevents his seeing the symbolism of the empty, convoluted figures he cuts.

What the skating episode reveals more generally is Levin's

fixation on the Feminine as innocent, pure, and pre-sexual, and quite out of touch with the real world where little girls cannot avoid becoming grown women. It is not difficult to see that he can only contemplate female figures whose underdeveloped sexuality cannot constitute any kind of threat to the hallowed place occupied by the maternal image. The next event in his day demonstrates equally clearly how far, and how similarly to Olenin, Levin has also reconstructed the identification of Mother with Nature, although in his case the mode of telling is closer to ridicule than to the trauma of the emergence from the stag's lair. For Levin Nature still represents the Good Mother, where virtue is expressed through the idyll of the countryside, where life is wholesome, authentic and – natural.

The city he dislikes and disdains must be endured in order to woo Kitty; but he makes very clear that he prefers his own life-style and value system, whose semiotics are scattered throughout the description of his dinner that evening in a restaurant with Oblonsky. He will not drink any vodka, not because he is abstemious, but because the vodka is served by a Frenchwoman with false hair and too much make-up; he would have preferred cabbage soup to the fancy food that is on the menu, and he is especially uncomfortable that he is immured in a restaurant with private rooms, where men take women to 'dine'; but he is almost as much offended by the too-long fingernails and too large cufflinks that symbolise the sybaritic lives of the city-dwellers.

Aware that he is faintly absurd in his priggishness towards these somewhat trivial matters, Levin is still monumentally serious about his feelings for Kitty. In the same words as those used by his antecedent Olenin, he talks of being 'seized' by some external force, which must not be equated with the sinful fleshly loves of his past life. 'Try and realise,' he tells Oblonsky, 'that this is not love . . . '. It cannot be, to his mind, because the word has become sullied by past encounters with women less virtuous than Kitty; Oblonsky's story of his escapade with the governess is both unpardonable and contaminating. Levin extends his black and white picture of womankind ('There are two kinds of women. . . . Well, no . . . it would be better to say that there are women and there are . . . ') into a general moral system in which there are also two different kinds of love, platonic and erotic, and two different kinds of men; if each keeps to the kind of love he understands, there will be no problem – no 'tragedy' as he puts it. The pragmatic Oblonsky however recognises that such neat divisions are unrealistic:

You want all the facts of life to be consistent, but life is not like that. . . . You want . . . love and family life always to coincide – and that doesn't happen either. All the variety, charm and beauty of life are made up of light and shade.        (*SS* 8, p. 55)

The problem of the hedgehog and the fox has been temporarily solved by the allotting of the two conflicting codes of behaviour to two separate characters; and perhaps it was not only an artistic solution. Perhaps the schizophrenia involved in creating multiple characters was for Tolstoy therapeutic, postponing for a long time the enactment of his own personal tragedy. But speculation causes depression. Let us return to Levin, on his trip to town, anxious to establish for himself the family life which characterised and enhanced his childhood. The necessity of a wife in this dream of a family romance does not escape him, but the order of priority is clear. Although 'Levin could scarcely remember his mother' [note that this is the second time this statement is made] he is nevertheless persuaded that his parents . . . had lived a life which appeared to him ideally perfect, and which he dreamed of renewing with a wife and family of his own.'

The connection between dead mother and future wife is then spelled out: 'In his imagination his future wife was to be a repetition of the enchanting and holy ideal of womanhood that his mother had been.' Indeed, 'not only could he not imagine loving a woman outside marriage, he first imagined to himself a family, and then the woman that would give him that family . . . ' (*SS* 8, p. 115).

At this point, both Levin, and this thread of his story, have reached an impasse. He has selected Kitty as the future mother of his children, proposed to her, and been rejected. According to the surface narrative this is because the proposal was mis-timed, Kitty being in love with Vronsky. Deeply humiliated and somewhat morose, Levin has returned to the country, convinced he must give up all thoughts of marriage.

It takes little insight however to recognise that Kitty's preference for Vronsky over Levin has as much to do with the immaturity of the latter as with the glamour of the former. Still obsessed with the maternal figure, yet quite unconscious of its insidiously inhibiting effects, Levin must, whether he knows it or not, shake off this strait-jacket and, somehow, grow up. Not until he has broken through the inhibitions caused by the perpetuating of that remembered ideal will he be able to be any kind of partner to Kitty.

Thus we see him fretting his time away, getting occasional enjoyment from shooting game, from Oblonsky's visit, from the duties and pleasures associated with the work of his estate. Nothing really improves his mood until the famous mowing-scene, which, much more frequently than the passages in *Childhood* and *The Cossacks* referred to in Chapter I, has been singled out time and again by critics for its extraordinary vividness and power. Yet its real significance can only be appreciated through an understanding of what is going on in Levin's psyche – and this is considerably more interesting than a mere celebration of the rural work ethic, or the virtues of physical exercise.

Once Levin has mastered the technique of handling the scythe and is able to immerse himself in the activity of mowing, he is literally transformed. The text is studded with a new set of words which now replace those used previously to denote the recalled innocence of childhood – all associated with his mother but recently transferred to Kitty. The new vocabulary reveals the change that has taken place in Levin's inner aspirations:

> *Those instances of unconsciousness* when it became possible *not to think* of what he was doing recurred more and more often. The scythe seemed to move of itself. These were happy moments. . . . Then came the *ecstasy* of the slow walk, one hand resting on the scythe . . . the longer Levin went on moving, the oftener he experienced those moments of *oblivion* when his arms no longer seemed to swing the scythe, but the scythe moved by itself, aware of itself, and infused with the life of his body; and as if by magic, *without thought for itself*, the work regularly and visibly accomplished itself *of its own accord*. These were blessed moments.'
> [My emphasis]                                      (*SS* 8, p. 297–8)

The scythe in this passage acts as a kind of 'transformational object' – as the term is used by Christopher Bollas (Bollas, 1968), quoted by Bernheimer. Bernheimer writes:

> Bollas observes that the infant identifies the mother's active alteration of his environment to meet his needs with the early integrations of his ego (cognitive, libidinal and affective) that constitute his final experience of subjectivity. Thus the mother is experienced as a process of transformation that the infant feels to be a function of his own emergent ego capacities. The mother

lends her substance through symbiotic relating to the infant's
feeling of polymorphous omnipotence. . . . Bollas argues that
the adult's search for an object that will metamorphose the self
(an ideology, person, job, product) is based on a kind of existential recollection of this earliest experience of the maternal function.                    (Bernheimer, p. 70, quoting Bollas, pp. 97–107)

The scythe creates for Levin the lost sense of union, although the
adult he now is interprets the recaptured ecstasy in terms of the
joys of physical labour – a practice Tolstoy never tired of extolling.
What is significant here, however, is not the recollection of the
maternal function, but the displacement of that remembered sense
of union on to something else. The transformational object that is
the goal of the *adult's* search is also the indication of a maturity
which, without being entirely true of the maternal impress, recognises that it is now appropriate to centre attention on aspects of the
world that exist at a remove from the memory of the mother.

The mowing receives heightened significance not just from the
extraordinary vividness of its recounting nor even from the underlying effect of its veiled transformational power, but from its last
fateful sentence: 'He felt as if some external force were urging him
on.' This is the third time we have encountered this sentiment, but
the first time that it has involved something other than women. It
was first used of Olenin's love for Marianka; but in this case the
urge was misplaced and the affair turned out to be abortive. On the
second occasion – in conjunction with Levin's pursuit of Kitty – the
misfortune of bad timing again resulted in failure. But in both
these situations the lack of success can also, in part, be ascribed to
a deep-seated prohibition based on the hero's normal retention of
the mother-image, which co-exists with and supports the external,
social reasons for the unsuitability of those projected unions advanced at the level of plot. If Marianka's upbringing prevented her
from developing a permanent interest in an outsider, Olenin is
ultimately relieved; and though Kitty is distracted by her infatuation with Vronsky, it is no less true that Levin in himself failed to
engage her interest, or arouse her virginal sexuality.

Now however, at last, the metamorphosis has begun; Levin is
on the way to that stage of emotional maturation when he will
contemplate partnership with a female figure who is now seen
as an acceptable replacement, rather than an ousting rival, of
his mother. In the mowing scene the narrative highlights the

transitional activity which enables him to become detached from his lost Mother to the extent minimally necessary to ensure the relief of his paralysis.

The process of objectifying the maternal attachment has been initiated by the consideration and testing out of replacement relationships, all rejected because premature; then, during the gestation period (when Levin must wait for Kitty to be ready for him, as well as for his own resolution to strengthen), Levin contemplates from a distance other, more pragmatic unions. For example, when he visits Dolly on the Oblonsky country estate, he finds her surrounded by her children and offering 'one of those pictures of future family life he often imagined to himself' (*SS* 8, p. 313). This scenario is rapidly spoiled by the realisation that not only do children quarrel but, worse, they can be made 'unnatural and false' by such worldly affectations as being taught to speak French rather than Russian. Levin realises that the innocence of childhood as he understands it can only be preserved by combatting the insidious influences of society. Similarly the inspiration effected by the 'strong, young, newly-awakened love' shining in the faces of the peasant-lad Vanka and his rosy young wife marks another step forward. Although Levin discovers, on questioning Vanka's father, that the couple have been married for over two years, they still have no children. The embarrassed father explains that, 'All the first year he didn't understand anything; and we used to tease him.' The implication that it is the sexual breakthrough that has occurred during the second year that makes the relationship between the young couple so strong also has a powerful impact on Levin. Intellectually, however, he cannot accept that message in its raw state. He euphemises it by letting it slide into that other version of union with an Other that he finds easier to entertain:

> Now, for the first time, especially moved by what he had seen in the behaviour of young Ivan Parmenich towards his young wife, Levin clearly realised that it was up to him to change the dreary, idle, and artificial personal life he was leading into that pure and attractive life of common toil.
>
> (*SS* 8, p. 324)

Quite simply, the audacity of the kind of union implied by the word 'common' – that is, common to a male and female joined together – is only made acceptable by its juxtaposition with the word 'toil'. The purifying properties of work so closely associated with the earth, with growth, with all things natural, which Levin had experienced so powerfully when mowing, are now used to justify that particular state with another which is constituted by marriage.

The oblivion achieved by physical work can be said to be parallel to the 'aesthetic moment' defined by Christopher Bollas and quoted by Bernheimer, when the 'subject is held in reverie with an object, be it a text, painting or landscape, and this reverie abolishes the need for cognitive or moral discrimination by evoking an existential recollection of the symbiotic relation to the mother's holding environment. Bollas claims that recollection is existential, because it is not a memory of something cognitively apprehended but rather of an ontogenetic process "where being handled by the maternal aesthetic made thinking irrelevant to survival"' (Bernheimer, p. 88, quoting Bollas, 1978, p. 388).

Seduced by this notion of union through common toil, though naturally unaware of its more sophisticated interpretation, Levin, as if he has not assimilated the lesson learnt by Olenin about the impossibility of crossing class barriers, toys with the idea of joining a peasant commune and marrying a peasant girl. But that vision has none of the power of Olenin's fantasy, and Levin remains disconsolate and uncertain, unaware that the maturation process of breaking away from the lost Mother is nearly complete, despite the apparent impasse. The break-through occurs only a few minutes later when, unexpectedly and momentarily, he meets the eyes of Kitty herself, travelling in a coach to stay with Dolly.

'No', says Levin to himself. 'However beautiful that simple, hardworking life, I cannot return to it. I love *her*.' (*SS* 8, p. 326)

One might think that the coincidence of this realisation with the proximity of Kitty's stay on an adjoining estate, especially when Kitty has recognised him from her travelling coach and her face has been lit up by 'joyful surprise', would urge Levin over to Dolly's house to make a second attempt to gain Kitty's now marriageable hand. In fact, Levin is paralysed to the point of not even paying a courtesy call; he refuses to hand-deliver, as requested by Dolly, the side-saddle he lends her for Kitty's use. He puts distance between them by going to stay with a friend, and upon his return is preoccupied by a visit from his dying brother, Nikolai.

The surface reading of this next, highly significant, episode merely suggests that Nikolai's persistent coughing *reminds* Levin of his brother's frail health, and by extension puts him in a gloomy frame of mind: 'There was only one thought filled in both their minds now – Nikolai's illness and approaching death' (*SS* 8, p. 408). However, it is not simply Nikolai's death which oppresses Levin, but its power to remind him of his own. 'It was within himself too – he felt it . . . '. The thought of the inevitability of death now becomes an obsession, constantly repeated for several pages. Levin quarrels with Nikolai, who leaves, and Levin himself within three days goes, most untypically, abroad. Even at the railway station he is still prey to a neurotic moroseness, telling a young Shcherbatsky cousin whom he meets there that it is time for him to die. The boy laughs. 'What a crazy idea! I'm only just starting to live!'. 'Yes', answers Levin, 'I thought so too, till lately; but now I know that I shall soon die' (p. 413).

He is not, in fact, going to die; but at this point in his life Levin is faced with three unarguable, despairing situations. He has been deeply and lastingly humiliated at being rejected by the girl he loves; his brother is truly dying; and his ideas for changing the running of his estate in favour of the peasants – a plan intended to challenge the whole national tradition – is not welcomed by the intended beneficiaries, the peasants themselves. It seems an appropriate moment to consider an alternative thesis to the one we have been pursuing: that is to ask whether Levin's obsession with death is attributable less to a critical change in his obsession with the Lost Mother – rather like the last convulsive shudders of a chrysalis about to break through into a new phase – or to some more immediate, obvious, and common-sensical causes. Rudolph Binion, in *Soundings Psychohistorical and Psycholiterary* (Binion, 1981) has persuasively argued that we must be ready to 'leave Freud behind', and allow for the possibility that *adult* traumas may equally induce behaviour which is essentially a replay of that traumatic event. He does not rule out-of-hand Freud's working formulation, specifically the locating of the source of emotional troubles in childhood, and the centrality of the Oedipus complex for all emotional life; but he does suggest that these working formulations became for Freud, and for posterity, fundamental laws whose application is now too rigid. To demonstrate his point he has produced several essays tracing both behaviour and creative writing to the unconscious re-enactment of adult traumas, as, for example, in the histories of Leopold III of Belgium and the

playwright Pirandello. In the former case, the tragedy concerned
the death of Leopold's wife Astrid in a car accident in which
Leopold was the driver; in Pirandello's, it was a drama arising out
of an alleged incestuous passion for his daughter, Lietta. The wife
so turned against the daughter that the latter tried to shoot and
drown herself, while the mother ended up in a mental hospital.
Both of these events (and they are not the only cases cited by
Binion) would seem to justify his claim for the effects of adult
trauma; but it also seems doubtful that the unhappy events in
Levin's adult life can properly be called traumatic – they are simply
frustrating and painful; and thus to understand fully his preoccupation with death we cannot avoid returning once again to Tolstoy's infant loss and subsequent idealisation of his mother.
However, Binion's wider perspective does serve the purpose of
prompting us to interweave the childhood fixation with the profoundly distressing, even if non-traumatic, period of his later life,
in order to arrive at a plausible hypothesis as to why his thoughts
at this time are so dogged by a preoccupation with death.

Freudian theory would argue that Tolstoy's early loss of his
mother, followed as it was by the death of his father less than eight
years later, must have resulted in the boy's bypassing the Oedipal
stage by which male children normally attain emotional detach-
ment from their mothers; and similarly Levin can also be surmised
to have failed to resolve the Oedipal triangle of desire for the
mother and prohibition by the father. In other words, the circumstances of parental loss meant that he never learned to accept that
as a son he could be like his father in possessing a woman (even if
the woman in question was other than his first love, his mother).
Having therefore retained into adult life a sublimated desire for the
mother, and having felt punished at least once for entertaining the
thought of a rival love, the composite Tolstoy–Olenin–Levin cannot make another attempt to establish a supplanter (Kitty) and
thus effect the final separation from the mother without hesitation
or profound side-effects. The text therefore shows us a Levin suc-
cumbing to an unprecedented anxiety, just as it showed us an
Olenin seized by inexplicable despair upon emerging from the
thicket. We can accept that such an obsession may well be caused
by a situation of deep inner conflict; but we still need to understand the link between the reluctance to replace an idealised
mother and the specific symptoms of Levin's behaviour. We want
to understand *why* Levin loses all interest in his farm, goes

uncharacteristically abroad, and is haunted by the (unlikely) immi-
nence of his own demise.

In his brilliant and apposite study *Life and Death in Psychoanalysis*
(Laplanche, 1976) Jean Laplanche distinguishes between Freud's
principle of constancy, which he associates with the binding function of the system of Eros, and the principle of reduction to zero, or
the return to an earlier state of quietude, which is death. However,
Laplanche also argues that the death instinct is already at work in
the first autoerotic, sexual satisfaction derived from sucking at the
mother's breast. Simultaneously with its life-giving function, the
breast presents the infant with a source of erotic stimulation,
becoming an object of fantasy when it is absent. Hence Laplanche
writes:

> Sexuality, in its entirety, in the human infant, lies in the move-
> ment which deflects the instinct, metaphorises its aim, deplaces
> and internalises its object, and concentrates its source on what is
> ultimately a minimal zone, the erotogenic zone.          (p. 23)

In Bernheimer's gloss, 'Autoerotic sexuality arises out of disunion and is sustained by fantasy.' In a further step derived from
Lacan's famous account of the *'stade du miroir'*, Bernheimer adds
that if, during the mirror stage, the ego is constituted by seeing
itself reflected as an imaginary other, this split ego can be said to be
subverted by alterity – 'a metaphoric structure made up by successive identifications with external objects and their subsequent
interjection' (p. 27). The ego, he could be paraphrased as saying, is
a double helix, one strand of its composition consisting of bodily
sensations whose purpose is life seeking, the other constituted by
the death instinct – 'the spirit of discontinuity'. Associated with the
death strand are the notions of punishment and castration. 'The
fear of death', wrote Freud in *The Ego and The Id*, '[is] a development of the fear of castration' (quoted by Bernheimer, p. 28).

Returning now to Levin, we realise that both these factors are in
play. Unable in his childhood to pass through the Oedipal situation because of the consecration of the image of his mother, and
having failed once to extricate himself from the embrace he
ascribes to her, it is not surprising that he should feel full of fear
and apprehension at another escape-attempt – this time a far more
serious one.

For Kitty is both the desired erotic object *and* the female who has already rejected him – confirming all his self-doubts, annihilating his self-confidence – in a word, castrating him. Caught between a desire which, if successful, will forever replace the mother with a new significant female other, and the memory and terror of Kitty's power to undo completely his zest for life, Levin (no wonder!) 'feels like death.' Given, however, Tolstoy's ignorance of psycho-analytic theory, we can only applaud his attempt to make sense of Levin's behaviour by introducing the dying brother – a naturalistic detail founded in his own autobiography (his brother Nicholas having died in his presence several years earlier), but a plausible, if superficial, explanation of Levin's anguish.

On his return from abroad, about three months later, Levin's preoccupation has not changed. He tells Oblonsky at their first meeting in Moscow that everything he does is but a distraction to prevent him from thinking about death. But Oblonsky invites him to a dinner at which Kitty is present, cured long since of her infatuation with Vronsky, and ready to find in Levin her husband for life. The outcome is both predictable and known to us all, but there are two salient points about the description of the courtship which deserve attention. The first is that despite the well-known similarities between Levin's story and Tolstoy's life – such as the unspoken exchange of vows conducted by way of the initials of the crucial words chalked on the green baize card-table, their common determination to display the true story of past sexual involvement by thrusting their diaries into the hands of their shattered brides, the reluctance to go through with the pre-wedding confession and communion required by the church, and the groom's tardy arrival at the church because he had forgotten to provide himself with a clean shirt – there is a new and noticeable distance between narrator and protagonist, revealed through the mocking tone now used of the hero. For example, Levin's naive joy at being loved and accepted by Kitty is shown on several occasions to rebound indis-criminately and rather foolishly upon all and sundry. Egor, the hotel attendant, of whom Levin had until now taken no notice, suddenly turns out to be 'a very intelligent, good and above all very kind man'; meeting with a group of men at the Town Council Levin recognises 'the soul of each and clearly [sees] that they were all kind, and in particular, were all extremely fond of him' (*SS* 8, pp. 468–70). The explanation for this clear and new separation of writer from hero is that here not Tolstoy's *un*conscious, but his only too cynical conscious is operative. Brilliantly capable of *re*telling the emotions of his own courtship of Sonya Behrs, he cannot totally approve them and hence does not fail to ironise his recreation of them in Levin. Thus, although Levin's now requited love usefully banishes his thoughts of death and allows the plot to move on, Tolstoy signals that marriage may be only a temporary and impermanent distraction from the oppression of the death-wish – the other strand of the double helix.

Secondly, the force of the previous argument should make us curious as to the extent to which Levin has successfully allowed Kitty to displace the image of his lost mother. She is no longer referred to in terms of childlikeness, but epithets such as 'innocent', 'pathetic', 'truthful' and 'mystic' still abound, and the wordlessness of the young couple's declaration of mutual love is not without significance. (Levin even cuts his brother's congratulations short because the words are too 'ordinary', 'insignificant' and 'inappropriate to his feelings'.)

This state of ecstasy is ambiguous. The heightened sensitivity of most people when they fall in love, however temporarily, is, one supposes, normal and human; Tolstoy seems to be suggesting this when he makes Levin's exultation infectious, at least to the 'wonderfully kind' Egor. But immediately after Egor's departure Levin sits by an open window and gazes at a gilt fretwork cross on the dome of a nearby church, and an ascending bright yellow star. The cross in particular is described as 'full of meaning' for him. The comment is anomalous, for there is little reason why a church cross should be full of meaning to a blatant agnostic who feels fraudulent at having to go through the rituals of confession, absolution and Holy Communion. One guesses that the piety of his mother, whose elevation and proximity are expressed through the ascending star, is not completely effaced from Levin's mind, that somehow as a being co-habiting heaven with stars and holy personages, she is being drawn in to approve of her son's recent step. Although at long last the mysterious power of the Lost Mother appears to have been successfully invested in another woman, the emphasis placed on the episodes of the star and the cross cast doubt upon the degree and permanency of the apparent displacement. This suspicion is further strengthened by the recollection of another little scene, which takes place the next day in the parental drawing room of the Shcherbatsky house. When Levin comes to seek approval for the engagement, we find that in the words used twice before, when Olenin was inappropriately drawn to Marianka, and

Levin unsuccessfully to Kitty, Kitty does not 'walk but [is] borne toward him by *some invisible force*' (*SS* 8, p. 473). As in all fairy-stories the third attempt yields success, but the repetition of the same words suggests that the underlying ideology has not changed. Success must be crowned by the approval not only of the living parents but also of that mysterious 'force' which may emanate variously from God, Nature or Mother, and which cannot be totally eliminated, even by the chosen object of desire.

The canny reader, sensing the potential future conflict between usurper and usurped, if the Mother is only down, but not out, will be wary of the apparent counter-evidence paraded in the example of the Shcherbatsky parents. The charming picture:

> The princess went up to her husband, kissed him and was about to go, but he stopped her, embraced her, and tenderly, like a young lover, kissed her several times, with a smile. The old couple seemed to have become confused for the moment, and not to know whether they were in love again or only their daughter. (*SS* 8, p. 475)

is soggy with sentimentality, while similar embarrassment is created by the ominous allusions to the conflict between domestic happiness and personal freedom expressed by a guest at Levin's pre-wedding bachelor lunch – and perhaps also by the sense of panic that Levin experiences both before and during the wedding ceremony, dispelled though it soon is by Stiva's heartiness. There is in fact a long description of that ceremony with its ritual, prayers, and intense emotions which emphasises the impression of a rite of passage; but this contrasts strangely with the very little that is said about the engagement period, whose whirl of arrangements is skated over with undeserved haste.

The honeymoon itself is flatly described as 'the most difficult and humiliating time of their lives'. The text continues, 'Afterwards they both tried separately to erase from their memories all the ugly, shameful circumstances of that unhealthy time' (*SS* 9, p. 60), and then leaps over to the third month of marriage, when life is running 'more smoothly'. Running smoothly means, insofar as the story is concerned, sublimating any discussion of the sexual side of the Levins' conjugal life to accounts of Kitty's absorption in the organisation of her new house, or to Levin's perseverance with his indoor and outdoor work while trying to accustom himself to close day-to-day living with another individual of very different temperament. There is a hint of some sense of mystical union – 'He could not now tell where he ended and she began' – but unlike the case of Levin's cogitations on the peasant Ivan Parmenich and his young wife, curiosity about the source of this union is avoided. It would appear that Levin's maturation is incomplete, or at least that for Tolstoy the issue of sexuality within marriage, that is, legal sexuality, was a paradox too difficult to confront; its erasure from the text has to be read as a repression, and one which he gives no evidence of being aware of. Predictably, however, in a situation where the sources of repression go unacknowledged, guilt comes to the fore. Within two minutes of enchanted conversation with Kitty in which Levin asks why such happiness should have come his way – 'It's not natural, it is too good', he protests – he is subject to feelings of disapprobation and remorse. 'There was something shameful, effeminate, Capuan, as he called it, in his present life.' He is sure he is not working hard enough, either at his book on agriculture or on his own estate. He is losing his 'independence as a man'. To his shame he cannot help projecting this guilt onto Kitty, whom he now blames for not being sufficiently interested in the farm work, or the peasants, or music or books. In contemplating this unsatisfactory state of affairs the relation between author and protagonist once again becomes one of veiled interplay. Not only does Levin project upon Kitty his own sense of guilt, but Tolstoy compounds the obfuscation of the real issue by explaining that Kitty's 'doing nothing' is justified by the 'period of activity which was inevitably coming, when at one and the same time she would be her husband's wife, the mistress of the house and would bear, nurture and educate her children' (*SS* 9, pp. 60–4).

Now, in the first place, Kitty is simply not inactive. Only a few pages before we have read that, 'Levin, like all men, forgot that [Kitty] too must work; and was surprised how she, the poetic, charming Kitty, could during the very first weeks and even days of married life, think, remember and fuss about table-cloths, furniture, spare-room mattresses, a tray, the cook, the dinner, and so forth.' She orders new furniture from Moscow, rearranges rooms, hangs curtains, and supervises meals and fills the storeroom to an extent that Levin feels to be quite unnecessary. The contradiction that Kitty is both too active and too inactive at the same time is only explained by the realisation that when Kitty is being 'inactive' she is playful and flirtatious. They have to jump guiltily apart when someone enters the room unexpectedly. In other words, Kitty seems to have capacity for sexual provocation which embarrasses Levin and which Tolstoy appears loath to write about. The only solution for him is to move Kitty on as swiftly as possible to what he has already anticipated – her metamorphosis into a 'bearer, nurturer and educator of children'. This acceptable female role emulates that of the Lost Mother, instead of displacing her with an adult, fully sexual, rival.

Why else would Levin feel such anxiety at the thought of Kitty's accompanying him to his dying brother's house, where the thought that she will be in the same room as his brother's mistress, 'a girl off the streets', makes him shudder 'with repulsion and horror'? Even nineteenth-century sensibility cannot rest too much on the issue of impropriety; Levin's overreaction comes from something which the text cannot admit – that the sight of Kitty, still etherealised despite her marriage (and, as it happens, her pregnancy, though that is as yet unannounced), side by side with a mistress makes too powerful an assault on the barriers that Levin has all his life erected between one woman – his mother – and the rest. The rest are tainted by carnality; Kitty, as the replacement mother, is by definition, pure. He would prefer to close his eyes to any semblance of similarity between Kitty and one of 'the rest', especially one unredeemed by legal marriage.

The same passage points to another disadvantage under which poor Kitty labours in relation to the absent mother. This is, quite simply, her actual physical presence. Apart from the issue of Nikolai's companion, Levin is irritated that Kitty will not let him go alone to meet his brother and is annoyed that his independence is threatened by Kitty's determination to accompany him. The dangers of propinquity are expounded in the sentence, 'How strange it was to think that he, who such a short time ago dared not believe in the happiness of her loving him, now felt unhappy because she loved him too much!' The exclamation-mark signifies shocked surprise, but it should not – for one of the advantages of a dead mother is clearly that she can be both invoked and dismissed more easily than can a living wife.

Fortunately for her, in this instance Kitty justifies her presence at every level, playing successfully the roles both of competent nurse and spiritual comforter. She is an angel of such purity that she manages to remain undefiled by the contact with Maria Niko-laevna. Once forgiven, however, she also ceases to constitute a threat to her husband's independence, the withdrawn danger being expressed linguistically by an Alice-in-Wonderland-like reduction of her size, as she combs with a *small* comb the soft fragrant hair which grows from a *narrow* parting on her *small* head, and glances the while at her *tiny* watch.

Nikolai's death occurs within the next few days, but its effect on Levin is mitigated by two things – Kitty's redeemed presence, and her newly discovered pregnancy.

It is at this point, when Levin and Kitty have returned to Pokrovsk for the summer, that the Levin *persona* undergoes a significant and obvious split. It is as if Tolstoy is now dissatisfied with the hitherto fairly constant identification of himself with Levin, and wishes to project his dilemma on to two separate horns. To launch Levin upon the path of family happiness – and this is of course the salvation that he has always wished for his fictional self – Tolstoy must also burden him with the commitment of a wife-soon-to-be-a-mother. But recalling with hindsight Sonya's many confinements (seven by the time of the completion of *Anna Karenina*), plus the other notorious sources of division within their marriage, the reader cannot be surprised that Levin's vision splendid should be somewhat tarnished for his creator. The pinpricks of disquiet which are already evident in Levin's married life, such as his irritation at being swamped by Kitty's relatives and friends, and his unnatural jealousy of Veslovksy's attentions to Kitty (to be discussed further), are described faithfully, but in a spirit of determination to surmount them. After all, they must be bypassed if the dream of family life is to be realised. But their very existence is already a warning. Marianna Torgovnick claims that at this point 'lack of communication has become a way of life for Kitty and her husband' (Torgovnick, 1981, p. 73) and shows how Kitty detests Levin's absorption in the philosophical issues that intellectually engage him, because her horizons are limited to the details of domesticity.

Clearly, family life is by now an ambivalent concept, both retained as the shining ideal, and subverted not just by its own petty betrayals, but by the subtle inclusion of another, contradictory ideal, whose significance is masked by the fact that it is presented as a failure. The reader may choose his or her own interpretation of the following account of a *non*-marriage.

Levin has a half-brother, Koznyshev, who has already appeared several times as Tweedledum to Levin's-Dee. To Levin the country is where one lives and works, to Koznyshev it is where one rests and recuperates; Koznyshev cultivates a liking for the peasants, Levin is mostly exasperated by them; Koznyshev is an intellectual, Levin a man of heart rather than head; in particular Koznyshev likes to discourse on the beauties of nature, while for Levin words merely detract from their ineffable transcendancy. Although the two take oppositive viewpoints on almost every issue they discuss – medical care, education, local government – they become increasingly close during the course of the novel, and Koznyshev is in the background during all the main events of Levin's life – his first, unsuccessful wooing of Kitty, the mowing scene, the wedding day, and now during the awaiting of the birth of the first child.

Most importantly, Koznyshev has never married, having remained true to the memory of an earlier, lost sweetheart. Since then he has appeared to lack any romantic or conjugal aspirations.

It is at this point that Tolstoy's twin but incompatible ideals are split between the two brothers, with Levin choosing the path of family happiness, and Koznyshev a 'spiritual' life, befitting his 'pure and lofty' nature. Levin comes close to admitting that Koznyshev has chosen the better, because higher road; he has 'none of that weakness' Levin now defines as being an inescapable aspect of conjugal life. 'When I examine myself and compare myself with others, especially with my brother, I feel how bad I am.'

The guilt with which this remark is tinged denotes a nostalgia for purity that is still strong in Tolstoy's mind. He plays it out in a little drama of wishful thinking which undermines all Levin's declarations of happiness.

Among the other guests at Pokrovsk is Kitty's friend Varenka, who is attracted, and attractive, to Koznyshev. Kitty longs for them to be united, and is delighted when they are manipulated into going mushrooming together. But the scene of the longed-for proposal is another of those enormously potent passages in Tolstoy's writing when the subterranean waters move more powerfully than the ripples on the surface. Varenka is tremulous, waiting; Koznyshev has formulated a proposal in his head. It seems that expectation and intention are on the point of mutual ignition – but it does not happen. The words that come out are: 'What is the difference between a white boletus and a birch mushroom?' Both know the moment has passed. But only Kitty is truly disappointed – and perhaps, also, the reader brought up on paper-back romances.

The passage represents a major, well-veiled allusion to the guilt and regret Tolstoy could not escape at betraying the image of his dead mother. In *Anna Karenina* he contrives, on the whole, to avoid imposing that guilt on the autobiographical 'I', by transferring the alternative path to another character, but any readers still unconvinced that such guilt existed need only glance at the hostile references to sex and marriage in his diaries and letters to have their doubts roundly dispelled.

Koznyshev's relinquishing of Varenka represents a last gesture of homage to the image of purity and abstention; inscribed in fiction, the long-standing conscious, and unconscious, but always cherished memory lives on, lasting even longer than a fading photograph. But that very inscription, while little more than an apparently minor episode in the main story Tolstoy is telling, is as liberating as a confession; once made, it releases Levin from his single-minded dedication to the family ideal, and allows him to become the mouthpiece for other preoccupations of his creator – in particular the question of religious faith, which dominates the last chapters of the novel.

The transition to this new period of spiritual development takes place after the birth of the Levins' son Mitya, and it could no doubt be thought that this highly significant event might symbolise Konstantin's ultimate achievement of maturity. But his becoming a father has no bearing on what we have claimed to be the major formative experience of his life, whereas his status as a husband does. It is more interesting to note that between the expiatory non-marriage of Koznyshev, and Levin's personal graduation to more spiritual concerns, Tolstoy expends an inordinate amount of attention on another apparently trivial interlude – the visit of the fat, sensual and insensitive Veslovsky to Pokrovsk. Invited by Oblonsky, Veslovsky is gay, gallant and garrulous – and Levin cannot bear him. Kitty has to soothe her ruffled husband whenever Veslovsky spends more than a minute talking to her, but her efforts are ultimately in vain. Levin loses all patience with his guest's fatuous attentions to Kitty, and orders the carriage to be brought around so that Veslovsky can be sent packing without ceremony.

It is extraordinary behaviour from a host, and particularly so since the text has made it absolutely clear that Veslovsky is innocent of any evil intent. A self-indulgent, amiable *bon enfant* with undisciplined appetites – he eats all the provisions on the snipe-shooting expedition and at night makes love to the peasant girls – his attentions to Kitty have no depth or significance, as everyone but Levin realises. But Levin is aroused to jealousy beyond his control, and it is this stupid but hot-blooded jealousy that signals the final spurt of maturity into adulthood. No longer half-given over to the shadowy but tenacious embrace of the Lost Mother, Levin behaves in the way proper to any half of a pair-bonded couple whose mate is threatened with possession by an outsider. He is ridiculous and discourteous, but he has become a husband in the most primitive sense of the word. And, despite the negative and uncivilised side of this fierce display of possessiveness, we should be able to see that in terms of his *Bildung* it is an essential breakthrough.

The period between the white boletus and the seatless tarantas in which the unfortunate Veslovsky is ignominiously conveyed out of their lives marks a watershed, the point at which Levin becomes adult – even though, by the most human of paradoxes, his adulthood is exhibited by a ludicrous display of adolescent petulance.

Moreover, the emphasis placed on this almost farcical episode may stand as the last piece of evidence for the claim that Tolstoy's identification with his hero is not diminished, but rather convoluted, by his inability to comprehend the complex springs of his own behaviour. But that about which Tolstoy is silent, either through lack of understanding, or because of the wilful avoidance of uncomfortable issues, the text frequently reveals through its own voices and silences, or through those of characters such as Koznyshev. Chapter 3 will take this consideration further.

# 3
# The Returns of Reading

In the essay 'Freud's Masterplot', mentioned briefly in Chapter 1 of this book, Peter Brooks writes:

> Narrative always makes the explicit claim to be in a state of repetition, as a going over again of a ground already covered: a *sjuzet* repeating the *fabula*. . . . Rhyme, alliteration, assonance, meter, refrain, all the mnemonic elements of literature and indeed most of its tropes are in some manner repetitions that take us back in the text, that allow the ear, the eye to make connections, conscious or unconscious, between different textual moments, to see the past and present as related and as establishing a future that will be noticeable as some variation in the pattern. (pp. 97–9)

Repetition is thus essential to narration, in its role of creating meaning through the detectible interconnection of motifs. But the scope of Brooks' remarks is now extended to the domain of psychoanalysis. He is among the many theoreticians (like Benjamin, Bloom and Derrida, to name only three) who have quarried Freud's 1925 essay *Beyond the Pleasure Principle* in order to bring to light his latter-day explanation for repetitive acts which patently defy his earlier hypothesis of the primacy of instant pleasure – now cast into doubt by phenomena ranging from the recurrence of bad dreams to the repeated banishing of the mother in the *fort-da* game. One of Freud's answers to his own speculations was that repetition enacts a movement from passivity to control: to deliberately repeat, by choice, a situation to which one must submit, is to claim mastery over it. Brooks' well-sustained application of this hypothesis to narrative theory is that repetition is one of the devices by which story is transformed into plot:

> Narrative, as we have seen, must ever present itself as a repetition of events that have already happened, and within this postulate of a generalised repetition it must make use of specific,

perceptible repetitions in order to create plot, that is, to show us a
significant interconnection of events. An event gains meaning by
its repetition . . .                                              (p. 99)

But the question then poses itself – if repetition is a return in the
text, a doubling back, does this constitute a return *to* (origins) or a
return *of* (the repressed)? Brooks draws further on Freud's more
speculative passages in *Beyond the Pleasure Principle* to suggest that
repetition works to *bind* the freely mobile, unbound energy of the
primary process, which normally seeks immediate discharge, so
that postponement of that discharge is achieved, and a constant-
state energy situation arrived at:

Repetition in all its literary manifestations may in fact work as a
'binding', a binding of textual energies that allows them to be
mastered by putting them into . . . perceptible form: repetition,
repeat, recall, symmetry, all those journeys back in the text,
returns to and returns of, that allows us to bind one textual
moment to another in terms of similarity or substitution rather
than mere contiguity.                                            (p. 101)

An example of this effect that has already been noted is Levin's
nearly falling in love with the two older Shcherbatsky girls before
he finally attaches himself to Kitty. That information can now be
seen to be important at three levels of the narrative. It points to
Levin's extended psychological readying of himself to begin his
attempt to find the woman who will replace his mother; it establishes the moral ambience in which that search will be successful,
since it never departs from the pure and innocent precincts of the
Shcherbatsky family; and it exemplifies Brooks' remarks on the
narrative binding of textual energy, whose characteristic it is to be
'always on the verge of premature discharge, of short-circuit'.
Thus Levin has in the past nearly prevented his history as we
know it from being written, but the fact that we are told of these
'mistakes' in securing the object of his desire adds to the erotic
tension of the opening chapter. We now realise also, of course,
that even that erotic desire is not simple, and that what is repressed within it also constitutes a return to what 'he had been
deprived of by the death of his father and mother'.
But Kitty too must, for similar psychological, moral and formal

reasons, undergo the experience of repeat-performances in her search to find her true soul-mate. Having (necessarily) but recently emerged from the school-room and been able to attract Levin by the one quality – childlike innocence – to which he can allow himself to succumb, she must, within certain moral limits, experience her own maturation. But just as realism demands that she not remain forever an *ingénue*, so does her story, like Levin's, require a twist or two to hold her back from short-circuit, from a too-rapid catapulting into a marriage that would spell closure for both the narrative and the character.

Thus, if Levin's three caskets are labelled Natalia, Dolly and Kitty, Kitty's are called Levin,[1] Vronsky, and Levin.[2] The first fails partly, as we know, because it is mis-timed, and partly because of the presence of the rich, clever and distinguished suitor favoured by Kitty's mother – the Vronsky choice. For a few pages we see the events and characters only though the eyes of a socially ambitious prospective mother-in-law, who attributes Levin's awkward manner to pride; she considers his way of life in the country to be boorish and strange, although, ironically, he compounds these offences when he leaves all of a sudden, without proposing to Kitty. By contrast, so far as a match with Vronsky is concerned – 'Nothing better could be desired'. (In fact Vronsky had no intention of marrying Kitty even before he met Anna, and thereafter ceased to give the young girl a passing thought.)

The humiliation of losing Vronsky's supposed love wounds Kitty deeply, but also serves as a reason for her journey abroad, which both delays and brings about her readiness to perceive Levin as her proper mate. Interestingly, though, what Kitty learns at the German spa is also a repetition of what Olenin discovered after making his resolution to 'live for others'. Taking the natural do-gooder Varenka as her model, Kitty makes the same resolve, and comes to similar grief. In the affair with the Petrov family, Kitty's ministrations to the sick husband are resented by the wife, and she comes to understand, as did Olenin, that she must at all costs be herself. 'Let me be what I am, and not pretend', she prays (*SS* 8, p. 278). Though she still wears a spuriously simple dress, she now knows not to indulge in the pretention of false piety; and so through a formal detour essential to the postponing of the events of the main plot, Kitty's learning experience repeats Olenin's and thus makes double sense of their respective lives.

These relatively small, internal instances of the patterns of repetition occurring within Kitty's and Levin's stories are redrawn on a larger scale in the parallel between the disruption to conjugal harmony caused by the minor infidelity of Stiva Oblonsky and the greater transgression of his sister.

We shall return in a later chapter to the larger issue of Anna, but this is a good place to register that the Oblonskys have rarely been given their full due in the critical writing on *Anna Karenina*. The usual assumption, that it is a two-stranded novel revolving around Anna and Levin, ignores the Oblonskys' structural role in linking Anna (Stiva's sister) with Levin (Dolly's brother-in-law); their formal significance in the parallels foreshadowing the issue of Anna's adultery; and also the importance of an alternative theme which is related to, but distinct from, that of marital infidelity.

Dolly's part in the first of these considerations is not to be ignored. It is for her sake that Anna makes the first fateful journey from Petersburg to Moscow; it is Dolly with whom Kitty stays in the country, thus reactivating Levin's hopes; and it is she who visits Anna when the latter is living openly with Vronsky, also in the country. Despite this pivotal centrality, the wan, care-worn, and pathetic Dolly cannot equal, in terms of motivational energy, the integrating role filled with such kindness, vivacity and amplitude by her ne'er-do-well husband Stiva. His contribution to the life of the novel is epitomised by the words used to describe his arrival – 'very late' – at his own dinner-party. Without him, the guests have been stiff and awkward, and the conversation refuses to flow. As soon as he enters the room, however, Stiva sizes up the situation and in a moment has 'so kneaded all that society dough in such a way that the party took off, and the drawing-room was filled with animated voices' (*SS* 8, p. 447). Inevitably, it is this very gathering that facilitates Levin and Kitty's third successful attempt, each to find their mutual soulmate; it is here that the card-table courtship takes place. But if Stiva's enabling role in the plot is frequently underrated, his moral position appears even more equivocal. Most critics agree that he is drawn ironically, but there is a division of opinion as to whether Tolstoy has or has not done too much to redeem him. R. F. Christian, for example, sums up the less than even-handed treatment accorded to the various adulteries in the novel as showing 'little logic . . . but much truth' (Christian, 1968, p. 80).

On the surface, it is true, Oblonsky's conduct refigures that of his sister, and is, at the very least, reprehensible. His venality is indisputable, his lack of true remorse seemingly without defense. Yet Tolstoy's treatment of this reprobate is hardly severe. In the opening episode, for example, Stiva's feelings at being banned from the conjugal bed to the sofa in the study are comically empathetic: he has slept as well as ever, had a gaily licentious dream, and woken at his usual time. As he recalls the hot water he is in (school-boy slang sets the appropriate tone) he is rueful but not repentant. Not infidelity itself, but the discovery of it, has succeeded in disturbing a lifestyle which he believes should keep everyone happy – even the reader, who is asked to condone his adventure via the invitation to picture Mlle Roland's roguish back eyes, and to accept Stiva's somewhat feckless perspective: 'How good it all was until now, how happy we were! . . . ' (*SS* 8, p. 108).

The second point about this episode, after the surprisingly sympathetic rendition of a 'minor' adultery, is that it sets up certain moral standards that were not predictable. Stiva's many weaknesses go beyond the specific example of conjugal infidelity – to include an overall want of devotion to family life, and the propensity to seek pleasure elsewhere; lack of independent thought coupled with a facile readiness to adapt to current intellectual fashions; and a general leaning towards any form of self-indulgence. Yet the reader-appeal with which he is generously endowed is actually based on *moral* worth, enhanced though this may be by physical good looks and a charming manner. Notwithstanding these more suspect traits, the list of genuine moral virtues in Stiva's character is considerable: he is incapable of self-deception; unhappy when he causes distress to others; selectively fastidious (he will not sell his wife's forest unless their quarrel is patched up); kind and courteous to servants and acquaintances; disgusted by hypocrisy and falsehood; and in the end resolute in his determination to mend – not his ways – but at least the damage done to his marriage. For the reader, the urge to see the marriage saved, despite some challenging reasons against it (Stiva at least recognises that it can only be patched up by more hypocrisy and falsehood), is powerful; the conviction that things cannot, remain as they are is strong, and we are silently relieved when Dolly, in the middle of packing to go home to mother, announces that she cannot, after all, quit the conjugal home. Stiva's inexcusable act has by now become a peccadillo to be overlooked, and Dolly's reaction in its turn is seen as a passing anger; both express merely the temporary difficulties of a couple unwilling to tear apart the fabric of their family life. The reader rejoices that Dolly still loves Stiva, is confident she will get over her chagrin, and that things will soon return to their imperfect norm. As for Stiva, the inferred aspiration is towards greater discretion rather than pious reform. The text works, in other words, for the maintenance of the *status quo*, for the return to things as they were.

What has happened can also be productively looked at in the light of Peter Brooks' claims for the repetition principle. Obviously the rehearsal of a little drama of adultery sets up the critical narrative tension of the novel, but what is interesting is that its smoothing-out does not discharge that tension, since Stiva and Dolly are only stand-ins – part of a sub-plot whose role is to provide an alternative outcome, a varying commentary to the complications of the main plot, while at the same time, by virtue of their very existence, delaying the too-rapid advance of the latter to a premature end. The Oblonskys' decision to go on living together is like the first ratchet on a spring-coil that is not to be screwed up to the full until other actors appear on the scene. But the fact that the energies of vexation and disillusionment are soothed into forgiveness and reluctant repentance means that neither of the supporting actors takes the steps that lead Anna, the principal, towards suicide (an act which Tolstoy himself describes in Anna's last minutes as the shutting of a book). The fact that Dolly and Stiva anticipate but avoid that outcome – one of many instances of devolved action – serves the purpose of binding the initial energy of the text 'in order to make [the] final discharge more effective'.

So what has paradoxically emerged is that Stiva's peccadillo, by risking an explosion which does not in the end occur, constitutes not a breach but an affirmation of the moral principle of continuity, ensuring the ongoing life of the novel, both conjugal and narrative. And if Stiva were not so charming, the reader would be less glad of this continuation. For it is the requirements of textual flow which primarily preclude any condemnation of Stiva; but it is also the pleasure of his company that creates the will to overlook his failings and assure the reader of his continuing presence; he gives life to the novel in more than the obvious sense.

I mentioned earlier that Stiva's story-line also expresses an alternative theme which makes him as much as Levin the true son of his creator, though Tolstoy is not so ready to confess this identification. The clues lie, as so often, in the opening chapter.

Despite the vividly specific picture of chaos and disarray

conjured up by the second sentence of the novel – 'Everything was upside-down at the Oblonskys' (an effect partly achieved by the immediate designation by name of the family who find themselves in that situation) – Tolstoy continues throughout the second paragraph to preserve the anonymity and representativeness of his characters by using the words 'the wife' and 'the husband'. Moreover, he focusses not on the inner suffering and distress of the two individuals, but on the more general effects of the discovered infidelity. Because 'the wife' feels she can no longer live under one roof with her husband, no one else wants to stay. The servants leave, the husband goes out, the children are neglected. There is 'more unity between fellow-travellers finding themselves together at an inn than amongst them, members of the same household' (*SS* 8, p. 7).

The depersonalised picture seems to indicate a general point: that even within an established marriage – any marriage – the sense of united intimacy between individuals can be illusory, the seamless fabric may still require some patching of the rents and tears. Such information is scarcely a revelation, but it is important as an explicit register of the difficulties inherent in any attempt to use marriage, and/or its extension into 'the family', to satisfy the desire for unity with another person.

This sobering realisation was for Tolstoy the result of experience rather than an innate conviction. His early history is studded with instances of overwhelming attractions to other beings, with whom he sought exclusive intimacy. His first childhood love was generated at the age of nine by his cousin Sonya Koloshin, with whom he wanted to spend the rest of his life 'in the cupboard under the stairs' (*Childhood*, p. 97). He later conceived a passion for the daughter of a neighbouring family, Liubov Islavin, whom he pushed off a balcony in a fit of jealousy because she was talking to some other boys. (It is an odd coincidence that the same girl was to be the mother of his future wife.) He also confessed to being 'in love with' the two Musin-Pushkin brothers who were his frequent playfellows (*Diary*, 29 November 1851).

The idealising vision of the dead mother cast its radiance even over these childish relationships, however, so that the natural innocence of childhood acquired in his later memory a heightened aura of specifically sexual purity. In a letter written 66 years after the event (27 November 1903), to his correspondent and biographer, Paul Biriukov, Tolstoy confided, 'My greatest love was a childhood love – for little Sonya Koloshin'; and he had already noted in his diary of 24 June 1890 that he had thought of writing a book about love – 'like for Sonya Koloshin – a love that would could never fall into sensuality, that would be the best possible protection against sensuality'.

The pre-sensual love of the nine-year old was tested at a later date when he re-encountered another childhood friend, Zinaida Molostvov, during the week he and his brother spent in Kazan, en route for the Caucasus. Now aged 23, Tolstoy was greatly attracted to this girl, and walked, talked and danced with her without acknowledging his elated feelings. A few days later he wrote in his diary:

'Do you remember, Zina, the little sidepath in the Archbishop's Garden? A confession of love was on the tip of my tongue then, and on yours too. It was for me to speak first. But do you know why, I think, I didn't? I was so happy that I wanted nothing more. . . . That time will forever remain among the best memories of my life.' (*Diary*, 8 June 1851)

They can also be seen as the basis for the idealised negation of the Koznyshev–Varenka silence, discussed in Chapter 2.

With the passing of time, however, Tolstoy's diaries and letters record a growing realisation of the social structures that must provide the framework for even an ideal love; he wrote to Valeria Arsenev, the 20-year old daughter of a neighbouring family, that he felt 'not love, yet, but a passionate desire to love . . .' (9 November 1856) and spoke of his yearning 'for a healthy and peaceful' family life. But he still went on to elaborate his idealisation of the spiritual by proclaiming that it was the particular destiny of every woman to be a mother rather than a womb. He urged Valeria to raise her eyes to the higher aspects of their relationship with the exhortation, 'By the Grace of God, my dove, love me, love the whole world, God's world, men, nature, poetry. . . .

His emphasis on the ideality of the institution rather than on the desirability of the individual is equally clear from his diaries, which not only display the absence of any real affection for Valeria, but are severe, critical, and even contemptuous of her. The truth comes out in a letter to Aunt Toinette: 'The only feeling I have for her is gratitude for her love for me, and the thought that, of all the girls I have known, and know now, she would make the best wife for me' (5 December 1856). A week later he had enough courage to say to Valeria herself, albeit by letter, 'I think I must not be made for family life, even though it is what I most admire in the world' (12 December).

As we know, the urge to emulate a lifestyle which his mother appeared to him to grace like an angel finally appeared realisable when he met Sonya Behrs, fond though that belief might appear in the light of their future life together.

The mutual torment of the latter years and the ultimate breakdown of the marriage is common knowledge, but even in its earliest stages, Tolstoy admitted to loving Sonya most when he was away from home; usually hitherto the *amant* rather than the *amoureux*, Tolstoy had never before encountered the hazards of envelopment and suffocation. With Sonya he discovered for the first time the pendulum-swing of attraction and repulsion, of the fear of loss and the terror of union. Bernheimer remarks that, 'Maternal closeness can be as threatening as it is appealing' (p. 11) – and so of course can any relationship based on extreme intimacy. It was Tolstoy's unusual situation to discover and experience this truth not in adolescence, in relation to a living parent, but for the first significant time in his marrige. But escape routes to a freedom and autonomy that are still compatible with the continuation of a marriage are not easy to discover. Stiva Oblonsky epitomises the pursuit of one alternative that Tolstoy did not allow himself in his own life, but one to which his attitude is more ambiguous than the history of Anna's downfall would lead us to suppose.

In fact, if it is demonstrable that Koznyshev represents a higher level of Tolstoy's psyche, that which did remain faithful to the maternal image, it may also be argued that Stiva stands for that aspect of the human personality which is governed by the pleasure principle – a hypothesis about human nature which is too simple to explain all there is to be said about the destiny of man, but one which nevertheless stands for how we might wish life to be. I am not of course implying that Stiva's indulgences represent an unrestrained *id*, that the reality principle has no force in his life; but I would suggest that he comes as far as is acceptable to expressing that other wayward and wanton way of life in which Tolstoy was deeply embroiled, while fighting so hard to suppress its seductions, during his early years. The connection is not immediately apparent since the urbane and civilised Stiva is far removed from the *farouche*, unbridled adolescent who persistently broke all his diary resolutions. But the evidence accumulates if one looks for it.

Levin and Oblonsky are 'almost' the same age, and have been companions since early youth; but thereafter, it would seem, the characters of these chips from the same block are contrasted rather than compared. Oblonsky's interest in Levin's country existence is limited to the shooting it offers, while the high-minded Levin despises the 'town life of his friend'. Yet Tolstoy writes with clear envy that 'Oblonsky laughed with confidence and good-humour, while Levin laughed uncertainly and sometimes angrily' (*SS* 8, p. 17). And Oblonsky can get away with things:

> Although he was entirely guilty, and was conscious of it, almost everyone in the house – even the nurse, Dolly's best friend – sided with him.

He is constantly described in the most attractive terms – clean, sweet, healthy, physically bright, springy, joyful, smiling, shining with freshness and health; in sum, liked by everyone that knew him.

> There was something in his handsome and bright appearance, his beaming eyes, black hair and eyebrows, and his white-and-rosy complexion, that had a physical effect on those he met, making them feel friendly and cheerful. (*SS* 8, p. 23)

These epithets have all appeared within the first 25 pages, and seem only too obviously to express the fantasies of an author who as a boy was constantly preoccupied with his too-large forehead, his too-small, deep-set eyes and his unfortunate nose. (He even cut off his bushy eyebrows, as a boy – judging them, according to Troyat, to be too thick.) Tolstoy's overall ugliness was, he believed, so extreme that no one could ever possibly love him. But everyone loves Oblonsky.

At their restaurant dinner at the beginning of the novel, therefore, Levin's upright and virtuous ideas sound simply priggish, while Oblonsky's disarming metaphor for the delights of extra-marital relationships – 'Rolls sometimes smell so good one can't resist them' – makes even Levin smile. When, many pages later, Tolstoy comments that 'Oblonsky never could remember that he had a wife and children. He had the tastes of a bachelor and understood no others', we read the statement with the smile of understanding that it clearly demands. It certainly is not Oblonsky's fault, the text implies, if he was born with a few unfortunate proclivities.

The same challenge to any facile condemnation of Oblonsky is written into the many roles he plays in the narrative. On the one hand, despite his own dubious record, it is he who does most to facilitate Kitty and Levin's marriage. He goes out of his way to encourage Levin, to comfort him and revive his hopes after the first refusal, to physically bring them together again after Kitty's return from abroad. He steers Levin through the pre-wedding requirements and rituals and waits with him during the agonising time when Levin's wedding shirt cannot be found. In other words he appears to compensate for the shortcomings of his own conjugal front by showing in word and deed that he is totally supportive of the institution of marriage.

On the other hand, it is also he who undertakes to try to arrange a divorce between his sister Anna and her husband Karenin. Going to visit her when he is 'overflowing' with his usual high spirits, Stiva finds his sister in tears, and immediately falls into a 'sympathetic and romantic mood suited to hers'. It is he who sees that divorce is the only solution, despite its opprobrium in nineteenth-century Russia – and the even greater difficulty in regard to re-marriage after divorce. Karenin is reluctant to accept such an outcome, but for a while allows himself to be persuaded by Stiva's concerned pleading. When nothing comes of this initial attempt Oblonsky tries again, but his hopes that a divorce can still be obtained are thwarted by a spiritualist – and Tolstoy detested fake religious practices even more than he disapproved of flirtations with governesses. Oblonsky's arguments and efforts in fact declare every positive position in favour of divorce, to the extent that the reader heartily endorses both them and the possibility of Anna and Vronsky living 'happily ever after'.

The complex and profound reasons for the frustration of such an eventuality will be considered later; for the moment the focus remains on Stiva's ambivalent role, as upholder both of marriage and divorce, of the family *and* of the amorous adventure, of dinner *plus* rolls. The fact that Oblonsky is so attractive a character would seem to point to the proposition that the source of the ambivalence lies in Tolstoy himself, who also longed for 'rolls', but who, by contrast, refused to admit it. Further textual evidence for this suggestion is contained in the second shooting scene, when Veslovsky and Stiva go for a 'walk' at night, having heard the nearby singing of the female servants. The newly married Levin of course refuses to accompany them, but Oblonsky's careless argument puts the case that Tolstoy, like Levin, will not allow himself to listen to: the 'courting' of maid-servants *'ne tire pas à conséquence'*. Wives are none the worse for it and the husbands have a good time. 'The important thing', says Stiva, 'is to guard the sanctity of the home. Nothing of that sort in the house, but no need to completely tie your hands.' The scene that Levin glimpses is in fact extremely attractive:

> Through his sleep he heard laughter and Veslovsky's and Oblonsky's merry talk. He opened his eyes for an instant: they were standing in the open doorway, brightly lit up by the moon which had now risen. Oblonsky was saying something about the freshness of a girl, comparing her to a fresh kernel just taken from its shell; and Veslovsky was laughing his very infectious laugh . . .
> (*SS* 9, p. 185)

When Tolstoy consciously damns, he does so sharply and unmistakeably; here we are clearly being shown not the horrors but rather the charms of what might be called the other side of the fence. We are reminded that it is always one and the same individual who both reveres the home paddock and at the same time covets what is in the next pasture.

It is possible and necessary to take still further this unexceptionable demonstration of Tolstoy's ambivalent attitude to Stiva, if only to put into perspective Stiva's frequently asserted negative qualities. A modern critic, Sydney Schulze, for example, writing as late as 1982, sees Stiva as 'tainted with the malignancy' of high society and its evils (p. 152). She claims that he 'helps lead Anna down the path of ruin'; that 'his destructiveness extends to his own marriage'; and that although he means no ill, he 'causes harm wherever he goes'. Schulze admits Stiva's great charm, which results in everyone's readiness to forgive or simply not notice his nefarious activities, but she does not follow the threads which lead to the reasons for the duality. Nor does she acknowledge the possibility of the argument that, setting aside Koznyshev's choosing of the highest path of all, Stiva's life-choices are better adapted to survival than are

Levin's. We have already seen, in his case, on what shaky foundations is poised that most essential element of a true union – the mutual communication of one self to another. It is not that exchange between Stiva and Dolly is any better, for it is actually worse; but the *expectations* suggested by their pragmatic form of family life are so low that they can scarcely be threatened. Kitty and Levin, on the other hand, are already failing to live up to the ideal posed by Natasha and Pierre in *War and Peace*, who communicate 'as only a husband and wife can talk, that is, with extraordinary clearness and rapidity, understanding and expressing each other's thoughts in ways contrary to all rules of logic . . .' (*SS* 7, p. 325).

What is interesting about this splitting-off of both Koznyshev and Oblonsky from the original Levin block is the clarity with which it demonstrates how the principle of repetition works for both a psychoanalytic and formal analysis of the text. That these two methods of approach are inextricably linked has been asserted frequently enough, in relation to the various explications of Freud's own figurative language and to the tropes to which later exponents such as Lacan and Bloom have resorted in order to render their external visions of the workings of the psyche. Similarly, writers such as Dostoevsky have illustrated through the creation of actual characters various principles of psychoanalysis: the 'split personality' in *The Double*, the Oedipal complex in *The Brothers Karamazov*, the *mise-en-abîme* of the conflicting sides of one personality in the opposing projections (Sonia and Svidrigailov) of the central but schismatic character Raskolnikov. But I am not aware of these principles having been seen as illuminating Tolstoy's writing; hence it may repay us to go back to the basics of some of the formal aspects of repetition.

Where Peter Brooks is embarrassed at the somewhat obvious quality of his introductory remarks on this subject ('Now repetition is so basic to our experience of literary texts that one is simultaneously tempted to say all and to say nothing . .' .), J. Hillis Miller has no such inhibitions. He leads us from the apparently trivial matter of Tess's red hair-ribbon through more subtle allusions such as d'Urberville's inscription as the 'blood-red ray in the spectrum of [Tess's] young life' to the red-painted words 'Thou, shalt, not, commit' – on walls and fences, put there by the itinerant religious man. As Miller ludicly remarks, 'In a novel, what is said two or more times may not be true, but the reader is fairly safe in assuming it is significant' (Miller, 1982, pp. 1–2).

These kinds of repetition are recurrent throughout *Anna Karenina* and so obvious that most critics have picked them up and made a meal of them. Probably the two most famous are the dream of the muttering peasant who is tinkering at the wheel of a train with a piece of iron (which Anna and Vronsky both dream, Anna more than once), and the ubiquitous image of the train itself, which carries people from Petersburg to Moscow and thus conjoins shifting groups, even as its more sinister overtones portending Anna's death are played out in children's games where the train capsizes and the passengers fall off the roof, or where Anna's own Seriozha, within the space of a half-hour, both mimes a fall from a train and mourns his mother's absence, thus unconsciously prefiguring the form and effect of her later death.

A third is the recurring image of fire associated with the initial hopes for the Anna–Vronsky liaison. It begins when her smile 'burns' Vronsky at the ball; then there is a brief 'spark' that gleams when they part at the railway station; but the 'fire' is quenched when she is obliged to endure the conjugal attentions of her husband. Thereafter the word 'burn' or 'burning' is used in nearly every encounter she has with Vronsky, sometimes with gratuitous glosses from the author, as when Anna returns from Princess Betsy's, where she has met Vronsky: 'Her face shone with a vivid glow, but it was not a joyous glow – it resembled the terrible glow of a conflagration on a dark night.' At the same time there is a constant and associated repetition of the word 'animation', as though Anna's natural vivacity is now fuelled from a new source. Thus, in surreptitious ways, as well as by more overt announcements, the text builds up a double structure: the heightening of Anna's love for Vronsky, and the author's determination that we shall share in both its compulsion and its peril.

Miller insists that far from being trivial, such repetitions contribute to the way readers are enabled to interpret a novel; but they also underscore a more important theoretical issue. Two distinct, almost opposing conceptions of repetition have been postulated, one by Plato, the other by Nietzsche; these have been brought together and contrasted against each other by Gilles Deleuze in his *Logigue du Sens* (Deleuze, 1969). Miller's translation of the relevant Deleuze passage reads:

Let us consider two formulations: "only that which resembles itself differs," "only differences resemble one another" [*"Seul ce qui se ressemble diffère," "seules les différences se ressemblent"*]. It is a question of the readings of the world in a sense that one asks us to think of difference on the basis of pre-established similitude or identity, while the other invites us on the contrary to think of similitude and even identity as the product of a fundamental disparity [*d'une disparité de fond*]. The first exactly defines the world of copies or of representations; it establishes the world as icon. The second, against the first, defines the world of simulacra. It presents the world itself as phantasm.

(Miller, pp. 5–6; Deleuze, p. 302)

Miller's leap from the simplicities of recurrent colours – or, in our case, trains, – to his exposition of the two alternate theories of repetition, lands his reader with great suddenness in the infinitely more complex terrain of deconstructive thinking – and in particular Miller's own mode of it, which stresses above all undecidability. In fact he unobtrusively slips in among his ratiocinations one of the most radical statements imaginable to the Western mind: 'The relationship between the two forms of repetition defies the elementary principle of logic, the law of contradiction which says: 'either A or not-A' (p. 17). Yet he arrives at his statement by steps whose own logic is impeccable.

He outlines first the more commonplace, Platonic concept of repetition, which is based on pre-established similitude or identity and grounded in a 'solid archetypal model. . . . All the other examples are copies of this model'. It can be called a *mimetic* form of repetition, and is the 'reigning pre-supposition of realistic fiction and of its critics in nineteenth- and even in twentieth-century England' (p. 6).

Opposed to this stands Nietzsche's concept of repetition, based on the notion that 'only differences resemble each other'. Here, each thing is intrinsically different from every other thing. Similarities may be perceived, but they are nevertheless ungrounded. Deleuze, quoted by Miller, uses the word 'phantasm' to distinguish these instances of repetition from those which are copies of a recognised model. 'It seems that X repeats Y,' adds Miller, 'But in fact it does not.'

Miller turns to Walter Benjamin for further exemplification. In his essay 'The Image of Proust' (Benjamin, 1969 ), the latter argues that if Penelope unwove at night what she had woven by day, Proust's writing did the reverse, unravelling by day what was woven at night.

> The distinction is between the rational, willed, intentional remembering of the day time, and that kind of involuntary Memory which Benjamin calls forgetting. The first kind of memory constructs a lucid pattern from which the 'life' has disappeared. The second kind of memory constructs an imaginary 'lived life', as dreams make a strangely powerful affective 'memory' of things which never happened as such.          (Miller, p. 7)

Miller goes on to note two essential qualities of this second more elusive form of repetition. Firstly its opaque, dreamlike quality means that it cannot be defined logically, but only exemplified; secondly, it is dependent on the first, grounded, logical, form. In fact, 'each form of repetition calls up the other, by an inevitable compulsion. The second is not the negation or opposite of the first, but its 'counterpart' (p. 9). (Boris Eikhenbaum also makes a similar point when he writes of the earlier Tolstoy, 'It is not a matter of 'duality' as is customarily said, but of a dual process of consciousness, one of which works over the material supplied by the other. One, "daytime", is a process of observation which demands from the observer himself that he take part in the activity demanded at the given moment; the other, "night-time", is a process of recollection, acting freely on the material supplied.' [Eikhenbaum, 1928]).

Miller uses a very simple example to show the closeness of the two forms of repetition: he quotes from Hardy's novel *The Well-Beloved* the following passage, where the hero is indulging in his habit of seeing Rome as a repetition of his native peninsula, Portland Bill:

> The unconscious habit, common to so many people, of tracing likes in unlikes had often led him to discern, or to fancy he discerned, in the Roman atmosphere, in its lights and shades, and particularly in its reflected or secondary lights, something resembling the atmosphere of his native promontory.     (p. 12)

For Miller the shift from 'to discern' to 'to fancy he discerned' is enough to show the essential difference between seeing real instances of repetition and phantasmagorical, deceptive ones, and it enables him to elaborate further on the frequency with which many of Hardy's narrators and characters see likenesses in the unlike, or mistakenly read the recurrences of persons or situations as repetitions of the first kind. Miller categorises this mistake as a linguistic one in that the people and the things which should be read as signs are taken literally. A character doing this will live his life as a metaphor, while the narrator will tell the story as a false series of significant repetitions.

That same narrator, however, provides sufficient information for the reader to perceive the double operation that is at work: he 'de-mystifies' his own reading of life as well as that of the characters', although 'this insight does not constitute total understanding or total liberation'. Nevertheless, he 'preserves and lovingly records [the character's] illusions . . . Hardy's narrator demonstrates the necessary coherence, one in the other, of the two forms' (p. 14).

It is not difficult to see that Miller's exposition, although resting mainly on a theory of perception and the evidence of language, supports and enhances what has so far – on the whole – been a psychoanalytical approach to Tolstoy's relationship with his character Levin. The convention is that Levin *is* Tolstoy; I have tried to show that Tolstoy also expresses himself through Koznyshev and Oblonsky; it takes little to substantiate that view further through the insights of Miller and Deleuze. Levin is constructed as Tolstoy's projection of himself trying to achieve the family happiness he believed was associated with his own childhood. Despite Kitty's imaginations he is a conscientious and constant husband, who abhors 'fallen women', to the extent that in his presence Kitty turns the conversation away from 'distasteful' gossip about Anna Karenin, while Dolly is too fastidious to use her brother-in-law's horses when she goes to visit her disgraced sister-in-law. Yet Levin not only insists on her taking them, he later willingly gives Dolly financial support when Stiva's profligacy undermines the Oblonsky resources. In other words, Levin, whose sexual morals are succinctly expressed in his distaste for stolen rolls, is also as tolerant as he can bring himself to be of the faults of others; when Kitty has just given birth and Levin is conversing with a group of his peasants, 'he talked but never ceased thinking of his wife'; at the birth itself the new joy is so great it is 'insupportable'. While such moments of supreme happiness may be later qualified by the reluctant awareness of new responsibilities, we have no doubt that

Levin will be an exemplary husband; the limitations which hamper any deeper relationship with his wife are not grounded in ill will but in lack of imagination. Even when he is charmed by Anna, there is no basis for Kitty's outburst of jealousy, for Levin will not succumb even to a flirtation, let alone an infidelity. In effect, he repeats his lessons like a dutiful schoolboy, the lessons his master--creator has taught him to recite. In this sense it can be said that Levin is a repetition of Tolstoy – a copy of a model which existed in Tolstoy's head of an idealised version of himself. Levin is thus an image of an image; but it is one that is grounded if not in the reality of Tolstoy, at least in what Tolstoy wished that reality to be. The various copy-cat scenarios taken straight from his own diaries make that point unarguable.

However, we have already noted that Levin is frequently iron-ised, while Oblonsky is not. The most extreme examples of this treatment revolve around Veslovsky's visit to Pokrovsk. When Veslovsky eats up all the hunting provisions Levin is so disap-pointed he feels inclined to cry, while Stiva merely laughs heartily; but when Levin turns Veslovsky out because 'there was something impure in Veslovsky's attitude' (which the reader knows is a hypersensitive constatation), Oblonsky's voice is that of good sense and common courtesy. 'What nonsense is this?' he protests. 'What bee have you got in your bonnet? . . . He [Veslovsky] feels insulted.' Levin replies like a stage husband wailing with self-pity:

> 'And I feel insulted and tortured! I have done nothing wrong and I don't deserve to suffer.' (*SS*, 9, p. 200)

In this and many other instances Tolstoy parts company with his supposed replica, and in the distance he puts between the two there bubbles up the laughter of ridicule. One can say that Levin's presentation is subverted by the infinitely greater appeal of the ne'er-do-well Stiva – but we can now see that this is because Oblonsky no less than Levin is the product of Tolstoy's self-projection. But now it is a projection not of his daytime self, as it were, not of the public image, but of the private self that Tolstoy did not overtly indulge. The Tolstoy who secretly hankered *not* to find his personal happiness in the domestic circle, who had made himself abjure what had been a frequent and delightful practice in his youth – the bedding of maid-servants and peasant girls – allows Stiva, his supposed opposite, to satisfy vicariously all these banned appetites, and in doing so, not only to reconstitute them, but even to make their attraction quite perceptible, while at the same time implying that they are also unacceptable. Perhaps another way of illustrating this example of the two kinds of repetition would be to say that if Levin is like a photograph of Tolstoy in the attitude most designed to impress, then Oblonsky is no less a replica, but one that is produced from the reverse tones of a negative. What is different (Oblonsky) springs from, resembles both the original (Tolstoy) and the model (Levin), but in such a way as to challenge Tolstoy's image of himself by suggesting that there may be more than one clone.

Miller's further point, which is also of relevance here, is that it would be misguided to see *either* Levin *or* Oblonsky as in some privileged way representing the 'real' Tolstoy. Even though the two characters contradict each other, have opposing views, and lead radically different lives, it is only by seeing both of them as speaking for Tolstoy that we can begin to grasp the truth. And this is not to forget Koznyshev, who represents an even more intangible fantasy than does Oblonsky – a fantasy left over, as we have seen, from an earlier phase.

As well, however, as illuminating and being illuminated by this very fundamental aspect of our perceptions of the world, these three characters from *Anna Karenina* exemplify what Miller has postulated as a principle of deconstructive criticism, demanding the kind of reading that 'best account[s] for the heterogeneity of the text, its presentation of a definite group of possible meanings which are systematically interconnected, determined by the text, but logically incompatible' (p. 51).

We cannot say that out of Levin, Stiva, or Koznyshev one is 'right' and the others wrong. They are *all* right, despite the mutual incongruities that separate them one from the other. Similarly, of course, Kitty for a while strives to 'repeat' Varenka, and Varenka, much later, would give anything to be able to replicate Kitty's position as a wife. In the end it is their differences which determine their divergent paths, yet both, in opposing ways, can be said to repeat Tolstoy's memory of his dead mother.

One of the forms of repetition that Miller does not discuss, but which has been the subject of much recent work, is parody. (See especially Margaret Rose's *Parody/Metafiction* (Rose, 1979).) Miller notwithstanding, there is an excellent example of parodic repetition in Part 2, chapter 4, where Vronsky describes to his cousin,

Princess Betsy, his own efforts at reconciling an angry husband with his maligned wife. While this situation is far removed from that of Dolly and Stiva – it involves a couple of drunken regimental *bons viveurs* who pursue a pretty woman to her home, only to find she is both married and pregnant, and indignantly protected by an outraged husband who requires appeasing – Vronsky does act and describe himself as a reconciler, and, like Anna's, his mission of peace at least appears successful.

Yet the incident, which provokes much mirth when he recounts it to his cousin Betsy, a woman of indifferent morals who does her best to promote the liaison between Anna and Vronsky, in fact serves to undermine Anna's mission to the Oblonsky's. The fragility of both human nature and the institution of marriage is hinted at, being shown first in the similarity between two apparently unrelated episodes, and then, as it were, implying that good deeds in one area do not necessarily characterise a person's total behaviour. Thus the two parodically-linked incidents play an important role in that they constitute one of the many literary moves which prepare the reader for the contrast between Anna the ministering angel and her demonic transformation.

But before we embark on a full discussion of the eponymous heroine, it is practically incumbent on us to make our own journey back to the introduction to this chapter – even if only to reverse the terms, and sense, of Brooks' claim that, 'The sense of a beginning . . . must in some important way be determined by the sense of an ending' (p. 94).

We began, then, by noting the function and importance of some of the more normal and conventional devices of repetition in *Anna Karenina*, and from there moved to the extrapolation of different kinds of repetition – one based simultaneously on considerations of character (Tolstoy's procedure of repeating himself,' the same but different,' in not just one, but three of his male protagonists). But it now seems that all that adds up to a concept of repetition which does not quite fit either of the two principles of repetition distinguished by Deleuze and Miller. If Plato's repetitions are copies of a model which 'remains untouched by the effects of repetition' (p. 6), and the Nietzschean mode posits *apparent* similarity which actually arises against a background in which everything is intrinsically different, where does Tolstoy leave us? He draws attention to the repetition of himself in Levin by highlighting the many instances of Levin's story which are taken straight from his own; but *I* have equally called to the reader's notice the less obvious but powerful grounds for arguing that Koznyshev and Oblonsky are also repetitions of Tolstoy; but because they recall aspects of his character that he was either unaware or ashamed of, they appear as quite different from each other, from Levin, and from the public Tolstoy. They incorporate a repetition which exhibits difference while secretly stemming from the same source; they could individually be called homologous – if, collectively, their dissimilarities did not make nonsense of that formulation. Perhaps it is best to think of them as examples of the existence of what Miller has called 'structures of language which contradict the law of non-contradiction' – for each allows Tolstoy to truthfully say, 'This is the real me', just as the next gainsays the 'real me' of the former. No more powerful corrective than this could be produced, should we need to be reminded of the fact that literature is always a linguistic construction, whatever its provenance.

And so, *a fortiori*, is parody. While, as a mode, parody may serve a variety of functions (such as, in the case in point in this chapter, that of helping to prepare the reader for a profound alteration in a character and hence a change in reader attitude towards her), it is through language that the semantic changes parody seeks to bring about in the mental world of that reader are achieved. Since such a change also falls into 'the same but different' pattern advanced by Todorov and approved and modified by Brooks into a dynamic model of simultaneous resemblance and difference, parody is classifiable as a sub-division of repetition. It is clear that in the two cases of reconciliation referred to earlier, the central action remains the same, while the characters who enact it differ, as does the audience (in one case the reader, in the other another character in the novel – thus heightening the self-reflexive nature of the device), and, above all, the motivation of the two episodes. The author, however, remains constant; the target of this parody is his own, earlier, text and thus, to some extent, himself.

Margaret Rose's discussion of parody sets out clearly the two main theories about the nature of the attitude of the parodical to the text quoted, one claiming the motivation to be contempt, the other arguing for sympathy. Rose herself plumps for an ambivalence of motivation, finding support for her view in Tynianov's article on parody in Dostoevsky and Gogol; as she remarks of both parody and irony, their function is to 'confuse the normal process of communication by offering more than one message' (p. 51).

Thus not only our understanding that Anna is a compassionate and moral woman bent on propping up and maintaining the institution of marriage, but also the assumption that the salvation of this marriage – perhaps of all marriages – is *worth* putting so much effort into, is cast into doubt by the parallel of Vronsky's parodic imitation of her mediating role. The 'straight' text has already informed us that Vronsky has never believed in marriage, and the audience to whom he recounts the whole affair, including its happy outcome, see it as amusingly ridiculous. The episode exemplifies the point that Rose makes, although unfortunately only as an almost throwaway line, that 'parody is often a symptom not only of external but internal censorship . . . '(p. 33). In other words, instead of the 'truth' being contained in an assumed, generalised underwriting of, in this case, the value of an unbroken marriage, such a view is suddenly, through the satirical effects of the parodistic retelling of a similar story, stood on its head, and, with hindsight, Anna's action appears pointless, if not hypocritical. Tolstoy's underlying desire to enact the break-up rather than the patch-up of a marriage can thus be seen as evident from the very start, but it is only through a *return*, through using the ending and the middle to make sense of the beginning, that we can arrive at such an understanding. And, in the form of a clear pointer to this knowledge, the repressed wish returns in disguise, dressed up as a parodic episode which mocks the values of the apparent storyline.

The authorial attitude to Anna, speaking here strictly of the novel itself, is thus revealed to be one not of evolution, as is commonly argued, but of an ever-present ambivalence that is betrayed through various manifestations of the repetition principle. From here it is but a small step to the postulation that Tolstoy repeats himself, the same but different, not only in his male protagonists, but deeply, implicitly, and possibly unconsciously – how can we know? – in his heroine, Anna.

# 4

# The Roots of Passion

The story of Anna Arkadevna Karenin is but one strand in the novel *Anna Karenina*, but Anna's death under the wheels of a train is as familiar to the general reading public as the yearning of the three sisters to go to Moscow. Thus no one can begin to discuss the Anna case without the shadow of tragedy falling starkly over the page; the overriding question with this heroine is not, 'What will happen to her?', but rather, 'Why did she do it? Do we believe that it had to end like this?' Two more far-reaching and disturbing issues also begin to crowd in. What in Tolstoy drove him to create and then destroy? What in the human condition seeks death?

As to the first pair of questions, they can be dismissed fairly summarily, though each for different reasons. Quite simply we *do* believe the suicide is inevitable if only because it has been so carefully and relentlessly prepared; to rehearse Anna's inexorable progress towards her own last train would simply be to retell the story, though in doing so we would also be answering the first question about why. The more attentively we examine Anna's thoughts, feelings and actions, the more clearly we see where she is heading. And, in case we fail to do this, there is a host of critics who have commentated it all for us, all proposing their own interpretation and emphasis: some invoke God and the Divine Law, some accuse society and its hypocrisies, others simply blame the demon jealousy. As to the degree of acceptance of the inevitable, it is true that the tearful reading public of the day in Moscow and St Petersburg protesed that the ending should be changed; for them the successive episodes that appeared in the *Russkii Vestnik* (*The Russian Herald*) were not yet a *fait accompli*. But their appeals had no effect on Tolstoy, and the moment of sentiment was soon over. With regard to the broader issues, it makes more sense to attempt to deal with them in reverse order, for then we will have a larger overview into which Tolstoy may or may not be inserted – with the proviso, of course, the neater the fit the more cautious we should be of it.

Before embarking upon that course, however, there is one preliminary observation that is relevant. While every reader has agonized over the question of Anna's death, because it is natural to *wish* there had been an alternative that might have saved her, no one challenges the act upon which that death is contingent. No one wishes she had not met Vronsky, given the acid strokes in which the sterility of her life with Karenin is etched. Besides – *le beau mariage n'a pas d'histoire*. Without that meeting we would have only Levin's story – and a very unlikely best seller. In other words the reading public, despite its protestations, is either interested in death in itself, or willing to put up with a tragic ending for the sake of what goes before. As we shall see, both options have their own intrinsic interest.

What comes between Anna's meeting with Vronsky and her final act is an interlude of passion, followed by the visible transformation of that passion into something so neurotic, obsessional and destructive that we are uncertain whether it can still be called by the same name. The relation between passion and self-destruction must therefore be examined in the light of concepts which go well beyond the usual limits of literary criticism. Already I, in *The Novel of Adultery* (Armstrong, 1978) and Tony Tanner in *Adultery in the Novel* (Tanner, 1979) have both had recourse to a standard work on passion and death, Denis de Rougemont's *L'amour et L'Occident* (de Rougemont, 1956), variously translated as *Passion and Society* and *Love in the Western World*, and I do not propose to do more than summarize an argument which can now be no more than a brief preliminary to a study of another kind.

Proceeding from the myth of *Tristan and Isolde* in which the lovers are initially thwarted by external circumstances, but come to block their own mutual happiness by deliberately creating obstacles to its achievement, de Rougemont concludes that this hindering of the fulfilment of love masks a love of passion for its own sake, which in turn conceals a love for obstruction *per se*. Finally, 'it turns out that the ultimate obstacle is death and at the close of the tale death is revealed as having been the real end, what passion yearned after from the beginning'. This is dramatically summed up in the claim that, 'unawares and in spite of themselves, the lovers have never had but one desire – the desire for death' (p. 46).

Because the idea is so shocking, it has to be contained in a myth, of which *Tristan and Isolde* becomes only one emblematic example. The rest of de Rougemont's book traces the subsequent history of

that myth, including its going 'underground' and its re-appearances
in the European novel; but the essential point of his argument is
this:

> A myth is needed to express the dark and unmentionable fact
> that passion is linked with death, and involves the destruction of
> anyone yielding himself up to it with all his strength. For we
> have wanted to preserve passion and we cherish the unhappi-
> ness that it brings with it; and yet at the same time both passion
> and unhappiness have stood condemned in the light of official
> morals and in the light of reason. . . . The myth expresses these
> realities to the extend exacted by our instinct, but it also veils
> them to the extent that broad daylight and reason might imperil
> them.                                            (de Rougemont, 1962, p. 21)

If we accept de Rougemont's premise, then the rest of his
account is very persuasive. But we should note that his case is
based on circumstantial evidence only. The behaviour of the two
lovers is indeed strange, refusing as it does to make the story end
up like a fairy-tale; but the fact that they experience passion and
succumb to death is not in itself sufficient to link the two states.
This does not of course remove the possibility that de Rougemont's
linkage may have substance – it only indicates that for properly
*causal* arguments we shall have to look elsewhere.

Fortunately, as Tanner also points out, Freud has something to
say about the role of obstacles in love, which suggests a further
reason why Tristan and Isolde might place a sword between
themselves. (Most Romantic literature depends on the presence of
some kind of symbolic sword obstructing union, such as a blood-
tie between would-be lovers; it can also be a more direct intervention, as in the case of parental opposition.) In 'The Most
Prevalent Form of Degradation in Erotic Life' Freud writes:

> It is easy to show that the value the mind sets on erotic needs
> instantly sinks as soon as satisfaction becomes readily obtain-
> able. Some obstacle is necessary to swell the tide of libido to its
> height; and at all periods of history, wherever natural barriers in
> the way of satisfaction have not sufficed, man has erected
> conventional ones in order to enjoy love.
> (*Collected papers*, ed. James Strachey, vol. 4, p. 213; quoted by
>                                                          Tanner, pp. 88–9)

But this does not really help us, since in the first place it does not rule out the overcoming of those barriers, be they natural or artificial, so that love may yet triumph; and second, it makes no connection with a death wish. Not surprisingly, we shall have to return to *Beyond the Pleasure Principle* to see if there is any argument for a causal linkage such as we are seeking.

Several theorists working as much in the field of literature as of psychoanalysis have mined and commentated this essay, as we have already seen. Most of them have concentrated on the relation between the repetition compulsion and death, leaving the passion/death connection surprisingly untouched – or giving tantalizingly brief allusions to the issue, as elusive as a Derridean trace. But in attempting to come to grips with such an under-developed issue, it is important to acknowledge how blurred is the line separating the slaves from the masters. The lessons of Donne (on islands) and the deconstructionists (on intertextuality and the creativity of criticism) join in the recognition that the commentators' work is invaluable in making the more difficult master-texts not only more accessible, but inestimably more fertile.

Peter Brooks, for example, has only a line or two relating to the theme under discussion, and uses the word 'passion' only once in the essay 'Freud's Masterplot'. Yet what he says is a stimulus which sends us back willy-nilly, to 'origins' – to Freud. Brooks notes, almost in parenthesis, with what frequency the beginnings of novels – the beginning being the moment of stimulation from 'quiescence into a state of narratability, into a tension, a kind of irritation, which demands narration' – are characterized by a specifically erotic quality. He mentions the masturbatory reveries which introduce both Rousseau's *Confessions* and Genêt's *Notre-Dame des Fleurs*, but we think immediately, of course, of Stiva and his affair with the governess; of Levin's visit to town to court Kitty Shcherbatsky; and of Anna's arrival with the intention to make conjugal peace but instead, or as well, encountering first Vronsky's mother and then Vronsky himself. But not only do these triple excitations kick the plot into action on all sides, they also show something of interest to our new theme. Even at this point we recognize that we are going to perceive differently, and probably label differently, these three sources of generative erotic tension; and however we categorise Stiva's naughty pecadillo or Levin's honorable intentions, we do not lump them together with what we instinctively classify as Anna's incipient passion. Thus our investigation into the links between passion and death may also contribute to a much-needed definition of the former, whose difference from lust and 'love' is arguably more than a just matter of quantitative intensity.

It will be remembered that Brooks' description of narrative gives it as a state of tension or 'prolonged deviance from the quiescence of the "normal" . . . until it reaches the terminal quiescence of the end' (p. 103). The danger of reaching the end too quickly is prevented by detour, intentional deviance. 'Plot is a kind of arabesque, a squiggle towards the end' (p. 104). This *saisissant* formulation of the essence of narrative is arrived at from Brooks' realization that Freud's early belief in two opposing principles, one preserving life, the other terminating it is, in *Beyond the Pleasure Principle*, corrected and reformulated to the view that *both* the death instincts *and* the life instincts are conservative, that is, they tend toward the restoration of an earlier state of things. The 'complicated detour' of life leads back to death in a dynamic relationship in which premature discharge frequently threatens the forward moving urge to go on (read on, or be read, on).

The maintenance of the onward-moving plot is sustained by the energy generated by 'deviance, extravagance, excess' writes Brooks (p. 108), and it is obvious that if the start of a particular novel has been set off, as it were, by the excitement of an erotic impulse, then the extravagance and excess are also likely to operate in the same domain; thus there is already in plot itself – both in the desire to surge forward and in its sphere of operation – something of the qualities we associate with passion. And there is also, in the Romantic plot in particular, a tradition of obstacles which apparently forbid passion. However, de Rougemont's comments have shown us that it is more likely to be the consummation of passion which is at the same time both sought and prohibited, while it is the ongoing attempt to *attain* that is the lifeblood of literature. Brooks claims that fulfilment is interdicted because 'it would be too perfect, a discharge indistinguishable from death'. From the formal point of view his claim is unassailable; if for example a brother and sister were to ignore the incest taboo they could marry and live happy ever after. But this would as inevitably precipitate the end of the story as should their deaths. Brooks adds that where there is no real obstacle, such an incest, 'lovers choose to turn the beloved into a soul-sister so that possession will be either impossible or mortal' (p. 109). He quotes the example of Rousseau's Julie and St.

Preux in *La Nouvelle Héloise*, who do indeed do exactly what he says, with St. Preux also writing letters beginning, 'Mourons, ô ma douce amie . . .'.

It therefore seems that one characteristic of literary passion is that narrative sexual fulfilment discharges a total energy commensurate with the life of the novel itself. Afterwards there is but non-narratability – death – or Freud's state of quiescence, which all life seeks but plot postpones.

Further elaboration of this elusive linkage between passion and death can be found in Neil Hertz's essay 'Freud and the Sandman' (Hertz, 1979) which takes up Freud's notion of the uncanny. Once again the main interest centres on the relation between Freud's elaboration of the repetition–compulsion, both here, and in the two drafts of *Beyond the Pleasure Principle* which separately preceded and followed the publication of '*Das Unheimliche*', and his revised postulation of the death instinct. And, once again, off-focus and in the margins as it were, we find traces that may help to track down what is *our* central enquiry, even while the main purpose of Hertz's essay is to make the picture of repetition and the death instincts clearer and more distinct. Hertz contemplates the 'rambling and intriguingly oblique presentation' (p. 298) of 'The Uncanny' and playfully suggests that the impulse to write a second draft of the essay in 1919 might have been Freud's exclamatory response ('*Unheimlich!*') to the theory's strangeness. More seriously, he suggests that its obliqueness is due in part to the difficulties of dealing with a 'compulsion' whose very nature provokes uncertainty. Hertz asks whether one can speak of the repetition–compulsion 'itself' – or merely of Freud's theory of repetition, and how one comes to terms 'with a force that seems at once mobile and concealed in it operation'. He points out that in *Beyond the Pleasure Principle* Freud was obliged to acknowledge that evidence for a compulsive force such as the 'death instinct' underlying the compulsion of the repetition instinct was hard to find, for the drive was 'in his words, never 'visible', it 'eluded perception'. However in *Civilization and its Discontents* he attached a significant rider to this formulation, including now the excepting circumstance of when it (the death instinct) is 'tinged or coloured' by sexuality. Hertz paraphrases, 'Like certain substances that must be prepared before they can be examined under a microscope, it is only when stained that the death instinct can be brought into focus' (pp. 299–300).

Hertz uses this image as a launching-pad for speculation about the connections between figurative language and the reality it seeks to describe, based on the claim that 'Freud sees his figurative language as a means of lending colour to what is otherwise imperceptible' (p. 300). He is however cautious about the three-fold analogy that likens repetition to colouring matter to figurative language, on the grounds that it presupposes a real, pre-existent force that is merely rendered more *discernible* by the above processess. His caution is salutory in that it reminds us that the relation between the universal and the particular: 'All happy families . . . every unhappy family . . . ' is indeed problematic. Yet his own troping of Freud – the image of the death instinct becoming visible when 'stained' by sexuality – is so apposite to the particular history of Anna that is seems like a piece of the jigsaw that really does fit.

But how can it? Sexuality is conventionally associated with eroticism, the erotic with Eros, Eros with life. How can it partake of both life and death, Eros and Thanatos, Anna and Levin? What is its relation to passion? The greatest source of help is surely that most lucid and careful exposition of *Beyond the Pleasure Principle*, Jean Laplanche's *Life and Death in Psychoanalysis* (Laplanche, 1976). (The following remarks have *to a preliminary degree* been anticipated in the chapter, 'Tolstoy's Dead Mother', but since the present investigation is a different, though related one, I have thought it preferable to go over some of the same ground rather than deprive the argument of its premises.)

In the first paragraph of Chapter 3 of this work, which sums up the arguments of Chapters 2 and 3, Laplanche states:

Sexuality breaks out, in the human child, through *deviation from* and *autoerotic reversal* of the vital processes. And, on the other hand, sexuality – the term still taken in its 'generalized' sense – appears as *implanted* in the child from the parental universe: from its structures, meanings, and fantasies.                    (p. 48)

Laplanche is seeking to uncover the genesis of sexuality in the infant, and without arbitrating between these two perspectives, at least claims firmly that the 'vital order' is both infested with and sustained by the 'sexual order'. But the vital sources are themselves divided: on the one hand 'love' and sexuality, on the other, 'hunger' and self-preservation. Thus survival is apparently threatened by sexuality. But since Freud never in fact elaborated such a theory of conflict between the two functions, it is preferable, says Laplanche, to view self-preservation as the ground of the conflict, rather than as one of the terms of the opposition; and to understand that what is threatened is not the life of the child, but a certain sense of its integrity. That is, sexual pleasure (the pleasure the child receives through sucking as distinct from the nourishment it gets by imbibing milk) threatens to break down the child's total and purposeful concentration on assuring its life through sucking, and to make inherent in that activity a pleasure which can be detached from the maternal connection and obtained from, for example, the child's own body.

However it is essential to realize that the child's body is not the object of the sexual drive; there is no *object* as such. 'The sexual object is not identical to the object of the function but is displaced in relation to it.' (p. 20) The milk, already blurring semantically into 'breast' and 'mother', becomes a lost object, the object of self-preservation and hunger; the object that sexuality seeks to find forever after. Thus the search for sexual satisfaction is a fantasmatic one, although this does not prevent the ego from seeking replacement love-objects. (The same sort of distinction had been drawn by Freud when he elaborated the so-called Pleasure Principle. Since this 'pleasure' refers specifically to the complete evacuation of physical energy, the attainment of neuronic inertia, it has nothing to do with the principle of life or with the vital functions. 'It is a model of death and not of life', says Laplanche (p. 58). The confusion of the two associations of the word 'pleasure' is specifically identified here: the adaptive meaning of the psychophysiological context, and the level of identical representation, which, he repeats, has nothing to do with the functioning of a living organism.)

Freud's theory of object-choice is concerned with the paths by which a person comes to fix upon another as their particular object and desire; these are reducible to two: an anaclitic object choice, which, originating in attachment to the person(s) associated with the child's care and feeding, is identified in later life as being complementary to and associated with the person who *can ensure life*; and a narcissistic object choice, which, having its source in auto-eroticism, is required to be similar, modelled on the self. Freud stresses that this is not a simple situation, since 'self' can mean 'what one once was – what one would like to be – someone who was once part of oneself, all relating to a certain image of oneself' (p. 75). But whatever the refinements, what actually happens in the case of narcissistic object choice is that libido is brought at different times to both the ego and the object. 'The narcissistic object choice is thus effected through a global transference onto another site (from the "intersubjective" to the "intrasubjective" and vice versa) of energy and of the object-form which that energy maintains' (p. 77). These two paths, states Laplanche, are the two alternatives available to every human being, irrespective of whether, in a particular case or at a particular moment, one is preferred over the other, or whether they are combined.

Laplanche continues that Freud's description of love choices leaves no doubt on one point. 'The prevalence of narcissism, if not in every libidinal relation at least in every *love* relation, in the sense of passion: that state of loss he [Freud] calls *Verliebtheit*' (p. 77).

Although we characteristically realize our 'complete object choice according to the anaclitic type', the libidinal energy expended on it is always borrowed from the ego, and is always ready to return to it, revealing its true origin in 'the marked sexual overvaluation which is doubtless derived from the child's original narcissism and thus corresponds to a transference of that narcissism to the sexual object' (Laplanche, p. 78, quoting Freud 'On Narcissism'). Thus, affirms Laplanche, 'The impassioned blindness of Eros . . . is the undeniable and definitive stigma of the narcissistic element existent, for Freud, in every love relation.'

(We must deviate from the main argument for one moment here, to foreshadow an objection to the status of the word 'every'. It has been frequently, and noted that Freud's arguments procede almost entirely from a male-oriented position – whereas both in general, and in the particular case under discussion in this study, we should have been helped by a greater attention to the effects of sexual differentiation. However, that issue must be reserved, since the general analysis is indispensible – bias notwithstanding.) Laplanche continues:

We are even obliged to rectify the statement according to which, in the state of being in love in a man the form of the object, at least, would not be modeled on the ego. For the altruism of the lover, the 'expropriation' of his own narcissism by a person in search of the love of his object, has as its precise counterpart the captivation by another 'beautiful totality': the self-sufficient women, the beautiful narcissistic animal loving only herself.

Thus at the very moment in which man – and Freud – would yield to 'objectality', he shifts dialectically into another form of narcissism.                                                      (p. 78)

It seems appropriate at this point to see how well or inadequately this theory helps to 'explain' what is going on in Anna's initial attachment to Vronsky – that is, in her choice of love-object and in his choice of her.

Vronsky is introduced to us indirectly, first by Oblonsky, and secondly by Princess Shcherbatsky. Both speakers praise him highly: according to Stiva he is 'terribly rich, handsome, and well connected . . . and at the same time a very nice chap. '. . . He'll go far, that man' (*SS* 8, p. 52). Supposed to be 'head-over heels in love with Kitty', he also satisfies all her mother's desires: 'He was very rich, clever, distinguished, with a brilliant military career before him . . . a charming man' (*SS* 8, p. 27). Princess Shcherbatsky is also convinced of the seriousness of his intentions towards Kitty. We are thus led, by Kitty and her mother, into reading into Vronsky's inclinations an anaclitic motivation. Vronsky tells Kitty that he and his brother never take an important step without consulting their mother; she is expected in Moscow any day; thus Princess Shcherbatsky concludes that Vronsky has refrained from declaring himself to Kitty until his mother's approval has been obtained; she is confident that the mother will approve the son's choice. Even Levin, who next observes him, is impressed by Vronsky's 'extremely tranquil, firm face' (*SS* 8, p. 50), and the fact that he is simple and elegant – all qualities that conform to Levin's own moral standards. By extension, Vronsky is presumed to be the same kind of respecter of familial virtues as Levin himself.

However, Vronsky's first step into the limelight is counter-corrective: he tries to initiate a game with the Ouija-board, which Prince Shcherbatsky, to Vronsky's astonishment, quietly vetoes. The old prince throughout the novel is the designated though unconscious arbiter of morality – which is to say that his views coincide with Levin's and represent Tolstoy's. We understand this from the moment when he chides Kitty for wearing *false* hair in her chignon, and from innumerable other instances, including his preference for Levin over Vronsky. Vronsky's moral basis is thus established from the outset as shaky, and at variance with the superficial impression he gives. His hand denotes this ambiguity, for it is both small and broad. (Readers of *War and Peace* have already learned that men with small white hands are suspect – emblematically Napoleon, and also Anatole Kuragin – while the broadness of hand of both Pierre and Levin is designed to connote every kind of moral reassurance.)

The doubtful quality of Vronsky's basis is firmly slanted in a negative direction when the author gets down to his own direct presentation of the character. Despite appearances Vronsky has in fact 'never known family life'. The moral connotation of his position, so diametrically opposite to Levin's, needs no spelling out, but we can also interpret this remark to indicate that the anaclitic aspect of Vronsky's development is meagre, despite his claim to take notice of his mother. In fact, the unity of this mother and son can be seen to be highly narcissistic. Within the space of two paragraphs they are both described as 'brilliant' in terms of their roles in society; we learn that the mother has had many love affairs both during her marriage and after she was widowed; and, significantly, it is here that we are told unequivocally that Vronsky has no serious intentions at all in regard to Kitty. Tolstoy is now completely unambiguous, describing Vronsky's behaviour as 'one of the *worst* [my emphasis] forms of conduct common among brilliant young men like himself. . . . He would not have believed that what gave so much and such excellent pleasure to him, and – what was more – to her, could be wrong. Still less could he have believed that he ought to marry' (*SS* 8, p. 72).

The origin of this standpoint is made perfectly clear: it stems from his contempt for family life, and his tendency to regard families and husbands as alien, hostile and ridiculous. It is interesting that Tolstoy goes to some lengths to ensure that these feelings on Vronsky's part, which I have identified as at base narcissistic, are tinged with superficial manifestations of what we can now see as the remnants of an anaclitic foundation; suggesting the vestigal memory of a nurturing care, and linked in Tolstoy's mind to a forgotten but instinctive sense of morality. Thus Vronsky is not impervious to the perception of a 'secret spiritual bond' linking him to Kitty, even though contemplation of it results in further ambiguity: the agreeable feeling that he becomes 'better' when visiting the Shcherbatsky's, and the denying shrug, 'Well, what of it? Nothing, of course. I'm fine, and so is she' (*SS* 8, p. 57).

The scene at the Moscow railway station where he and Oblonsky both await the arrival, respectively, of mother and sister, which of course anticipates Vronsky and Anna's first meeting, is also pertinent. Vronsky unconsciously ranges himself further and further on the 'negative' side, by being critical of Muscovites (for Tolstoy all cites are morally less healthy than the countryside, but Petersburg with its connotations of 'a window on the [evil] West' is a great deal more compromised than Moscow) and by taking not a lover's but a 'conqueror's', delight in hearing of Kitty's refusal of Levin. At this moment not only does Vronsky *forget* that he is supposed to be meeting his mother (whereas for Levin Kitty constantly reinforces the memories of his childhood), but Tolstoy roundly informs the reader that Vronsky does not, in the depth of his heart, either respect or love his mother. In fact mother and son simply reinforce each other's dubious values. It is not surprising that certain physical similarities are shared between Anna, Vronsky and Vronsky's mother – particularly black hair, which in the case of both women, curls. And Countess Vronsky already has a habit which Anna will only acquire much later in the novel – that of screwing up her eyes.

Thus there are connections not only between Levin's dead mother and his chosen love-object, but also between Vronsky's mother and Anna. And I am claiming that, despite the inextricable meshing of the two origins that is inevitable in any 'real' situation, Levin's attachment can be classified as more strongly anaclitic, and Vronsky's as narcissistic. I believe such a distinction to be further justified on the grounds of Vronsky's more 'split' personality, which is suggested in the ambiguities already referred to, but emerges more strongly during the development of his relationship with Anna.

Anna is seen and heard by Vronsky as it were anonymously, in the first instance. *We* have heard of her visit as the conciliating angel who alone may be able to patch up Stiva and Dolly's marriage. But Vronsky, unacquainted with the background of Anna's visit, sees leaving the train a beautiful woman whose virtues are written all over her face, bespeaking her sweetness, tenderness and compassion. In this rendition Anna incarnates Eros – the spirit of binding, the principle of the preservation of the life-force. It is written into her very mode of being, constantly described in synonyms of 'life': her eyes are bright, her step brisk, her figure full; her face is enlivened by a subdued animation and she seems to be filled by an excess of vitality. When she is outside the carriage in which Vronsky is greeting his mother, Anna's voice is heard protesting another aspect of her personality: her views are 'a woman's views' – and sociologically, in that epoch and especially in that country, 'woman' was equated with 'mother'. She and Countess Vronsky have spent much of the journey talking about their respective sons.

However, ambiguity is hardly lacking in Anna's make-up. The first hint of self-interest appears when Oblonsky tells her they hope to marry Kitty to the man Anna has just met – Count Vronsky. Anna's answer is a soft 'Yes?', which questions that likelihood, instead of corroborating and celebrating the possibility for Kitty of that very special form of binding – the formal engagement. Secondly, Dolly reacts adversely to her memory of the Karenin household – 'She had not liked their house: there seemed to be something false in the whole framework of their family life' (*SS* 8, p. 83). But Anna's charm and her efforts to reconcile Dolly to Stiva win out over these low-key reservations, and the text itself reverts to the celebration of Anna's life-enhancing qualities: her wilfully curly hair catches at her hat, she is radiant with joy and health, her figure is flexible, her face fresh, natural and animated. Her nurturing love brings Dolly's children to her lap as if drawn by a magnet; and she succeeds in binding Stiva to his wife – more or less.

The direct opposite of this binding, life-enhancing effect is described only a week later at the ball where Kitty notices the elation at play in the interaction that has suddenly sprung up between Anna and Vronsky. She is of course more sensitive to it than anyone else in the room. But what is curious is the language that is used to describe this mutual excitation. What Kitty sees in Vronsky's face she also seens distinctly in 'the mirror' of Anna's. When Anna smiles, the smile passes on to Vronsky. When she falls into thought, he too becomes pensive. It is impossible at this moment not to be reminded of Lacan's *stade du miroir*. I do not at this point wish to rehearse the whole of his argument, especially as there are now many secondary accounts of it in works of literary criticism. But Laplanche's brief allusion to it in his chapter, 'The Ego and Narcissism', from which I have already quoted extensively, indicates its relevance:

The most elaborate attempt to fill in the gap left by Freud's notion of the ego, to describe that 'new psychical action' capable of effecting the transition from autoeroticism to narcissism, was proposed by Jacques Lacan in his theory of the 'mirror stage'.

(p. 81)

Lacan himself actually says (Lacan, 1977):

The *mirror stage* is a drama whose internal thrust is precipitated from insufficiency to anticipation and which manufacturers for the subject, caught up in the lure of spatial identification, the succession of phantasies that extends from a fragmented body-image to a form of its totality that I shall call orthopedic. (p. 4)

But Laplanche points out that Freud himself had already focused on specular identification in both 'Mourning and Melancholia' and *The Ego and The Id*, and Laplanche too had already used the specular relation in his own exegesis. Perhaps we can say that what occurs in the moment of incipient passion (*Verliebtheit?*), as evidenced in the case of what Kitty sees happening between Anna and Vronsky, is that each partner experiences a sense of loss of self as the object libido is brought to the object with the accompanying exhilaration of release as if from bondage, and, simultaneously, a re-identification of self with the other. But since that state is unstable, there is always the possibility of a transferal back to the ego of psychic energy or ego libido. Further, the terms involved in this triangle (subject, ego, total object) exclude the term 'object of self-preservation', present in the account of anaclitic object-choice, which leads Laplanche to remind us that 'sexuality, in effect, leaves life out of its field of operation, borrowing only from the prototypes of its fantasies' (p. 83). But life, of course, cannot leave out sexuality. Even 'in the state of being in love, when the subject seems to yield up his whole personality in favour of an object cathexis, the ego remains the site of a permanent stasis of energy, perpetually maintaining in itself a certain minimal level' (p. 73). Thus the ego maintains what Laplanche calls the 'vital order', while sexuality as it were ignores it; yet sexuality is present in both poles – in itself, by definition, and on the side of the ego by virtue of the ego's ability to 'bind' sexuality to its own purposes.

In relation to the novel *Anna Karenina* I have tried to show that even in the beginning of their relationship, Anna and Vronsky's love has several narcissistic elements, which are suggested by the mirroring of interest reflected on both their faces at the ball, and in Kitty's subjective experience of Anna's excluding her from her affection and conversation during the mazurka. Next day it is remarked that Dolly's children, formerly adoring of their aunt, sense a withdrawal of her all-embracing love, and leave off 'playing with their aunt and loving her'. How right is Laplanche to claim that, ultimately, the various propositions advanced in regard to the ego may be summarized: 'I live for my own love, for the love of the ego' (p. 85).

Despite Bloom's testy remark that 'the Lacanians have been a kind of disaster, with their simplistic over-reliance upon the metaphor/metonymy distinction' (Bloom, 1981, p. 225), an understandable reproof in the light of his six-fold rhetoric of the psyche displayed in *A Map of Misreading* – there are good grounds for introducing these two tropes into the life-death issue, for the reasons given by Laplanche in the appendix to *Life and Death in Psychoanalysis*. Having shown that there are two distinct but mutually supportive derivations for the modern usage of the word 'trauma', Laplanche simply states that what his study reveals is in fact quite banal, 'if one considers that continuity and resemblance [the two demonstrated paths] are the two fundamental types of association posited by every theory of associationism since the classical era' (p. 131). They are also the basis of the two principal rhetorical tropes to which all others may be reduced. Ever since Jakobson (1956) underwrote these terms by showing their usefulness to his physiological and mental study of aphasics, they have generated both repudiation and extremely profitable discussion. I do not wish to enter into that argument at the moment; but I do want to draw attention to the acknowledged source of Bernheimer's highly-developed extrapolation of the affiliation of metonymy and metaphor with Eros and Thanatos, which is Laplanche's categorization of the two movements by which infantile sexuality emerges from an anaclitic 'leaning' on the self-preservative functions:

> The two essential phases here are a *metaphorization of the aim* which brings us from the ingestion of food, at the level of self-preservation, to fantasmatic incorporation and introjection as actual psychical processes, this time at the level of drive – and, on the other hand, what might be termed, after Jacques Lacan, a *metonymization of the object*, which, substituting for the milk

which is directly contiguous to it (the breast), introduces that hiatus allowing us to say without contradiction that 'finding the object is refinding it', since the rediscovered object is in fact not the lost one, but its metonym. (p. 137)

While Laplanche's point is to suggest that metaphor and metonymy can be something more than 'pure figures of style', they remain tropes nevertheless; and this fact becomes the basis for drawing in style as a factor in the investigation of passion.

Although absences are usually less striking than 'features', though certainly no less significant, any reader who takes the trouble to examine the text of *Anna Karenina* will find that Levin's language – by which I mean that used to describe and discuss him, as well as that which he uses himself – is almost entirely 'untroped'; it is straightforward (which I suppose might be considered a trope in itself, in the sense that it is always ploughing onward), plain (like himself, another trope) and literal. (He has even forgotten that he once called the Shcherbatsky girls the Three Bears.) But there are three significant exceptions to this general rule, and all occur in moments when even Levin is in a state of heightened consciousness. The first is when he lies all one summer night on a haystack, and reflects that his views of life change as quickly and as indefinably as the clouds in the dawn sky; another is just before his wedding day and after his obligatory confession, when he feels like a dog that has learnt to jump through a hoop; and the last is when he has consciously embarked upon his search for faith. In this last instance, the new scientific ideas which seem in contemporary society to have replaced conventional religious beliefs give no guidance to his anachronistic quest and Levin suddenly feels like 'a person who has exchanged a warm fur coat for a muslin garment and who, being out in the frost for the first time, becomes clearly convinced, not by arguments, but with the whole of his being, that he is as good as naked and that he must inevitably perish miserably' (*SS* 9, p. 409). Graphic though these illustrations are, they are noticeable also for their rarity.

Anna's story, by contrast, is thickly scattered with metaphors, similes, and symbols, many of which have been dissected so often by critics eager to retrieve their meaning that I prefer to give just a few examples, and go on to discuss not what they stand for (their signified) but what they signify in the ordinary sense of that word.

Christian long ago claimed that playing 'hunt the symbol' with

*Anna Karenina* was one of the least rewarding things to do with the novel though he still draws our attention to candles, books, Karenin's ears, and loose wedding rings. Much later, Elisabeth Stenbock-Fermor discusses Anna's red handbag and the fact that in the train from Moscow to Petersburg Anna takes from this handbag a book, bidding her maid light the reading-lamp, so that she can see to read (write) a new life for herself. All critics of course discuss trains, railway stations and recurrent dreams of peasants beating something with a piece of iron. But there are some metaphorical implications on which, as far as I am aware, no one has commented. For example, it is obvious that the storm which rages outside the Moscow–Petersburg train that is carrying Vronsky as well as Anna is designed to reflect the turmoil in Anna's mind and to presage the tumultuous passion to which she will succumb, as well as the lashings she will receive from outraged society. But surely the words 'All the horror of the storm appeared still more beautiful to her now' (*SS* 8, p. 125), which occur immediately after Vronsky has confessed what she wants – and does not want – to hear ('I am going in order to be where you are. I cannot do otherwise'), has a significance deeper than mere symbolism. What Anna has done is to take what is innately sacred – Nature itself – and distort it, twist it, so that it has a special meaning for her, related only to her nascent passion. To appropriate an effect of Nature, such as a storm, so that it serves rampant, illegitimate sexuality instead letting it remain an obedient offspring of the great Mother, is Tolstoy's most aggressive manoeuvre in blackening the red of Anna's love for Vronsky.

It is also a strategy which appears to define passion as simply that which is illegal, in contrast to legal married love. Of course this is not really the case, for while there are numerous examples of illegitimate love affairs in the novel, there is only one instance of sexual passion. But we do have to allow that within this novel, as Tolstoy has set it up, moral values are introduced into the two categories discussed by Freud, Laplanche, and Bernheimer. If the name of Eros is associated with binding, mother, metonymy, transitional phenomena, and (to add Jakobson and David Lodge's extrapolation) realistic prose, it also, in Tolstoy's view, denotes what is right – because in a very circular argument, it also serves the family, motherhood, Nature, and the search for the lost object. The definition of 'wrong' is that which subverts all of these – whatever can be called unnatural, unmaternal, autoerotic, narcissistic – and metaphorical. (Vronsky's 'language' is also constantly figurative – during the train journey he looks at the nervous young man opposite him 'as at a lamp pole', and on seeing Karenin come to met Anna, experiences 'such a disagreeable sensation as a man tortured by thirst might feel on reaching a spring and finding a dog, sheep, or pig in it, drinking the water and making it muddy'. Further examples are legion.

However, it is not with the rights and wrongs of passion that we are concerned here, despite the fact that Tolstoy's moral viewpoint pervades and informs every aspect of the novel. In fact, so persuasive is it that it constantly urges one to digress in that direction; but this is a tendency that must be firmly avoided, since the question of the nature of passion, and its connections with death, is difficult enough without the involvement of ethics and/or personality. Let us return to the central concern.

As everyone knows, Vronsky achieves his 'purpose in life' of drawing Anna into adultery in just under a year. The brilliant yet terrible aftermath to that act is extraordinarily instructive in our slow progression towards an understanding of passion. Vronsky stands over Anna with pale face and trembling jaw; he feels like a murderer gazing at the body he has just killed; just as the murderer throws himself on the body and cuts it into pieces and hides them so that he can profit by his murder, so does Vronsky cover Anna's face and shoulder with kisses. Anna meanwhile huddles at his feet in a paroxysm of guilt and self-loathing; within a minute she has run from his presence. In the parallel scene between Vronsky and his mare Frou-frou, whose back has just been broken in a horse-race jump, he again stands over his 'darling' (by which endearment he repeatedly addresses the mare), pale, and with trembling jaw. First, in his disappointment at being put out of the race, he kicks her in the belly (just as he had had a feeling of there being something 'frightful and revolting' after making love to Anna); then he is filled with misery, pain and distress.

The second passage clearly repeats the message of the first: that Vronsky's love is destructive. In one case he has killed 'the first period of their love'; in the second, a gentle spirited creature who seemed always to understand 'all he was feeling when looking at her'. In both cases it appears that the destruction is accidental to some unspecified but larger scheme of things; thus, while it adds a deeply sombre note to both events, it seems also to exonerate Vronsky from any blame that might be attributed to him.

Nevertheless these passages are insistent: the horse-race is not *essential* to the plot, yet it is there, and highlighted; the consummation of Anna and Vronsky's love *could* have been described in terms of joy, ecstacy and union, but in fact stands as an ominously negative moment. It is also a very brief passage, as though the author dwelt on it only with the greatest reluctance. Any attempt to probe these impressions of negativity and distaste must again involve two approaches: one can attempt a more generalized understanding of what is going on, and one can look more closely at Tolstoy. Both avenues are essential, but we shall begin with the first, which is more difficult, but perhaps less speculative. I shall also, again, be extrapolating from Laplanche's exposition of Freud's notions of aggressiveness and sadomasochism, appropriating from his text only what is relevant to the interpretation of the scenes under discussion.

In this chapter Laplanche renews his insistence on the distinction between the 'sexual' and the 'non-sexual' – a point he has already made, and clarified, by making a similar distinction between 'organ pleasure' (as in auto-eroticism) and 'function-pleasure' (as in the satisfaction of hunger). This enables him to further categorize 'sadism' as sexual (i.e. involving, consciously or unconsciously, an element of sexual excitement or enjoyment) and 'aggression' (whether self- or hetero-) as essentially non-sexual. It will be remembered that the basic notion of anaclisis, or propping, implies that sexuality (organ pleasure) emerges from non-sexual, instinctual activities – from functional pleasure. Sexuality can thus be said first, to have a marginal genesis, and second to find that genesis in a moment of 'turning round upon the self'. He states, 'Sexuality appears as a drive that can be isolated and observed at the moment at which the nonsexual activity, the vital function, becomes detached from its natural object or loses it.' For sexuality, it is the reflexive (*selbst* or auto-) moment that is constitutive: the moment of a turning back towards self, an 'autoeroticism' in which the object has been replaced by a fantasy by an object *reflected* within the subject (p. 88).

Relating the theory so far to the Anna–Vronsky story, we have something like this: Vronsky, prone through upbringing to narcissism, is attracted, as is predictable, to an apparently self-sufficient and beautiful woman (Anna's apparent 'sufficiency' being manifested in her status as wife, mother, and leader of society.) The arousal of his sexual love for Anna is not an example of 'sexuality in general'; since it cannot contribute to the *social* vital order (as distinct from the biological vital order), it must represent that 'derivative' of general sexuality which is autoerotic and narcissistic. Its aim is clearly to *master* Anna (this is made quite clear from the text) and hence it has a component of sadism, even if he does not wish, at this point, to humiliate her, or as occurred with Frou-frou, to inflict pain on her. But this kind of mastery is close to, and inherent in, these other aspects of sadism, which *in the end* will lead to destruction.

As for Anna, her love is also narcissistic, partly because she and Stiva have similarly been deprived of proper family life, having been brought up by an aunt; and partly because, given the social mores of her time, it is a dead-end love, a love with nowhere to go. This situation obtains despite her attempts to gain happiness by living with Vronsky, which does not 'work out'; and is not ameliorated even by the birth of a child – for it is a child that she is unable to love. Her love for Vronsky eventually undergoes what Freud calls a vicissitude, that is, it turns around upon the subject (herself). We will see later where this will ultimately take her, but at the moment of which we are now speaking, the aftermath of its first consummation, it has become masochistic. It is clear that the moment is for her one of great suffering; her head droops, she sobs. She feels degraded, ashamed, naked. Indeed there are all the elements of rape, although we know this has not literally been the case. What has happened, it might be suggested, is that the mutual passion of Anna and Vronsky has first become an entity in itself which assumes the properties of both sadism and masochism. This 'entity' then plays out, *simultaneously*, what Freud (and Laplanche) would normally separate into three separate steps: the exercise of power upon some other person as its object (sadism); a turning round upon the self (self-infected torment which is an intermediate stage, not yet pure masochism); and the final stage of passive masochism in which the active aim is transformed into a passive aim, which implies the search for another person as 'object'; that is, object of the drive but subject of the action (Laplanche, p. 92).

This suggestion brings us a part of the way in our attempt to understand passion, having demonstrated from the case of Anna and Vronsky that it is a love with an element of destructiveness which can be both aggressive and self-reflexive (or sadistic and masochistic). But if we go back to Freud to remind ourselves that 'what is repressed' is never the actual memory of an event or situation, but the 'fantasy deriving from it or subtending it', we shall be in a better position to see where Tolstoy himself comes in.

There are many popular accounts of Tolstoy's married life, the most well-known probably being that of Troyat, whose extensive use of proper primary sources such as diaries and letters, embellished by a novelettish *insouciance* which allows him apparent *clairvoyance* into the minds of his characters, has already been noted. It is, I believe, largely due to his interpretation that the picture has been universalized of Sonya the martyr/harridan from whom Tolstoy was finally forced to flee, at the faintly ridiculous age of 82. Troyat's account is not free from distortion yet it is not without truth either, as the claims of both parties verify.

We may deduce that Tolstoy was at first haunted by a residual guilt at finally daring to replace the mother with the wife from a letter of 28 September 1862 (a few days after the wedding), which reads, 'I lived for thirty-four years without knowing it was possible to love so much and be so happy . . . I keep feeling as though I had stolen some undeserved, illegal happiness that was not meant for me.' But that guilt was for some time repressed by the strategy of refusing to acknowledge Sonya's status as rival. In his diary he is still referring to Sonya in terms which insist on her childishness or youth – 'I love her when, a little girl in a yellow dress, she lifts her jaw and sticks her tongue out at me. I love to see her head thrown back, her face solemn and frightened, her passionate child's face . . .' (*Diary* of 5 January 1863). Sonya foreshadows Kitty in being developmentally arrested (in Tolstoy's mind) at the moment of betrothal, and this condition lasts until she becomes a biological mother. But unlike Levin, Tolstoy exults in a kind of liberation resulting from the social legitimizing of his sexual activity. The censor found fit to excise from the above quotation the continuation of the sentence beginning 'I love her when . . . '. In sad contrast, Sonya's diary entries (Sonya Tolstoy, 1985) tell of an obsessional, dependant relationship, essentially emotional rather than sensual. 'All this commerce of the flesh is repellent' (8 October 1862). And, 'The physical side of love is very important for him. It's terrible; for me it's quite the opposite' (29 April 1863).

The point here is not the banal and perhaps impertinent retelling of the intimacies of the Tolstoy's tormented married life, but the fact that these diary entries record in jabbing pen-strokes everything that each felt, but, Levin-like, could not *say* to the other;

they play out with a torturous mutual hypersensitivity what Bakhtin was to characterize as the word with a 'sideways glance', here translated into so acute an awareness of the reader-over-the-shoulder that the 'private' outpourings end by being written deliberately for the other's eyes. It was a household in which the written word was, *pace* Derrida, privileged over the oral.

However, with dramatic suddenness, in 1864, Tolstoy's entries begin to fall off, and in 1865 they are terminated. The silence lasts 13 years – spanning the period of the writing of *War and Peace* and *Anna Karenina*. And what Tolstoy now writes, with numerous crossings-out and insertions, Sonya copies, gaining from this first-hand contact with her husband's trains of thought a sense of union and intimacy she apparently failed to find in sexual intercourse. It is even productive: sending off a package of transcribed pages to Tolstoy who was researching in a Moscow library, Sonya writes: 'I feel that this is your child and consequently my child and, as I send off this package of paper to Moscow, I feel I am abandoning a baby to the elements' (Letter of 14 November). This was in 1863, during the writing of *War and Peace*, a period of relative domestic calm, with the young Natasha Rostov modelled on Sonya's younger sister Tanya, and the epilogue scenes of Kinder and Kueche, all romanticism repudiated, on Tolstoy's idealized vision of unassailable domesticity. It has already been pointed out that this particular ideal is too idiosyncratic to appeal to the modern reader. Yet it is probably important to note that the epilogue to *War and Peace* allowed Tolstoy to write of how he wished married life to be without turning these thoughts into diary-recriminations against Sonya. And since *Anna Karenina* was also written before the resumption of the diary, it is fair to assume that it too was used to give projected form to Tolstoy's conscious and unconscious reactions to the ongoing vicissitudes of his own personal and marital situation. With only Tolstoy's letters (until 1881 when the diary was resumed) and Sonya's diaries to draw on, retrospective interpretation must admit to being largely conjectural, but a picture emerges of growing estrangement between the two. Fewer quarrels, but also few joyful reunions. When she was without any work of her husband's to copy, Sonya felt redundant; this diary entry is typical:

The autumn has brought on my usual depression. I sit here in

silence, stiching away at my rug, or reading. I feel cold, dull and indifferent to everything – and ahead lies nothing but darkness.
(19 November 1878)

In general Sonya felt unloved, while Tolstoy still protested an enduring devotion which he tended to express by being wherever she was not. When she was in the house they had brought in Moscow, he would either return to Yasnaya Polyana, or work all day in rented rooms in the house next door, prompting Sonya to write, 'Our two lives have separated. Is this still a life at all?' (3 February 1882) No matter how much Tolstoy reiterated that he loved her, and that her love was essential to him, Sonya did not experience his need of her, and a few months afterwards was still writing in the same vein:

I pray for death for I cannot survive without his love. I knew this the moment his love for me died. I love him as him as I loved him twenty years ago. My love oppresses me and irritates him. He is filled with his Christian notions of self-perfection, and I envy him.                                        (26 August 1882)

By 1884, when Sonya to her great humiliation and despair was pregnant for the twelfth time, Tolstoy was noting in his diary dissatisfaction with all his children and extreme fretfulness with family life. Of Sonya he wrote, 'Poor thing, how she hates me! God, help me! A cross would oppress me and tear me apart. But this twisting of my heart is awful, not just painful and sad, but difficult. . . . Help me!' (3 May) And two days later: 'I dreamt that my wife loves me. How relieved I was, and how simple everything became. But it's nothing like the reality. And that is what is destroying my life. I cannot even try to write. It would be good to die . . . '. Even the delivery of the last child produced no change: 'What should be the greatest joy and happiness for the family was like something pointless and painful . . . '. Yet a sexual life continued: 'She tried to seduce me with her body. I wanted to resist but felt I could not, under the present circumstances. And living with a woman who is alien to your soul – in other words with her – is quite disgusting. Until the day I die she will be a millstone around my neck and the necks of my children' (18 June 1884). The attempted resumption of sexual intercourse a month after the childbirth provoked physical complications and the midwife had to ban intercourse for a month 'at least'. Separation improved their relations as it always did, but further quarrels led to the final announcement at the end of a long, recriminatory and bitter letter from Tolstoy to Sonya, that, 'A fight to the finish has begun between us . . . .'.

The above account, compressed thought it is, is enough to show that Levin could only represent one strand of the Tolstoyan complex – a strand that Tolstoy liked to bring to the surface and let the lamp shine on. The underside contained threads that he cared less to examine by the light of day – the product of a personality who could father thirteen children with a reluctant wife yet, when his eldest son became engaged, sob with joy 'for a long time' at the young man's admission that he was still a virgin (Ilya was 22). By the time he was an old man this position had become rooted in his attitudes, and when called upon to give advice on matters of sex, love and marriage he had only this to say: 'Whatever the circumstances may be you will find only one answer: Chastity! How can anyone be afraid of chastity?' (Letter of 17 November 1907). To another correspondent he wrote a few months later, 'Chastity is an ideal for which we must strive, always and in all cases' (17 March 1908). And also in the same year:

> As to sexual matters, there has always been and there will always be, one ideal and only one – chastity. It is natural for men to slave after this ideal, seeing that the opposite is natural to the beasts. Since, however, it is hard for young people to attain perfect chastity, the next best thing is marriage, in which man and wife remain faithful to one another for the procreation and rearing of children, which is the only justification for the married state.

This is the sublimation of the self-disgust he felt at being unable to control his own body's physical desire for his wife, even when he was out of love and sympathy with her, unwilling to add to the ever-increasing number of children, and somewhat ridiculous because of his public stand on chastity and restraint.

Thus his first intention in regard to the creation of his heroine Anna, while expressly stated as being to make her pitiable rather than guilty, is also executed with some opprobrium. In the first drafts, Anna is unattractive, with a narrow, low forehead, and a short turned-up nose. Her dress is bold and provocative, her voice loud. Her vulgararity would seem to indicate a wish on Tolstoy's part to persuade himself and his readers that sexuality, like this personification of it, is ugly and demeaning. In the same early draft Karenin is depicted as sensitive, generous, and cultivated and not responsible for any contributing factor to his wife's blatant flirta- tiousness, while Vronsky is similarly portrayed as a victim rather than seducer, unwillingly decoyed from his firm and honourable intention of marrying Kitty into a shameful affair with a married woman.

The changes in all three main characters stem from the initial change in Tolstoy's conception of Anna. As she metamorphoses into the brilliant, beautiful and essentially good woman who comes to town to heal the breach between her brother and sister- in-law, Karenin in particular acquires the famously unappealing characteristics which are summed up in the sticking-out ears and cracking finger-joints. Similarly, Vronsky's treatment reveals in- creasing harshness, his underlying characteristics of venality and shallowness never obscured except to Anna.

It seems impossible not to agree with all those critics who, like Troyat and Christian, have interpreted these changes as an exam- ple of what J. Hillis Miller calls 'That strange phenomenon in which a male author invents a female protagonist and then falls in love with her, so to speak, pities her, suffers with her, takes her to his bosom, as Hardy did in the case of Tess, and Trollope in regard to Lily Dale' (Miller, 1982, p. 119).

So much is commonplace. What is interesting is to see what Tolstoy does with a heroine with whom he has fallen in love (as the critics concede) but whom he loves with what must be called a *passionate* love, since what he loves in Anna is also his own sexuality. Inherent in this must be a significant element of rep- ressed narcissism, expressed initially by an inversion, then later by blatant delight. Despite the image every reader must carry in his or her head of Anna's wondrous charm and total appeal at the beginning of the book – qualities which can still captivate Levin long after her deterioration has begun – we should note that from the start Kitty detects another quality in Anna which she categor- izes as 'diabolical' and 'cruel'. Naturally Kitty is hypersensitive to Anna's charms, since she has at just this point registered that Vronsky's sudden attraction to Anna has rendered him indifferent to the younger girl. Kitty can in fact be said to be rehearsing those reactions of 'fear' and 'despair' which Tolstoy himself suffered when in the grip of the overt physical lust which many women, but most successfully his wife, could arouse in him, forcing him to break his 'resolutions'. It is not surprising that, with that battle lost, Kitty fades into the background for several chapters, leaving Anna to become both the subject and object of her creator's sexuality. Both Anna and what she stands for are simultaneously repellant and enthralling to Tolstoy.

The hidden reasons for this lie in the very nature of passion, for the 'pleasure' that is associated with the satisfaction of sexual desire is automatically problematized the minute one recalls that sexuality itself is split between that which is associated with the continuance of the vital order, and that which is associated with narcissism, and its concomitants, sadism and masochism. In the latter two cases there is, alongside pleasure, an element of pain, suffering, or 'unpleasure' which seems to invite the 'persistently disquieting equation pleasure = unpleasure' (Laplanche, p. 104). 'The subject is masochistic only insofar as he derives enjoyment *precisely there where* he suffers.' This is already a paradox. Yet Freud, claims Laplanche, always considered *the pleasure of causing suffering* as more *enigmatic* and requiring a more complex explanation than *the pleasure of suffering*: two paradoxes!

Laplanche attempts to unravel the puzzle of an equation with 'unknowns' – or rather 'not-completely-understoods' – on *both* sides, by positing first of all a negative side (pain, suffering and unpleasure), and a positive side which is less simple. The term 'pleasure' is capable of being broken down into two alternatives, for which he uses the terms 'satisfaction' to denote the 'appeasement linked to a reduction of tension', and which is thus situated within the vital register; and 'enjoyment' or *'jouissance'* (he falls back on the French word that Barthes was to take up) which he interprets as frenetic pleasure, including lust. Laplanche stresses that 'satisfaction' and 'enjoyment' are *in opposition* to each other so that 'positive = negative only if the "positive" is not quite a positive and the "negative" not quite a negative'. This leads Laplanche by a somewhat Derridean manoeuvre to locate 'pleasure' at either pole of a fundamental opposition: 'Either it is situated in opposition to functional satisfaction . . . (what Freud called organ pleasure) or it is opposed to frenetic 'enjoyment' [*jouissance*] (and in that case pleasure would be situated on the side of constancy and homeostasis)' (p. 105). It is at the level of 'enjoyment' (which includes lust) that primary masochism is located – the 'lust for and/or the

enjoyment of pain'. Laplanche continues, 'It is intimately connected with the notion of fantasy as an alien internal entity and
with the drive of an internal attack, so that the paradox of masochism, far from deserving to be circumscribed as a specific "perver-
sion" should be generalized, linked as it is to the *essentially traumatic
nature of human sexuality'* (Laplanche's emphasis).

In order to understand what lies behind that remark we must
now undertake what was skirted around in Chapter 1, that is, a
more detailed follow-through of Freud's concept of the death
drive. Once again Laplanche is our guide as he recoups from
Freud's poetic and speculative text the three recurring elements
whose energy 'serves to propel the concept of the death drive'
(p. 112).

The first is priority of the reflective phase, manifest in the theory
of autoeroticism, but implicit also in the 'presupposition' of primary narcissism, which Laplanche describes as a state which is
totally closed in on itself, and present both at the level of self-
preservation and at the level of sexuality, where it can be self-
aggressive (masochistic) or heteroaggressive (sadistic).

The second element is the priority of zero over constancy, that
is, the priority of the tendency to reduce or remove excitation over
the tendency to keep it constant. The former is a principle of
discharge of free energy, by the shortest path; the latter a principle
of the binding of a quantity of energy 'sufficient to meet the
demands for specific action'. The 'pleasure principle', associated
normally with the discharge of energy, can only be situated on the
side of constancy insofar as it undergoes a displacement as modifi-
cation into the reality principle, constancy being introduced
as an adaptation of the principle of inertia on account of 'the
necessity of life'. Only in its most radical form, its 'beyond', does it
reassert the priority of the tendency towards absolute zero, or the
death drive.

The third aspect of the death drive is also the strangest. For,
contrary as it may sound, Freud insists on the *'necessity of inscribing
the two preceding priorities (the priority of the self-phase, the priority of
zero) within the domain of the vital'* (p. 117). The biological domain, in
other words, is 'infested' by the immanence of a tendency to zero.
This is because the ego accumulates to itself both the power of
self-preservation (Eros) *and* the power of sexuality, which is always
inhabited by narcissism. Eros seeks to maintain, preserve and
augment the cohesion and 'synthetic' tendency of living beings; on

the other hand, sexuality is essentially hostile to binding, it is a principle of unbinding. Sexuality can only be rendered bindable through the intervention of the ego; thus *with* Eros there appears the *'bound and binding'* form of sexuality, the form of sexuality that will henceforth sustain life and yield satisfaction. But there is also a sexuality which is anti-life, which is *jouissance*, that is, negative and operating through the repetition compulsion. In this sense, sexuality must be seen as subversive of life, as a death drive; but the death-drive does not possess its own energy, it uses that of sexuality – libido. The death drive uses, is constitutive of, libidinal circulation. The pleasure principle serves the death instincts.

To see the way all this is put in *Anna Karenina* is only an exercise of application. The chiasmus or crossing-over is dramatized when Anna's *jouissance* is temporarily converted to the uses of the life principle by the conception of Ani – the daughter fathered by Vronsky – and, in reverse, in the conflict she experiences in regard to Seriozha, her son by Karenin, conceived in an act which must have been empty of pleasure for her, yet 'erotic' in the sense of life-affirming.

Because of her alienated relations with Karenin, and in the abence of any sexual excitation before the appearance of Vronsky, Anna has for most of her adult life played the 'partly sincere but greatly exaggerated role of a mother living for her son', and she attempts to hold on to this role even after the conception of Vronsky's child. The identification between Anna and Seriozha seems almost parodic in the scene where she determines to put her son before both Alexei's, for in this episode Seriozha, dressed all in white, is like Anna – outwardly impeccable but inwardly corrupt, being in disgrace with his governess for eating forbidden fruit. But the apple to which his mother succumbs proves a greater influence in her life than her much-vaunted and 'partly sincere' love for her son. Encouraged by Vronsky, who has no grasp at all of maternal bonds, Anna abandons her first- born and thus loses all connection with the love-object who generates in her the kind of love that nurtures and sustains. The interview in which she and Vronsky decide on this plan of action is innately and overtly passionate:

> Without thinking or noticing whether there was anyone else in the room or not, he embraced her and began to cover her face, hands, and neck with kisses. Anna had prepared herself for this meeting and had thought what she would say to him, but she

had no time to say any of it. She was seized by his passion. She wished to calm him, to calm herself, but if was too late. His feeling communicated itself to her. Her lips trembled so that for a long time she could not speak. . . . A month later Karenin and his son were left alone in the house, and Anna went abroad with Vronsky – not only without obtaining a divorce, but having decisively rejected it.                              (*SS* 8, pp. 508–9)

Technically, though not dramatically, this is the weakest point in the novel, for Tolstoy has not succeeded in showing any convincing reason why Anna should refuse a divorce. The attributed motive is Anna's wish not to accept Karenin's generosity; the real intention is of course that author and reader should both be enabled to follow the path of passion to its very end, to find out, vicariously, 'what happens' with a drive as yet not properly identified, but recognized in a way that must, inevitably, be described as the uncanny return of the repressed.

What happens in regard to her maternal love is of course that it dries up, sacrificed to her narcissism. Seriozha whom she had loved is no longer available to her, nor she to him; but Ani through no overt cause, she simply does not love. 'Everything about this little girl was sweet but for some reason she did not tug at the heart' (*SS* 9, p. 725). The later picture of Anna's unnatural motherhood is put together through Dolly's acute observation of the nursery that houses little Ani, which is furnished with the latest children's apparatus ordered from England by Vronsky, staffed by a slovenly Russian wet-nurse and an unpleasant, 'impure'-looking head-nurse, and rarely visited by a mother who does not even know that her child has two new teeth. Anna's use of birth-control, shocking to the naive Dolly, is the final gesture in her deliberate rejection of 'functional' love; thereafter Ani is merely a weapon in the ploys she uses to make Vronsky return home.

Anna's relationship with her children is thus symptomatic of the changes in her psychic state brought about by the birth and progress of her love for Vronsky. Until now, it has been argued, the narcissistic element that is part of any love is merely stronger than usual in Anna and Vronsky, this situation being attributable to their unfamilial childhoods. Now, as their passion progresses, despite its intensity and the havoc it causes in several lives, it is shown to be unsustainable because it is always destructive of the ego the harbours it. It fails Anna, it fails *in* Vronsky, the preposition expressing a good deal of the difference between two forms of annihilation.

In Vronsky it is fairly simple. We read that 'in spite of the complete fulfilment of what he had so long desired, [he] was not completely happy. He soon felt that the realization of his longing had given him only one grain of the mountain of bliss he had anticipated' (*SS* 8, p. 39). Tolstoy comments that this realization demonstrates to Vronsky 'the eternal error men make by imagining that happiness consists in the gratification of their wishes. . . . Soon he felt that there was arising in his soul a desire for desire – boredom'. While Tolstoy uses this new-found knowledge on Vronsky's part to introduce a new activity (painting) for his character, and hence a disgression on the nature of art as expressed in painting for the author, we should see in it a little more than the truism it also is. Laplanche (p. 106) reminds us that Freud wrote in 'The Economic Problem in Masochism', 'The subject derives enjoyment from [the] excitation', and comments that this statement situates Freud in the ancient line of thought which has always claimed that man prefers the hunt to the capture (or perhaps that to travel hopefully is better than to arrive). But Freud also wrote, in the *Three Essays* of 1905, that the concepts of 'sexual excitation' and 'satisfaction' can to a great extent be used 'without distinction'. Laplanche's linking of the two statements leads him to remark that while the inherent satisfaction that can almost be equated with excitation means in the first instance that the hunt entails the fantasy of the capture, we must realize that the fantasy is not just the simple reflection of the capture, but is derived from it through a complex series of displacements.

This seems to imply that the *sense* of the hunt is as it were larger than any one object can be. The fantasies that throng in Vronsky's mind embrace more than just Anna, though naturally she becomes the ideational representative of what he is himself unable to express. This explains Vronsky's unsuccessful and somewhat half-hearted suicide-attempt which occurs after Anna's illness and near-death. Because at that moment Karenin has been briefly magnanimous, because the drama of the bedside has made Vronsky feel no longer like a hunter gleefully nearing his prey, but rather like an unworthy and beaten opponent for whom the goal is decisively out of reach, he can no longer sustain the fantasy of capture. Without it life no longer seems worthwhile and he attempts to shoot himself. The fact that he *should* have been able to bring it off – he is after all a career soldier – indicates not only that his urge to kill himself is half-hearted, but also that Anna is not the whole object of his life, though his fantasies can make it seem so. And the period when he does have her to himself, night and day, in Italy, is precisely the time when the apparent satisfaction of desire is also seen to be only a part of that greater desire which Lacan would tell us is by definition unappeasable. Yet we should note that Freud had already remarked in his essay, 'The Psychology of Love' Part 2 (*PF 7*), 'We must reckon with the possibility that something in the nature of the sexual instinct itself is unfavourable to realization of complete satisfaction' (p. 258).

In the novel there is of course a social situation which accentuates Vronsky's difficulties in filling in sixteen hours a day – somehow. He has left the army, is in a foreign country, and is completely cut off from previous activities, both social and professional. These tribulations are real enough, but Vronsky's reactions are a salutary reminder of the fact that the superficial social behaviour of the characters of fiction masks – and betrays – motivations at once both deeper and more universal than is obvious. Vronsky, who epitomizes the more lustful aspect of passion, also shows the limitations of *jouissance*, whose apparent satisfaction is chimeral, since *jouissance* partakes of sexuality, and the sexuality that is associated with *jouissance* is based in fantasy.

This insistence upon the fantastic element in sexual enjoyment has a by-product, in that it unwittingly repudiates de Rougement's assumption that all love is but a death-wish in disguise. For, although the word 'passion' is used of Vronsky's feeling for Anna, we now understand that passion comprises both destruction and fantasy, the latter being frequently expressed as lust – an effect of sexuality that is caught up with the hunt and its fantastic satisfactions, but does not of itself seek death. This is of course partly due to the ambiguity of the word 'hunt', which as J. M. Holquist has shown in his article on the mythologisations in *Crime and Punishment* (Holquist, 1974), succeeds in reconciling the life–death opposition by generating myths of hunter–warriors who ensure the life of the tribe precisely by killing. Thus when Vronsky is 'on the hunt' he feels vital, alive; when the hunt seems abortive he wants to kill himself. We seem to have come back to a rephrasing of Freud, for what we want to say here is that it is the hunting-quest for death which makes life worthwhile.

Why then is Anna's fate, and the feelings we have about her, so different from everything to do with her partner in passion? The contrast with Vronsky is greatest during the Italian episode where Anna, having recovered from illness, and achieved her goal of living with her lover, regains the right to all the terms of her first appearance in the novel. Once again she is energetic, vital and full of the joy of *life*. She glories, gratefully and humbly, in the sacrifice made for her sake that Vronsky's diminution of activities has required of him. She gladly accepts what are even, for her also, the constraints of being loved; even though 'The intensity of his attention to her, the atmosphere of solicitude with which he surrounded her, weighed on her at times . . .' (*SS* 9, p. 39).

In Italy then Vronsky experiences a sense of reduction in his life, Anna a sense of expansion and fulfilment in hers. But while her feelings are, like his, based in the sexuality of *jouissance*, Lacan's understanding of that word seems more apt for Anna than does Freud's 'In his [Lacan's] account', claims Jacqueline Rose in *Feminine Sexuality* (Mitchell and Rose, 1985), 'The drive [of sexuality] is something in the nature of an appeal, or searching out, which always goes beyond the actual relationship on which it turns. . . . The drive touches on an area of excess (it is "too much")' (p. 34).

Thus, whereas Vronsky begins to search for the 'extra' that is missing in the *beyond* that lies outside his relationship to Anna, she looks for it only within, and associates the object of her search, mistakenly, with the person and 'love' of Vronsky. That both quests are in Lacan's perception always already doomed to frustration goes without saying; but the interest of the novel still lies with the working out of two very different ways of discovering the essential lack that activates desire.

All readers of the novel know that Anna's fears that Vronsky has suddenly ceased to love her are groundless. While he may seek diversion in politicking, or in the company of male friends such as Yashvin; and while he may feel constricted, even suffocated by Anna's excessive need for his company, Vronsky has no thought of being unfaithful to her, nor even of ceasing to love her. Yet Anna invents this possibility and dwells on it more and more obsessively. Tolstoy does not try to explain it, but he does show it as unwarranted: 'Suddenly a strange idea crossed her mind: what if he ceased to love her?' He shows Anna irrationally laying the blame for this imaginary motivation on quite independent courses of action, such as their occupying separate apartments when return from Italy to Petersburg – a measure Vronsky believes to be a social requirement once they are back in their own *milieu*.

One might attribute the unfounded insecurity on Anna's part to two alternate sources; but perhaps 'alternate' is not the right word. For they can both be (and probably are) co-existent. On the one hand, one might say that since Anna's passion has a strong underlying element of narcissism, she dreads the loss of Vronsky's love because she has already ceased to love and respect herself. This theory is supportable from the text, for just prior to her final formulation of the thought that Vronsky's love might have dried up, she has explicitly turned away from the baby Ani, and frightened herself by her thoughtless but unconsciously symbolic act when she uses a photograph of Vronsky to push her son Seriozha's photograph out of her album. In fact Vronsky's 'regard' for her *has* to some extent diminished, or at least it does so temporarily when she flaunts convention by going to the Opera and is publicly snubbed; in their interview after that disastrous evening Anna becomes shrewishly accusatory and spiteful, until comforted by Vronsky's harrassed assurances of continuing love. But by the time they are living in the Russian countryside, such 'scenes' have become the 'usual thing' – with Anna recognizing that they are caused by the humiliation of her utter dependence on her lover's presence and protestations of devotion. Her possessiveness appalls her, but not even shame can alter her conduct. Possessiveness turns to jealousy, jealousy to the desire for revenge; she is displayed to us as manipulative, counter-suggestive, untruthful and finally even vulgar, as she sticks her little finger out while holding a coffee-cup.

Yet by now Anna has lost the capacity to judge herself. She ceases to reproach herself and lays the entire blame – both real and imagined – on Vronsky. 'All the cruellest words that a coarse man could say he, in her imagination, said to her, and she did not forgive him for them, as though he had really said them' (*SS* 8, p. 368). It no longer makes sense to accuse her of narcissism because self-hatred has by now destroyed self. Self now only exists when it is recognized that no recognising response seems adequate or even, in Anna's case, visible. Despite the Hegelian formulation, we are talking about a Lacanian Demand, which 'constitutes the Other as already possessing the "privelege" of satisfying needs, that is, the power to deprive them of the one thing by which they are satisfied. But as Lacan has already claimed that it is in the nature of the Other to be situated *"some way short* of any needs which it might gratify", the privilege of the Other "thus sketches out the radical form of the gift of something which it does not have, namely, what is called its love"' (Mitchell and Rose, p. 80).

This explanation is helpful, but it does not take us as far as the alternative formulation of the problem, for what it does is to describe a kind of existential impasse which is a statement not just about a particular case, but about the human condition. We are all subject to it, if Lacan is right, but we do not all throw ourselves under trains.

It is my belief that the most fruitful way of arriving at an explanation of what is going on in Anna's mind and being during the latter part of her story is suggested by Harold Bloom, following (appropriately) Lionel Trilling in the collection of essays edited by Perry Meisel under the title *Freud: a Collection of Critical Essays* (1981). Both these commentators, although Bloom's account is the more developed, focus on that strand of the complex Freudian text which is concerned with the repetition compulsion; both take that concept further than do the considerations of textual repetitions produced by Brooks and Miller. If Trilling can see the *fort-da* game as an attempt to promote the fear of absence in order to learn to cope with or master it, Bloom interprets it as an attempt 'to master a stimulus retroactively by first developing the anxiety' (Bloom, p. 216). Anna invents Vronsky's failure of love in order to create and develop, through anxiety, the effort to control that very fear. Hers is an anxiety that precedes both threat and event. But anxiety motivates also the repression of the force that calls it into existence; thus Anna persists in calling forth her anxiety – that is, in provoking Vronsky to anger or irritation, which she then experiences as the cessation of his love. Thus, for her, Vronsky *has* ceased to love her, and at these moments she feels she has nothing left to live for. Although, in the narrative, they several times make up after their quarrels and continue to live together, the compulsion to repeat grows stronger as Anna seeks vainly to control what cannot be controlled, since her very anxiety creates what it pretends to allay. 'Defence produces what it defends against by presuming it', as Meisel summarises in his introduction to the collected essays (p. 33).

Bloom speaks later in his article of 'an anxiety narcissistically intoxicated with itself, an anxiety determined to go on being anxious, a drive towards destruction, in love with the image of self-destruction', and relates this 'blocking-agent' to the romantic poets (p. 228). But that *Anna Karenina* is a novel of persuasive realism (as well as of tragic irony), is precisely what I have tried to show, in relating the events of the plot to a more masterful theory of the workings of the human psyche.

Anna persistently tells herself that Vronsky no longer loves her – which the reader knows to be an unfair accusation – and, towards the end, just as insistently castigates Vronsky for it, even though he never fails to reassure her that such is not the case. These scenes are peculiarly painful to read precisely because Anna's accusations are manifestly untrue; yet they speak a latent truth in terms of Anna's experience of her own situation. She personalizes the universal in a radical and acute form by finally announcing:

> I want love and it is lacking. So everything's finished. It has to be.

Suddenly she understands 'what [is] in her soul' – the thought that will solve everything. The thought is of course that of her own death; but what lends this final outcome its inestimable sadness in the end defies universalisations, whether they be the myth of the death wish as promoted by de Rougemont, or the pessimistic Lacanian perception of the human condition. The 'case' of Anna Arkadevna Karenin, who threw herself under a train, effectively transcends theory precisely because it so graphically individual-izes. Yet it is only through a theoretical attempt to unravel the nature of passion that we can come to any understanding of *why* she came to such a dead end. If the lesson of this chapter has largely been that sexuality shuttles back and forth, 'infesting' both life and death, we can also say that literature is equally mercurial as it too flirts with both theory and example, with the general and with the particular. Can it too not tell whether it is a hedgehog or a fox?

We have been trying to gain some undertaining on the nature of passion by looking at it in the light not of mythology (a task already undertaken by de Rougemont) but of psychoanalysis – basically Freudian psychoanalysis, but with a great reliance on one particular commentator, and one central essay – Laplanche's pre-sentation of *Beyond the Pleasure Principle*. Proceeding from the idea, shared by both de Rougemont and Freud, that passion thrives on obstacle, it seemed that plots are precipitated into action or life by the excitement of an erotic impulse, and avoid closure (the end) by maintaining a series of obstacles to the too early fulfilment of the erotic desire. The life of a particular novel depends on the maintenance of some level of sexual energy which must not be discharged prematurely. The question of whether a death instinct lurks, invisible, beneath the play of plot, inevitably drawing it towards its own extinction, was raised in relation to the attempts of various authors to come to terms with the repetition principle postulated by Freud as imperceptible except when tinged with sexuality. This seemed to make sexuality serve both the life and the death instincts, as does the pleasure principle itself – a model of death (since it demands the evaluation of psychic energy) which apparently only *happens* to produce life.

The hypothesized double nature of sexuality is substantiated by Freud's account of its initial production in the human infant: it is born of an autoerotic reversal of the vital processes, but at the same time appears to be implanted from the parental universe, in that it accepts a handling-on of the life force (and will of course be necessary to the perpetuation of that universal). As the child turns away from anaclitic or 'function-love' (i.e. love associated with the maternal life-giving figure) and back towards narcissistic or autoerotic love, the latter seems to become a not altogether adequate substitute for the former, as does every future replacement love-object that may be encountered in later life. There is a narcissistic element in every choice of a love-object, even when it is realized according to the anaclitic model.

This point was 'tried out' in application to the personal histories of Levin, Vronsky, and Anna; the textual evidence corroborated the categorisation of Levin's attachment to Kitty as more strongly anaclitic, and Vronsky's to Anna as narcissistic; Anna, who appears initially to be on the side of Eros (of binding, of maternal love etc.) displays more and more narcissistic tendencies as the novel proceeds. And these claims are supported by an examination of the rhetoric associated with the same three characters. Levin's language (both that which he uses and that which is used of him) is basically untroped, while Anna and Vronsky are persistently figural, subscribing to the Jakobson–Laplanche–Bernheimer belief that metaphor is associated with substitution, fantasy and death.

The consummation of Anna and Vronsky's love is also seen as an event of great significance to the understanding of passion, because of its demonstrable elements of sadism on Vronsky's part and masochism on Anna's, which now appear to be its constitutive elements.

However, Tolstoy himself comes into the argument at this point, because of the evidence supporting the notion that he fell in love with his own heroine. In doing so he experienced that split between fascination and repulsion, between 'function-love' and 'organ-love', or anaclisis and narcissicism, and inevitably also experienced in regard to this last the qualities of pain and unpleasure associated with its sado- and masochistic elements.

Pleasure breaks down into two possibilities – the satisfaction associated with a reduction of tension (which is situated within the vital register); and enjoyment (frenetic pleasure, lust). Satisfaction and enjoyment are in opposition to each other, enjoyment comprehending primary masochism – the lust for and enjoyment of pain – and linked with what Laplanche has called, after Freud, the 'essentially traumatic nature of human sexuality'.

This statement provides a further clear link with the death drive itself, if death is the ultimate pain. Laplanche reminds us that Freud insisted both on the priority of the self-reflective phase, and on the priority of the tendency to reduce or remove excitation by the discharge of energy. Yet he further insists on inserting both these priorities within the domain of the vital. The biological domain is 'infested' with the tendency to zero because the ego accumulates to itself both the power of self-preservation and the power of sexuality, which is always inhabited by narcissism. Sexuality is both life-preserving, and self-destructive (a death-drive); the death-drive is a drive without energy of its own, having to use that of sexuality. It is thus that sexuality serves both the life and the death instincts. In the case of Anna the paradox is expressed symbolically in that her maternal love for Seriozha is swallowed up by her narcissistic passion for Vronsky, which also stifles any potential love she might bear for Ani. However it is precisely the narcissistic quality of passion that makes it unsustainable – in Vronsky because the 'capture' of Anna does not preclude fantasies which exceed satisfaction; and in Anna because she centres *all* desire on Vronsky, not understanding that desire is by nature incapable of complete satisfaction. She invents Vronsky's failure of love in order to create and develop, through anxiety, the effort to control that very fear.

# 5
# Executing a Figure

The attempt of Chapter 4 to explore the nature of passion and its relation to the so-called death-wish was based on a psychoanalytic reading of the novel, with Anna the principal object of the analysis. But proceeding from the belief of several critics that Tolstoy 'fell in love' with his own heroine, we should now turn from the opaque depths of his unacknowledged subconscious to Tolstoy's social construction in the 'real' world and his open engagement with the famous 'woman question'.

The main sources regarding Tolstoy's development and social-isation as a young male aristocrat are naturally much the same as those already referred to in the discussion of his psychological formation: his semi-autobiographical writings, his own diaries and letters, and those of his wife. There are also several biographies and innumerable works of criticism and historical background; and there remain, of course, on the open market, whatever attitudes that can be justifiably gleaned from the works of fiction. In other words, there is no shortage of either primary or secondary material surrounding almost any issue that Tolstoy chose to take up – indeed, there is no shortage of issues either. As a highly influential writer of his time, Tolstoy's trenchant views on the social and spiritual role of women have been paraded many times over, and sufficiently corroborate each other for us to be able to accept, without quoting every available chapter and verse, that at the time of writing *Anna Karenina* Tolstoy was unquestionably ranged with the conservatives. The question of the rights of women had al-ready confronted him in the fifties, having been carried to Russia in the novels of George Sand, and in socio-philosophical writings such as Proudhon's *De la justice dans la révolution dans l'église* and Michelet's *De l'amour*. Both these treatises appeared in 1858 in the defence of unconventional marriage. (It should be noted that despite her reputation George Sand advocated freedom of female choice in regard to strictly monogamous relationships; in cases where legal marriage was not a possible solution she depicted faithful couples living exemplary lives in far-away places where they would not affront the society from which they had fled. However, many Russian readers saw only her advocacy of freedom and used her novels to fuel the demands for a more radical female liberation.[1])

In response partly to this current issue and partly to his own failed attempt to 'be married' to Valeria Arsenev, Tolstoy had written the novella *Family Happiness* (1858), and in 1864 a comedy-farce entitled *A Contaminated Family*, which savages the idea of the emancipation of women and also those who held it, particularly the Nihilists. Although much of *Family Happiness* is written in an amazingly convincing first person, the last part of the novel is forced and unpersuasive. The heroine describes a visit to a German watering-place where her seduction is attempted by a lecherous Italian marquis; she subsequently retreats from both Europe and St. Petersburg to conjugal subordination and domestic happiness in the Russian countryside. The unease that most readers feel for the motivating episode in Baden and the 'happy-ever-after' ending is sensitively summed up by Edward Wasiolek, in a paragraph which glancingly underwrites the contentions of the present study:

> There is a third courtship in the novel – the coarse and mechanical attempt at love by an Italian marquis. The fact that only 'sex' remains when real feelings have been killed may be already an indication of Tolstoy's later identification of sex and death. The scene in Baden amongst the ruins is not very well done, nor is it really necessary. . . . The best one can say for it is that Masha needs some blow to move her back to the country, to Sergey, and to natural domestic love; and Tolstoy does not have the patience to wait – as James does characteristically – until the consciousness of what she has experienced in the city matures and moves her.          (Wasiolek, 1978, p. 46)

As in the case of Kitty, Tolstoy's talents were more than adequate to express his ideals of family life through the lips of a young girl; but the writing seems ill at ease when dealing with a threat to the stability of marriage. Masha (the heroine's) submission to a deromanticised marital pact implies Tolstoy's apprehension that the real-life Valeria might not have conformed so easily to the kind of 'family happiness' he envisaged. The novella appears to offer him the reassurance that he had indeed made the correct decision when he jilted her.

Confident in this view of happy marriage, he continued to preach it in *War and Peace*, whose First Epilogue, as we have noted, portrays a now stout, thoroughly practical-minded Natasha, careless of everything about her person from her clothes to her once exquisite singing voice – presumably the ideal portrait of a woman concerned only with what Tolstoy called her 'mission':

> Man's mission – men are the worker bees of the hive of human society – is endlessly diverse, but the mission of the queen bee, without whom reproduction of the species is impossible, is without question one and the same. And in spite of this a woman frequently does not see this mission and chooses imaginary ones, other ones. The dignity of a woman consists in knowing her mission.    (Quoted by Eikhenbaum, 1982, p. 96)

Although he adds that the mission goes beyond simply bearing eggs, Tolstoy's picture of Natasha is an inordinately limited one, in which even conversation about the rights of women is described as unnecessary; it is not surprising then that he was greatly excited by the general polemic aroused in 1869 by the publication of two separate Russian translations of J. S. Mill's *On the Subjection of Women*. It was in fact through correspondence on this topic that Tolstoy began his lifelong friendship with a somewhat sycophantic admirer, N. N. Strakhov. Despite the spice of minor disagreements Tolstoy and Strakhov were trenchantly ranged on the same side, that is, against the progressives and with reactionaries such as Alexandre Dumas *fils*, whose arch-conservative *L'homme-femme* now appeared (1872). Here Dumas wrote in advice to an imaginary son:

> If you have joined to your life a creature unworthy of you; if, after having vainly tried to make her the wife she ought to be to you, you have not been able to save her through maternity, that earthly redemption of her sex; if, wishing no longer to listen to you neither as a husband nor as a father, nor as a friend, nor as a teacher she not only abandons your children but goes off with the first man she meets and brings other children into the world . . . if the law, which has taken upon itself the right to tie together has refused itself the right to untie and declare itself helpless, declare yourself . . . the judge and executioner of this creature. She is not . . . a woman . . . she is simply animal, she

is the monkey from the Biblical land of Nod, she is Cain's female;
kill her.                                          (Eikhenbaum, p. 103)

The burden of the correspondence is reproduced, as Eikhenbaum points out, in a gently satiric conversation conducted by old
Prince Shcherbatsky: if women are hampered and oppressed by
their inability to achieve independence, then, says the Prince, 'I am
hampered and oppressed because they will not take me as a wet
nurse in the Foundling Hospital' (*SS* 8, p. 456).

From almost any point of view, then, Tolstoy invites adjectives
like 'patriarchal'; from the standpoint of modern feminism his
treatment of his wife (the last few of the 13 children fathered while
he publicly preached the virtues of chastity and continence) and
the extremity of his views regarding what he called 'the tragedy of
the bedroom', have left him a target of horror, ridicule, or both.

Nevertheless, the quantity of female writings on this male-
authored, male-criticized, and male multi-produced novel (if we
include the many film, television, opera and ballet versions of
*Anna Karenina* that have appeared over the years) is noticeably
small. And not even the most rabid feminist has, as far as I am
aware, tried to argue that it would have been a better novel had it
been written by a woman. Such a thought should rightly be
considered absurd. But precisely because the political thrust of the
arguments of feminism frequently tends to marginalize the role of
more strictly literary analysis, let us attempt some investigation of
the former without forgetting the latter. Bearing in mind the fact
that we are *all* time-conditioned, culture-specific and gender-
constructed, let us consider *Anna Karenina* in the light of one
recent, partially formal essay in feminist theory.

In her study of feminism and semiotics, *Alice Doesn't* (de Lauretis,
1984) Teresa de Lauretis refocuses the formulations of Lévi-Strauss
to argue that women inherit a double status in society. As the
natural bearers of children and gatherers of food, they are allotted
a positive economic value; but they are also assigned a sign value
derived from the place they occupy in the social system maintained
by kinship and exchange. Girls are *given* in marriage by their
fathers, in a system which is independent of dowry (historically
dowries can be either paid *or* received by the bride's father, de-
pending on whether the bride is considered an asset or a burden).
In Western society, too, they usually take their husband's name.
Their value is conferred from an already existent hierarchical

sexual division which makes women's semiotic value one of difference (in the Saussurean sense), of negation, of inferiority.

This picture could be borne out by a superficial reading of any of Tolstoy's novels: the male characters indeed occupy positions of social leadership and deal with more significant issues – philosophy, politics, agriculture and, occasionally, economics – while the females, headed by Natasha, Masha and Kitty, are confined to the social mores and apparatus pertaining to the rituals of courtship and marriage, and to the practicalities of food-preparation and the rearing of children. By feminist standards this second register must indeed be counted as restrictive and hence declared to be socially as well as semiotically negative. But it will also be evident to any reader that for Tolstoy these activities are clearly endowed with authorial approval; they are *morally positive*. Kitty, whose behaviour conforms impeccably to that code, is 'good', while Anna, who in the latter part of the novel performs her female role either indifferently or quite inadequately, is 'bad' – as their respective rewards proclaim.

The further notion that men can actually learn from 'good' women is expressly stated in Levin's admiration for Kitty at his brother's death-bed, and in his admission that the secret of an inspirational religious faith comes to him partly from the peasants, but partly also from some of the innately devout women of his acquaintance. At every level he asserts an intuitive, personal approach over the dogmas of institution and establishment, and allocates this quality to (good) women also. It seems that it was Tolstoy's personal wish to praise highly, and even appropriate to his own use, certain of the values of the subjugated female culture, *without* elevating the hierarchical status of the females (or peasants) who held them. His views accord perfectly, in fact, with the received Russian tradition which has always allowed women a special affinity with wisdom (Sophia) and the *Bogoroditsa*, or Mother of God, who barely overlaid the pagan *persona* of Mother Earth with selected Christian values. They also echo the world-picture of literary Romanticism, in which the Romantic heroine (as the Russian theoretician Iuri Lotman has pointed out) exists to complement the hero; 'she is his ideal, his Other', providing what he lacks in wisdom and spirituality (Lotman, 1977, p. 40).

Kitty thus acquires her positive semiotic value from the place she occupies in the traditions of the national culture. She is a figure produced by Russian history, in the sense that she occupies a prepared place in the line of virtuous female figures running through from the spirited but pious Olga, widow of Igor, to the celebrated Decembrist wives – perhaps even anticipating the mother–poet Akhmatova. In this regard she partakes of the mystic, religious Romantic qualities that the male culture seems willingly to allow to the female on the grounds of complementarity – although it is not to be confused with equality. At the same time she (Kitty) has a personal history within the novel – she is Tiny Bear, youngest of three daughters. Her family background ensures both her exchange value and her moral authenticity. She is, in sum, the shining product of traditional, romantic and familial ideals from which she does not deflect and which make her the perfect helpmeet and handmaiden. Her positive value will prevail so long as she does not challenge the hegemony.

By contrast, Anna is not a product of Russian tradition, based as it is on the premise that 'all social life is shaped as the extension of family life' (Fedotov, 1946, p. 16). She can better be described in the more modern terminology of the contemporary feminist Laura Mulvey as a *visual object*. Mulvey is in fact discussing cinematic codes, which, she claims, 'create a *gaze*, a *world*, and an *object*, thereby *producing* an *illusion* cut to the measure of desire' (Mulvey, 1975, p. 17). But her categories are equally applicable to Anna, who is born in the first instance of the gaze of horror that Tolstoy let travel over the mutilated body of the governess Anna Pirogov as it lay on a table in the station waiting-room; and in the second, of Vronsky's gaze, when, after 'a single glance' (which registers Anna as belonging to the world of high society) he is 'compelled to have another look' at the lady about to enter the railway-carriage (*SS* 1, p. 18). Laura Mulvey's concept shows how differently we *perceive* Anna in contrast to the other females. Kitty's story, for example, is a long series of sequential and consequential actions (the rejection of Levin; the ball; the break with Vronsky; the events of the German spa) which lend it the essentially metonymic quality of linear narrative. By contrast, Anna is viewed in a series of vivid but still frames: Anna in the whirl of snow at the railway-station; Anna gazed down upon by the trembling Vronsky after their first sexual encounter; Anna, pregnant, resting her hot forehead against the watering-can on the day of the race. It is not surprising, given narrative's predisposition to comment on its own practices, that there are in the novel two allusions to portraits of Anna – one in her marital home, and another painted by the artist Mikhailov, which seduces Levin even before he meets her. Thus the tension between image and narrative projects different emphases in the parallel stories of Anna and Kitty, the significance of which would be seen all the more clearly if some feature film version of *Anna Karenina* were to begin with a shot of Anna Pirogov's crushed body, hauled out from under the wheels of a train. If that film were made, its opening scene would predict with banal certainty not only that Anna Karenin was destined to die, but also the means of her destruction. But, taking us outside the claustrophobic circle of Tolstoy's unacknowledged sexual preoccupations, it might also show us why there are external reasons for the co-existence of two major parallel and contrasting plot-lines in the novel.

Propp's claim in 'The Historical Roots of the Folk-tale' (Propp, 1984) that plots arise from the clash of different social orders as they overlap with one another, verifies the suspicion that Kitty is there not simply to provide a life for Levin, but also to defend and justify the whole patriarchal system which Tolstoy believed to be under siege from the influx of the new feminist ideas that were infiltrating Russia at that time. His fears were not unfounded. There was a growing number of real-life girls demanding a more rewarding lot than that of the bitterly clear-sighted heroine of Turgenev's novella *A Correspondence*, whose life is blighted by the dashing of her hopes of love and marriage. The were actual women for whom the enterprising and free-thinking (if still somewhat confused) Olga, heroine of Chernyshevsky's *What's to be Done?* was the representative and spokeswoman. The turning of the tide, in effect, towards the emancipation of women as well as of the serfs, places the author of *Anna Karenina* at a socio-historical cross-roads, and impels him to take up an embattled and defensive position. If Kitty was drawn as a figure in a historical series, she appears to be dangerously close to the end of the line.

In this light the suicide of the governess Anna Pirogov should be read not as a repetition of the fate of Karamzin's *Poor Liza*,[2] but as an act of protest, a newsworthy event (these words will acquire a particular significance later in this chapter) at once sensational and symptomatic of the contemporary cry for female emancipation. Her image remains one of the sources of the Anna strand in Tolstoy's novel, but it now contributes to a female figure whose death is as much an act of confrontation as one of despair.

Support for this new viewpoint is suggested indirectly by several of Lotman's articles (on some of which, interestingly enough, de

Lauretis also draws, although to reach rather different conclusions). In his discussion of what he believes to be inherently
spatial features of all 'world-pictures', Lotman talks of the capacity
of these spatial structures to organise 'all other levels of any
world-view' (Shukman, 1977, p. 94). For example, he argues in a
1965 article that to the medieval Russian mind ideas of geographical space were frequently bound up with ideas of morality (Shukman, p. 88). People leaving the parental home could be interpreted
as journeying towards Paradise (via places such as monasteries or
holy lands) or towards Hell (via houses of sin or impious lands).
On this basis Lotman later reiterates his belief that all 'world-
pictures' have spatial features, but he makes some new distinc-
tions. The world over which travel takes place is of itself static – as
must be the texts which describe it. But texts describing man and
his place(s) in the world are dynamic. There is thus a basic opposition between the movable and the immovable, but one which
does not simply parallel the land/person opposition. Characters
totally fixed to certain places belong to the *immovable*. The hero, on
the other hand, is essentially mobile.

Lotman makes clear that the fixed world is, notwithstanding,
capable of interior differentiations, expressed in the form of oppositions of the good/bad, believing/heathen, own/other type. In fact,
within this world there is a basic boundary which virtually divides
it into two: *etot mir* and *tot mir* (*this world* and *that world*). We shall
return to this concept.

In the third section of his book, *The Structure of the Artistic Text*
(Lotman, 1977, p. 211), Lotman cites the example of *Anna Karenina*
as the story of a particular woman in a particular time and place,
but says that it is also the story of every woman, or even every
person. Both concepts, he asserts, are essential if a work is to have
more than mere historical interest. He writes: 'In literary plot
[*syuzhet*] (and in any narrative) one can distinguish two aspects.
One of them, by which the text models a total *universum*, may be
termed mythological, and the second, which represents some
episode of reality, the story.' The mythological aspect, according to
Lotman, is a *sine qua non*, though the reality aspect is dispensable.
However, the modern literary text is 'as a rule, constructed on the
conflict between these tendencies, on the structural tension between them'. (p. 259). Plot is therefore neither confined to something taken directly from life, nor something 'passively passed on
by tradition'. Its primary element is the 'event', defined as 'the

shift of a character across the frontier of a semantic field'. Only mobile characters, of course, have the right to cross frontiers. The movement of a plot, an event, is the crossing of the forbidden frontier which the plotless structure affirms. . . . Plot is a 'revolutionary element' in relation to the 'picture of the world' (p. 288).

We next turn to yet another relevant article of Lotman's, one published originally in 1973, which takes up and rephrases several of his earlier assertions regarding the origin of plot 'in the light of typology' (as the translation by Julian Draffy puts it). Lotman now describes the 'mythological text' as subject to cyclical–temporal motion, wanting in the categories of beginning and end, and synchronized with the processes of nature such as the seasons of the year. In this framework, human life is a recurrent phenomenon; death is not the end but rebirth; and the purpose of such texts is to perform a 'classifying, stratifying and regulating' role, reducing the world of 'excesses and anomalies' to norm and system (p. 162).

In the mythical text mechanism, as Lotman had already stated in the previously discussed articles, 'a certain plot-space is divided by a single boundary into an internal and an external sphere, and a single character has the opportunity to cross that boundary . . .'. But further, 'The elementary sequence of events in myth can be reduced to a chain: entry into a closed space – emergence from it' (p. 168). Lotman uses this single mythological invariant as the paradigm for the life–death–resurrection (or renewal) cycle, which is expressed by images of closed space such as 'a cave', 'the grave', 'a house', or 'woman' – all with corresponding features of darkness, warmth and dampness. Birth – emergence from the space – is contingent upon death – entry into it; both events can be endlessly varied and repeated.

The counterpart of this central, cyclical, text-generating mechanism, that is, the one dealing with story rather than myth, is organized in accordance with linear temporal motion and designed precisely to accommodate issues and anomalies – what might constitute 'news'. (Hence the significant 'newsworthiness' of the governess Pirogov's suicide.) Lotman envisages that whereas news is always about someone else, myth correlates the microcosm of 'my' internal world with the macrocosm of the surrounding universe. While myth, his first category, 'organizes the hearer's world, the second adds interesting details to his knowledge of this world' (p. 163). It is the reciprocal interaction between the two

categories of text that produces the effects he had already anticipated, such as the fragmentation of the original 'hero' figure into a
number of independent characters, each with an individual name,
yet often revealing a common origin through pairings and repetitions (such as the cross-identification in many of Shakespeare's
comedies – notably, *As You Like It*). Another already foreshadowed
outcome was the division of characters into the mobile and the
fixed. The latter are now said to be 'given-off' (i.e. produced,
generated) at and by the fixed boundary between the two worlds –
'this one' and 'that one' – characterised by the inner/outer,
familiar/alien, cultured/barbarian, etc. oppositions. Lotman now
clarifies that since the spatial frontier (which can of course be
mental or symbolic) is dominant in any plot, it is at this boundary
that the oppositions are apparent.

Despite some repetition, these theses now provide the ground-
work for an extremely fruitful examination of the previously mentioned conflict between mythological structure and linear narrative,
which, he claims, is representative of the modern literary text. *His*
example is the two contrasting spheres of Dostoevsky's novels: the
field of ideological conflict and the world of social action; ours is
the two worlds of traditional feminine conformism and erupting
female autonomy. But before we turn more specifically to that
issue, it is interesting to note that the preoccupations of modern
feminism have led to more rebarbative reactions to Lotman's
arguments: they prompt Teresa de Lauretis, for example, to interpret mythical structuration as established on biological sexual
difference. 'The hero, the mythical subject, is constructed as
human being and as male; he is the active principle of culture, the
establisher of distinction, the creator of difference. Female is what
is not susceptible to transformation, to life or death; she (it) is an
element of plot-space, a topis, a resistance, matrix and matter'
(p. 119). And this negative postulation of woman as merely 'non-
man' carries over, in de Lauretis' view, to modern plots interpret-
able as a 'two-character drama in which the human person creates
and recreates himself out of an abstract or purely symbolic other –
the womb, the earth, the grave, the woman . . .'. De Lauretis
reproaches Lotman for the implication that all of these can firstly
be interpreted as mere spaces, and secondly thought of as 'mutually identical'.

But she somewhat misinterprets Lotman in this gloss. To begin
with, he nowhere uses the words 'mere spaces'. On the contrary,

he expressly describes caves, graves, houses and wombs as *places* that are dark, warm, and damp – that is, possessing the characteristics of the mystical, deeply revered *persona* of Mother Earth, whose connotations in Russian mythology are both profound and inspirational. In no way can they called negative or inferior, as the following passage indicates:

> In Mother Earth, who remains the core of Russian religion, converge the most secret and deep religious feelings of the folk. Beneath the beautiful veil of grass and flowers, the people venerate with awe the black moist depths, the source of all fertilizing powers, the nourishing breast of nature, and their own last resting-place. (Fedotov, p. 12)

It is moreover the *acts of returning* to these places (rather than spaces) for the common goal of renewal, renaissance, and resurrection, that are 'mutually identical' – not the places themselves. However, it is primarily the failure in de Lauretis' argument to take account of historical change in both human and literary history that I take issue with. For, by remaining preoccupied with what she interprets as Lotman's negative pertinence to that sphere of feminist thought which is concerned with the privileged production of male power, she has ignored its more interesting application to the production of text – which is, after all, the point of his argument. What is more wonderful, however, is that this exercise vindicates the Feminine in a way which renders de Lauretis' protests somewhat short-sighted.

Tolstoy began *Anna Karenina* during a period of deliberate withdrawal from a world apparently headed in a direction he fundamentally disagreed with. His clearest form of protest against the liberal attempt to westernize and the radical move towards revolution was to bury himself at Yasnaya Polyana and to refuse to receive any magazines or newspapers. His reading, partly designed to feed a Primer intended for use in schools, was largely confined to Russian folk literature. He wrote in a letter to Strakhov that if he were to return to literature (we are speaking of the period of the early 1870s between the completion of *War and Peace* and the commencement of *Anna Karenina*), he would write works 'where there would be nothing superfluous, which would be just as pure, as elegant, as all ancient Greek literature' (3 March 1872). The first visible result of the premediated return to myth and epic was *A*

*Prisoner of the Caucasus* (1872), largely inspired by his reading of
Homer (who had also had an effect on *The Cossacks*, published in
1863). At the same time, he wrote another letter to Strakhov telling
him that by this withdrawal into his own 'atmosphere', 'all living
phenomena begin to fall into place as they ought to do . . .' –
words significantly similar to Lotman's description of the regulating, normalising role of mythology. Boris Eikhenbaum writes of
this period in Tolstoy's life – the gestation years of *Anna Karenina* –
that 'his Primer, his attack against the pedagogues, and his article
'On Public Education' – all this was preparation for the change in
Tolstoy's life and work that came about in the eighties and at the
base of which lay a resolute denial of any historical progress'
(p. 63).

In his new current plan for a novel, he did not go so far as to try
to reconstruct a Greek myth, but he did imagine that his new work
would go backwards in time to the epoch of Peter the Great, which
he described as the 'knot' of Russian life. But 'the work does not
move' he wrote on 7 March 1873, and, as we all know, apparently
unpremeditated, 'suddenly, unexpectedly, 'as Sonya put it in her
diary, he began, instead, *Anna Karenina*.

Lotman's theory of the twin origins of the modern novel are thus
easily assimilated to the double impetus of the new work, which in
its two strands epitomises the opposition between the mythological and the eschatological systems. Levin, the male hero, the
obvious active principle of the story, is also the reincarnation of the
heroes of *Childhood* and *The Cossacks* (unconsciously illustrating
Lotman's claim that a hero figure could have many names). He
willingly enters the 'closed space' of marriage with Kitty, and is not
only reincarnated himself in his baby son, but can also be said to
emerge from that space in order to seek spiritual rebirth in religious faith. In his story de Lauretis' reading is justified, for Kitty
is, at different times, obstacle, receptacle, matrix, mother – all in
relation to Levin. Her independent life is virtually confined to
introducing her own recipe for making raspberry jam, in spite of
the disgruntlement of Levin's housekeeper.

In strong contrast, Anna is by definition a transgressor. She is
even a usurper. But in Lotman's context to transgress (cross over)
boundaries is constitutive of being a hero. Despite her sex, Anna
seeks to be mobile instead of fixed, to be the active principle rather
than the passive, to assume mobility to the extent of trying to
operate her own exchange (Karenin for Vronsky) instead of simply
being given in marriage.

In her attempt to assume the mobility of the hero, she is, of course, ultimately defeated by the rules of the game she wants to buy into. Even though she confronts and even crosses a boundary, her training, her basic formation as a nineteenth-century female have not prepared her to live successfully in freedom. The move to Italy gave her the illusion of acceptance, but this was based on the anonymity conferred by living in a foreign country, and the presence of one or two visitors. The barriers that her own society had not lowered after all are shown at their most intransigent in the scene at the opera, when Anna is snubbed and ostracised. It simply proves impossible in Moscow society to move from the world beyond the pale to the drawing-rooms of the 'insiders'. Branded as an outcast, Anna now wanders around the plot-space until the social barrier turns into the final frontier of death itself. 'The text which had separated itself from ritual and acquired independent verbal existence automatically acquired in its linear disposition a marked beginning and end', writes Lotman (1973, p. 168), as if summing up an inevitable fate. He then concludes, 'Plot represents a powerful means of making sense of life.'

If Tolstoy was trying to make sense of two conflicting tensions in his own situation – his desire to evade the modern world by retreating into an ancient, mythological world in tune with Nature and the seasons, and his need to give some external form to his very immediate preoccupations with the woman question – then the recently established *genre* of the novel (which 'rose' much later in Russia than in the West) was an extraordinarily apt vehicle. With its formal ambiguities and double origins, its tension between 'truth' and 'news',[3] it was well able to justify its displacement of Tolstoy's former preference for autobiography, novella and epic. The succession of discrete plot units in *Anna Karenina* became a means by which Tolstoy (but also, by extension, every writer and reader) could attempt to make sense of his own life and times, particularly the threat of feminism, in and against the macrocosm of non-discrete, mythologized life, represented by the Nature idyll on native Russian soil.

Paradoxically, it is also in the light of Lotman's theory (*pace* de Lauretis) that a feminist defence of Tolstoy can be mounted – provided, that is, that one accepts as unnegotiable both his historicity and the psychology of his early formation. Such a defence, it must be admitted, would not attempt to salvage either Dolly or Kitty. They do indeed exist in a relation of difference to their sister, as that which Anna is not. They have to be cast as the classic objects of masculine desire; as the legitimate replacement of the mother; as 'negative semantic space'; as Propp's princess of the thirty-first function (the one the hero marries before he ascends the throne); as the socialized good wife and mother at the end of every romance. The two sisters have identical semiotic values and collectively contribute to a patriarchal construct of 'woman' which was almost the norm in the nineteenth century and is not yet extinct.

But Anna, as we have partly seen already, does not come out of the same mould. It is precisely through grasping that she is a *hero* in the mythological sense elaborated by Lotman that we can also appreciate Tolstoy's amazing boldness in grappling with the issues and conventions of his society, both literary and historical, and his courage in forcing himself to go some way along a path of excruciating self-exposure. But the status of hero is not unambiguous. The heroes of antiquity originally distinguished themselves from the ordinary people by their god-like attributes; in time they were anthropomorphized into hybrid figures, half-god, half-man; and ultimately they became completely human, although usually retaining some mark of outstanding superiority. Thus the heroes stood above the common mass – wherein of course lay the dangers of *hubris*, and the risk of divine wrath.

Obviously Anna is supremely invested with this quality of 'extra'. Not only does she outshine every other woman in the novel, she is also more vital, more noticeable, more commanding of attention than any of the males, including Levin and Vronsky. Indeed, it has been suggested by R. F. Christian (p. 176) that one cause of Anna's tragedy was simply her inability to find an adequate male counterpart. But this is to assume that conventional marriage is her only 'proper' destiny, and to give Christian his due he does not really think that Anna's case can be so easily solved. And it is equally clear that containment is not what Tolstoy wants for his heroine. He endows her with great beauty and irresistible charm, but it is above all by such epithets as 'vitality', 'energy', and 'animation' that he defines her difference from all other characters. She simply has more *life* than any of them. This is not to deny the social constraints that dog her everyday existence, forced as she is to *watch* Vronsky while he races, to *wait* for him to return from political meetings. But it is as if the mobility denied to the nineteenth century female heroine bursts out in Anna in the form of a super-vitality that makes her metaphorically larger than life, as were the heroes of antiquity. It is in this sense that I categorise

Anna as 'hero', while leaving it to Kitty, Masha and Natasha to remain mere heroines. In other words, Anna transcends the constraints of her gender, to provide the counter-illustration to de Lauretis' too *parti-pris* interpretation of Lotman's thesis.

Of course, this claim has not yet dealt with the counter-issue of the dangers of *hubris*, to which we shall return. Let us just say for the moment that it is one thing to become a hero, even if it means being struck down by the gods, and quite another to remain confined to the jam-pot on the terrace, doing battle with a recalcitrant housekeeper.

While the events leading to Anna's downfall are still taking their course, other contrasts between Anna and Kitty emerge, all of which emphasise the essential difference in their status. To start with, Kitty is the object of Levin's desire, but she herself is portrayed less as desiring Levin than simply wanting to be married. She is anxious to find her role in life by exchanging the status of daughter for that of wife, and thus sharing with her husband dominion over a small domestic world. Anna, on the other hand, actively desires Vronsky; he is as much the object of her desire, her 'significant other' as she is his. Even though the narrative reflects the conventions of the society in sentences such as: 'That which for nearly the whole year had been the sole and exclusive desire of Vronsky's life, supplanting all his former desires . . . had been fulfilled . . .', Tolstoy does not pretend that consummation was not Anna's desire, equally with, perhaps even more than, Vronsky's. For her, the possibility of sexual intercourse with her lover was a 'bewitching dream of happiness', and thereafter she willingly risks marital and social opprobrium by engineering meetings with him; her 'blood is fired', and soon she is writing imperious notes, urging his presence because she needs him.

This is not supposed to be typical 'feminine' behaviour, nor are the activities she takes up in *lieu* of child-bearing and jam-making. For example, we find her showing an unexpectedly informed (masculine?) interest in architecture, buildings, and farm machinery during Dolly's visit to Vronsky's country-house. When they visit the site of the hospital Vronsky is building, Dolly enquires about a maternity ward, but Anna displays her knowledge of the proper depth to which foundations should be poured.

Thus not only through her transgression, but also through her desire and her intellect, Anna is constituted as an active principle. And the more we pursue that line of inquiry the more positive it becomes. However there are at least four more important ways in which she stakes a claim to be subject rather than object.

One is the fact that, unlike Kitty, no institution guarantees her position as Vronsky's partner; all depends on her own powers – which she of course ends up by misusing, but that is not the point. Anna controls the relationship, and even controls Vronsky. He sometimes arrives later than she requests, but nevertheless comes, because the request is an imperious command. One could also make a similar point about her power over her author; for in the creation of two characters to fill the roles of hero and heroine (as the words are conventionally used), Tolstoy ensured that it was the former who occupied more space – on Sydney Schulze's analysis, 126 chapters are devoted to Levin, and 113 to Anna (Schulze, 1982, p. 20) – but it was Anna who claimed the title role.

Secondly, and more importantly, Tolstoy allows Anna one supremely 'male' activity: he endows her with a pen, the instrument to which many theorists have appended an 'is', so great is its phallic power. She does not remain the reader figure depicted in the early chapters, the train-passenger who finds it hard to concentrate on what is being recounted in her English novel because she so longs 'to do it herself' (*SS* 8, p. 121). During that prelude she can only read, because there *is* 'nothing to be done', other than to follow vicariously the career of the hero of the novel and his attainment of 'English' happiness. But much later, when she has taken control of her own destiny, she not only continues to read a great deal, but is described as *writing* a book for children – an activity to which Tolstoy was deeply and seriously committed immediately prior to embarking on *Anna Karenina*, but also the ultimate symbolic activity of someone seeking to impose her own patterns on the chaotic raw material of life (turning *fabula* into *siuzhet*).

The use of the adjective 'English' to qualify both the novel Anna reads, and also the happiness of its hero, is significant. It seems to dignify for Tolstoy a freedom that he believed was impossible and wrong in Russian society. For example, when old Princess Shcherbatsky is worrying over how to arrange a match for Kitty without imposing too much constraint or allowing too much latitude, she rejects 'the English way of giving a girl perfect freedom'. For her, it is tantamount to giving loaded pistols to a five-year-old to play with (*SS*, p.58). Yet in Part 7 we find that not only has Anna carved out an 'English' path for herself, she has taken into her house a little English girl and assumed financial responsibility for the child's family. It can be said that Hannah (the English girl) replaces Annushka (the obedient maid-servant) as an extension or projection of Anna, since both bear variants of her name: in the reading scene in the railway carriage, Russian Annushka was shown sitting with Anna's red bag (which Jakobson argued is a metonym for Anna's passion so far held in check) clutched firmly on her broad lap. But she is already half-asleep. Perhaps the future of Anna's daughter will depend on etymology – that is, on whether she will live up to her name as transliterated into the English 'Annie' or the more Russian Ani (as the Oxford and Penguin paper back translations respectively offer).

Unfortunately, the last factor which constitutes Anna as subject rather than object, or as 'hero' in Lotman's use of the term, is more problematical and also more pessimistic, for we come back yet again to the central but ultimate fact that *Anna kills herself*. Does this make her agent or victim? Actant or acted upon? The answer is of course that she is both. As Terry Eagleton writes of Clarissa Harlowe, 'The final exercise of "free" individual choice is in fact tragic self-extinction' (Eagleton, 1982, p. 87).

The barbed irony of Eagleton's comment points up the essential dilemma very nicely. But not every critic has found themself caught by it. Several commentators of Anna's act of self-destruction construe her solely as victim, emphasising her as acted *upon*. Their argument sets up and answers their own next question – who, if not she, was responsible for her death? Society, said D. H. Lawrence (Davie, 1965, p. 141). People, claimed Viktor Shklovsky: 'It was people, not God, who threw Anna under the train', (Shklovsky, 1963, p. 473). But 'Vengeance is mine, I will repay.' says the epigraph. Was Anna God's hapless, helpless victim?

Considerable debate has ranged over the question of whether Anna's death should be seen as a willed authorial intervention, or simply as the ineluctable outcome flowing inevitably from the initial premises – the natural *dénouement* to a story 'prepared by the bitterness' she had experienced. 'The point is not in the suicide itself . . . but precisely in the fact that passion led to suffering', writes Eikhenbaum (p. 143). But what makes one uneasy about these apparently oppositional lines of argument is that they both deprive Anna of her autonomy. In one case she is the powerless object of punishment, whether it is meted out by God or man; in the other she is caught in a chain of cause and effect – suffering being the 'inescapable' result of 'evil' in Eikhenbaum's assessment of Tolstoy's moral position.

If we as readers are to avoid the equally doomed alternatives of such a choice, we must remind ourselves that it is simply the case that Anna was not in fact killed or murdered, as was the wife in *The Kreuzer Sonata*, the true victim of a paranoid husband. Anna Karenin took her own life. By exercising that ambiguous final choice, she does, despite the irony of Eagleton's constation of Clarissa's fate, procure a kind of meaning for herself. For one thing, she outdoes in death the males (Vronsky and Levin) who fail to bring off their own suicide attempts. Neither in her life nor in her death was there anyone to hold a candle to her – to appropriate the famous symbol of that very death.

Given this impressive list of queenly attributes on Anna's part – her mobility, desire, intellect, imperiousness, creativity, and 'Englishness', and not excluding her final 'success' in taking her own life, it seems more appropriate to marvel at the extent to which Anna creates and embraces her own fate than to make an issue of its inevitability or injustice. By pushing passion, punishment and pity to their limits, Tolstoy truly throws an arc-light on the concept of female subjectivity; and although Anna withers under it, we learn as in a laboratory. Had she not exposed herself to all this, and hence to us as readers, we would know considerably less about woman as subject, even if in the process we also learn a good deal about Tolstoy and the complexities of subject–object relations. Dramatised before us is an example of one of the many crises that arose in nineteenth century Russia when entrenched patriarchial patterns clashed with the radical convictions of the progressive 'New People'. The hierarchy appears to win only if we read Anna's story as one of retribution against an isolated individual who tried to pit herself against the system; but in reality the triumph of the 'fallen woman' is proclaimed in the power she exerts over author, reader, and text. The insistences of today's sexual politics require that Anna's career be understood as an unconscious assault on the very forces that were victorious in obtaining her downfall. For while Anna is inevitably defeated at a number of levels, some internal, as we shall discuss further, but many arising from by the religious, moral and social conventions of her own society – in other words because of localized issues of psychology, morality and history – it is important to see her story as a milestone in the female struggle to become subject rather than object, to be her own agent rather than a mere passive space. And it is particularly important to do this in the light of Tolstoy's subsequent retreat from that courageous and challenging expedition into an area he preferred to ignore. In later works he still gnaws at the problem of sexuality, but no longer is the woman the centre of interest. *The Kreuzer Sonata* depicts an innocent, unjustly murdered, but shadowy female figure, a victim only; 'The Devil' posits alternative endings (murder and suicide) as solutions to a husband's guilt, but neither ending depends on or even alters the portrayal of the female protagonist; the hero of *Resurrection* finds his salvation in destiny and reading the Gospels, while the infinitely wronged heroine cleaves to someone else. Thus, paradoxically, the later stories absolve the female of guilt, which is laid in each case upon the male protagonist; but they do her an immeasurably greater disservice than is done to Anna Karenin, because in them the female is relegated once more to the position of object. Without them the male heroes could not play out their own supremely absorbing dramas of transgression and guilt. And this renewed objectivisation is quite as dismissive as in any modern screen depiction of women 'cut to the measure of desire'.

Standing out from the rest of the conventional female characters, Anna is seen to be untraditional, a-historic, and episodic rather than mythological – an event on the surface of Tolstoy's preferred depiction of cyclical time. And because she is mobile, heroic, active, she is also a transgressor of boundaries; a reader who becomes a writer; a Russian who seizes English freedoms. The effect of the 'killing' of Anna Karenin is undermined by the power of her presence, which appears to have unnerved her patriarchial progenitor since he did not repeat that act of creation ever again. Eikhenbaum truly remarks that *Anna Karenina* was the 'last word' in the line of the Russian family novel; but Anna herself was a one-off trip up the Amazon.

# 6

# The Daughter's Reduction

*La reine est morte. Vive la reine.* We have been arguing not so much a replacement queen as some kind of vivid, enduring presence who is created during the novel, and lives on after it. But the fact remains that in order for this to happen, Anna had first to die. Her death may well have been the inevitable destiny of an extravagantly passionate character, and it may also in part have been the result of the affront she caused to the society in which she lived; but both of these issues occur after the primal event of her creation. They are the symptoms rather than the causes of a situation that is already posed as irremediable. So the triumphalism which attempts to claim Anna as victor rather than victim, as able to vanquish her own death through that very death, must probe a question which comes from further back. We should now be wondering by what right Tolstoy created her *at all*. To what extent *can* a male author assume a feminine *persona* and write her 'from the inside'? What are the conditions and limitations of such a presumptuous act of creation?

Of course the male writing of female characters has been going on since before *The Widow of Ephesus*; rather less often, and on the whole more recently, though not necessarily with any less confidence, has the reverse been practised. Often the only question asked is the degree to which we judge a male author successful in demonstrating some kind of extra-temporal, prophetic and intuitive coincidence of understanding with the 'facts' and hypotheses put forward not only by the new discourses of psychoanalysis but also by the even newer ones of feminism. But neither the commonness of cross-writing nor its ready acceptance should prevent some questioning of whether, how, and why it might be a different creative process from homo-genetic writing; and, clearly, the Anna strand of *Anna Karenina* is an obvious target for the beginning of an investigation.

'Theories of women's writing', writes Elaine Showalter (Showalter, 1985), 'presently make use of four models of difference: biological, linguistic, psychoanalytic, and cultural' (p. 249). Perhaps

any full-fledged account of woman-written-by-man should also go
through these categories in the sequential and overlapping order
proposed by Showalter. But this study has already declared its
need and intent to be selective, and thus makes no apologies either
for restricting its interest to the last two models, or for not leaving
psychoanalysis behind when continuing to discuss the feminist
issue. If what is written by any author depends partially on the
earliest formation of their psyche, we must wonder whether, and
to what extent, the formation of a male ego precludes anything but
a borrowed and superficial grasp of what it is to be female. Despite
claims like Eagleton's, that Samuel Richardson's *Clarissa* is 'arguably the major feminist text of the language' (Eagleton, 1983,
p. viii), much feminist criticism seems simply to take it for granted
that the writing of female heroines by male authors is merely one
of the more common examples of patriarchal phallogocentrism –
though none the less heinous for being 'the norm'.

Fortunately there are now many sophisticated considerations of
the way sex and gender affect text and writer; indeed, there are so
many introductions, overviews and polemical articles in print that
to select from this abundance of what might be called the femmeta-
critical answer to phallogocentrism is probably to invite attack from
one's own side. A possible course is to take one of the wittier and
sharper pieces of work in this area and hope that the insights
gained from it justify the choice. Jane Gallop's first, powerful
explication of the writings of (mainly) Lacan (Gallop, 1982[1]) draws
attention to two footnotes to *Civilisation and its Discontents* in which
Freud privileges the visual impact of the male genitalia over the
less visible female sexual organs, despite the stronger olfactory
stimuli of the latter (Gallop, p. 267). In Gallop's own succinct
words, 'The penis may be more visible, but female genitalia have a
stronger smell'.

This scent leads her to the work of the French feminist Michèle
Montrelay, who, in a review of a book on female sexuality (Montrelay, 1977), postulates a relation of anxiety between the female's
'more immediate, primitive, olfactory sexuality, and [the] mediated, sublimated visual sexuality' of the male.

> The unbearably intense immediacy of the *'odor di femina'* pro-
> duces anxiety, a state totally threatening to the stability of the
> psychic economy, that stability which is achieved by means of
> representation. The visual mode produces representations as a

way of mastering what is otherwise too intense. The '*odor di femina*' becomes odious, nauseous, because it threatens to undo the achievements of repression and sublimation, threatens to return the subject to the powerlessness, intensity and anxiety of an immediate unmediated connection with the body of the mother.                                                                          (p. 27)

Thus Gallop through Montrelay sends forth immediate and powerful resonances which immediately remind one of Tolstoy, enabling a speculation something like the following: There can be no doubt that all his life the '*odor di femina*' produced an anxiety of guilt in Tolstoy, whether it was triggered by tension emanating from the loss of his mother, the inordinate appetites of his youth, or the legal but shameful lust that for him characterised his marriage. Translating the role of 'visual representations' to the register of narrative, we would certainly allow that Tolstoy was able to come to terms at least superficially with the issue by writing the stories of Olenin and Levin, and through this activity achieve a degree of sublimation. Of course even that representational stability was seen to have its fissures; but nevertheless both heroes amount to an attempt at projected self-mastery. In the case of Levin, however, that attempt is subverted by the presence of an insistent co-protagonist, redolent with femininity – by Anna herself, who becomes not so much odious as oppressive; not nauseous, but neurotic; and who indeed threatens to undo 'the achievements of repression and sublimation' that Tolstoy aspired to in both his life and his writings.

Montrelay's last few words enable us further to see why being to close to Mother [-Nature] undoubtedly constituted a threat for Olenin. But Gallop's rendering of Montrelay opens the argument to the possibility that Tolstoy's insistent idealisation and enshrinement of his mother, which we saw as a hidden motivation, was also a displacement, the repression of a repression. By such a move Tolstoy could avoid confronting the possibility that the disgust he felt for his own sexual appetite might be rooted in the horror with which he experienced the 'powerlessness, intensity and anxiety' of his infantile dependency on the mother who died. The difference between Levin – whose story is after all a tale of love, courtship and marriage – and Anna, who pursues passion and death, is similar to the difference between the 'more mediated, represented, mastered form of sexuality' (Gallop, p. 28) and its raw, unsublimated, unmastered counterpart which has the capacity both to fascinate and terrorise its progenitor. The double story of Levin and Anna, in other words, *represents* what Freud theorised in another footnote to *Civilisation and its Discontents*: the belief that,

> The sexual function has been accompanied by a repugnance which cannot further be accounted for, and which prevents its complete satisfaction and forces it away from the sexual aim into sublimations and libidinal displacements.
>
> (Gallop, p. 28, quoting Freud)

On Gallop's account, the sacrifice of complete satisfaction is a necessary concomitant to the acquisition of adult sexual identity (the term *Bildingsroman* has already been applied to the Levin story); or, to put it another way, true male adulthood (since Freud spoke only for his own sex) would consist in the recognition and acceptance that desire will always remain both unfulfilled and excentric; displacements are always required.

An obedient Kitty, her sexuality contained in wife- and motherhood, becomes for Tolstoy the sublimation and displacement of the mother whose closeness is highly desirable, but whose tooscloseness is threateningly repugnant. In that dialectic what cannot be sublimated in Kitty is displaced onto that monster of rampant femaleness, Anna.

Paradoxically, the combined efforts of Gallop and Montrelay are both illuminating and frustrating, for the light they throw shows the issue to be even more imponderable than it already was. The question of whether a male has (a) the right and (b) the capacity to create a female character has now come to turn upon the question of whether he can overcome his repressed fastidiousness sufficiently to 'become' that which he may actually find odious. The enterprise is even more hazardous when one considers that girl and boy infants may experience different ego-formations, stemming from a gender-differentiated relation to the mother.

In a process which must admit to something of an excess of intersexuality, Gallop quotes Montrelay who quotes a further source – the essay by Béla Grunberger entitled 'Outline for a Study of Narcissism in Female Sexuality' (Grunberger, 1970). In order to avoid compounding the dizzying effects of these constructions, we shall now work directly from this last article.

Grunberger begins by doubting Freud's tacit assumption that

boys and girls endure *identical* sexual sensations during their first infantile contact with the mother, that is, during nursing and bathing. However, concrete – or rather 'visible and verifiable' – evidence for either view is, he admits, neither sufficiently available, nor, in his opinion, adequate to explain female sexuality, which in any case 'goes beyond biological facts'. So, with considerable justification from Freud's own insistence on its importance, he uses the theory of narcissism as his starting point.

Speaking in a generalised way of the initial mother–child relationship, Grunberger claims that this effects a 'narcissistic confirmation' of the child's instinctual needs (that is, the child comes to recognise them and accept them as his own) through the mother loving *'her child and all expressions of his life'* (p. 72; his emphasis). But the mother as a sexual being and object has a different value for the girl than for the boy, since, firstly, 'we have every reason to believe' that all mothers, no matter how loving, are ambivalent towards their daughters; and secondly, according to Freud, 'a true sexual object can only be of the opposite sex'. The mother cannot therefore be the satisfactory sexual object for the girl that she is for the boy; the maternal object is for the girl only a *substitute* for a true sexual object. The girl is thus in an essentially frustrating situation, which leads her to seek narcissistic confirmation by taking over the role of her mother (when a little girl plays with dolls, for example, she identifies herself both with her mother and with the doll), while the boy is content simply to bask in his mother's love. The girl becomes *'essentially narcissistic* [Grunberger's emphasis] in an effort to make up for maternal deficiency' (p. 73). Yet the love she can give herself is equally deficient by comparison with the maternal love she seeks – which only leads her to her over-evaluate all substitute love-objects. Although in the Oedipal phase she will probably come to focus upon her father as her true love-object, the waiting period between infancy and the Oedipal period has allowed her narcissism to develop, while her love for her father will be contaminated by the guilt arising from her experience of an inauthentic pregenital satisfaction (inauthentic because it has its source in a substitute object). During the parallel period the boy, unable to satisfy his Oedipal desires, suffers a narcissistic wound which he represses in favour of a 'precocious, pregenital sexuality', but which leads him to despise his narcissistic needs. Thus, when the girl looks for someone (her sexual partner) to provide the missing narcissistic confirmation she has never had, the boy has come to despise narcissistic needs.

Grunberger calls this a 'tragic state of affairs'; nevertheless he still believes that it is possible for a woman to achieve a synthesis between narcissistic satisfaction and instinctual gratification, even though her need for self-confirmation will lead her to try to satisfy the first at the expense of the second. In 'satisfactory instances' she will manage to achieve both instinctual maturity *and* an adequate degree of narcissistic confirmation; but Grunberger admits that such success is not common. To seek this harmony through a multiplicity of sexual partners, for example, is counter-productive, since Grunberger insists (and is supported in his view by Gallop) that narcissism is marked by singleness; women have an image of an ideal object-choice who can bring together 'all the elements belonging to their various models of identification designated by narcissistic cathexis' (p. 76). But any real-life partner is unlikely to fill all such requirements, and thus disappoints. (Grunberger adds that the woman will accept her disappointment so long as she can count on the essential condition of being loved.)

It is important to remind ourselves here that Grunberger is examining *tendencies* which he believes may help to give an account of characteristic female sexuality; he does not wish to claim that no sexual satisfaction between partners is possible, but rather attempts to specify that aspect of disharmony in male–female relations that stems from what is perceived as the male inability to fulfil female expectations. Thus the generalised view that 'women need their narcissism satisfied and men seem unfit to do so' (i.e. to satisfy it) is predicated on the belief that women are narcissistic 'before all else', for reasons which go back to the fact that neither mother nor daughter can be satisfactory objects for the other. A woman thus cathects her own ego, and invests everything in self-love, in substitute love-objects, and in love itself. A man, on the other hand, may choose a woman – and her love – as the first object of cathexis; but when there he moves on to a 'hierarchy of realities', with, moreover, the narcissistic aspect of his cathexis subordinated to the instinctual. He is thus less fully engaged in 'love' than is the female.

That this should be simply the *normal* situation in male–female relations might be considered sad enough; it goes a long way to explaining a good deal of what goes on even in Kitty's mind in the earliest days of her marriage to Levin. But in neurosis, according to Grunberger, there occurs a disturbance of the normal synthesis of 'narcissistically cathected instincts . . . what should be synthesised becomes a source of interference'.

That is, whereas in normal relations object–love intensifies in proportion to the growth of narcissism, in neurosis the inverse occurs: as narcissism grows, the importance of object-relations decreases, because less libido is available to be invested in the instincts (including the sexual drive). It can therefore be said that Tolstoy gives us a heroine whose inscription can be read as an extreme example – an *un*satisfactory instance – of the inadequacies put forward by Grunberger as deficiencies in the ego-formation of *any* female.

Moreover, the outward coldness, dryness and general sterility of Karenin's nature makes reasonable the corollary that in the marriage-bed with him Anna's sexual instincts were frustrated further, rather than induced towards that synthesis which Grunberger postulates as normal and desirable. Hence Anna's overreaction to Vronsky's courtship – a courtship he certainly conducts in his own interest, to obtain sexual satisfaction for himself, but which is construed subconsciously by Anna as an opportunity to obtain narcissistic confirmation and through that, self-recognition and identity. The intensity with which she seizes upon his 'love' is a product of her own sense of need *and* demand (blatantly expressed in the cry of 'I need love!' as she awaits Vronsky's return from Yashvin's); and truly, as that insatiable urge inevitably remains unsatisfied, so does her narcissism grow in itself and in ever increasing demand. It is perhaps the inevitability of this psychic economy of inflation (of the ego), and devaluation (of the object), which endows Anna's degeneration into jealousy, possessiveness and despair with its dimension of tragedy. The rules of this system obtain, apparently, not just for her, but for the entire female species, making new sense of the old cliché that 'the woman is always the victim'.

The foregoing, very necessary addition to the classical, Freudian, and male-orientated account of ego-formation has parenthetically extended our understanding of Anna's situation; more relevantly to this chapter, it has also provided reasons for the feminist doubt that any male can ever truly write a female protagonist. But Grunberger himself admits that there is no experimental evidence for his hypothesis; and perhaps because of the innate obscurities of this kind of investigation, it does not constitute the most frequent form of attack on the enigma of the male *production* of the female. A more common and contentious issue is the question of how a male author *relates* to this creature to whom he has given form and a kind of life.

The French feminist Luce Irigaray (Irigaray, 1974) suggests that a father 'desires to have a daughter *in order* to seduce her. That he wishes to become an analyst in order to exercise . . . *a lasting seduction upon the hysteric*' (Gallop p. 75, Irigaray's emphasis). From these assertions, the conceptual jump to the idea that an author may equally desire to seduce his heroine is but a small one; it is rather the assertions themselves that are startling enough to require further substantiation.

In life the biological father must ultimately rely on the mother's *word* that the child is his; thus the effort to enthrall, or seduce, the daughter is the product of anxiety. The 'word' normally of course belongs to the Symbolic Order, where, in the Name of the Father, it both serves and implements the Law. But in that one case where the Father must depend for his mental comfort on the say-so of the Mother, one can say that she, however temporally, appropriates the Word. However, the word can be restored to the Father if he can exercise not the dubious hold of paternal assumptions over his daughter, but a more dynamic thralldom. In other words, it is more subtle, more tempting and more effective to bind her by the power of seduction than by the supposed claims of kinship. As Gallop points out (p. 56), 'the dichotomy active/passive is always equivocal in seduction'; the question of the complicity of the victim suggests itself as not only justification but flattery for the seducer.

Of course paternal seduction of the daughter is not countenanced in either life or literature; but this does not prevent its being fantasised – by either party. Irigaray (1974, p. 106; Gallop, p. 70) claims that the daughter also desires the father because 'the only redemption' of the daughter's value as a girl is her ability to seduce the male hero of the family romance. Possession of the phallus confers value; therefore the daughter needs to feel that the Father, possessor of the phallus, desires her if she is to have any sense of her own value. And, conversely, the more worthy the daughter (that is, beautiful, desirable, admirable in every way – as Anna is depicted at the start of the novel), the more enhanced is the father, or author, who lends her her value. In the end, though, the father does not want to actually engage in the seduction of the daughter, since to do so would be to partake of her otherness, to be weakened in his maleness. It is better, after all, to avoid dependence on both the claims of biology and the undoings of seduction, and retreat to the strength of the law – to make the daughter submit by doing his bidding; to let her 'seduce' him by pleasing and obeying him. 'The only way to seduce the father, to avoid scaring him away, is to please him, and to please him one must submit to his law which proscribes any sexual relation' (p. 71) – or, by extension, the triumph of any sexual relation with a substitute male. Precisely, then, because of the beautification of Anna (as contrasted perhaps with the beatification of Kitty) which enhances her creator's interest and investment in her, it is all the more essential that he should deny her her power, her attraction, her possible mastery – in other words he must protect himself from her. Gallop extends the significance of this prohibition by noting that fathers who desire their daughters can no longer exchange them: it loses them the 'commerce in which women are exchanged between men, in the service of power relations and community for the men' (p. 76). This may be a pertinent comment in regard to society; more relevant to Tolstoy is the consideration that fathers who desire their daughters upset the relational economy of the family, which for him is more sacred than its parts. Hence the sacrifice of a daughter who seduces her father by an attraction which exceeds the mere revelation of her obedience and wish to please contributes to the interests of both the family itself and of patriarchal authority in general. So what lesser fate should befall a heroine who tempts her author beyond his strength? Anna's 'suicide' thus becomes ineluctable on yet another account; she dies not only by her own hand, but also by that of her author, who loathes this creature taken from his own rib. Ultimately perhaps the two issues do reduce to the same; but because of the 'blindness of insight', what Tolstoy and the superficial reader perceive to be the motivating causes are separable from those produced by the underside of the divided subject.

Thus Tolstoy's interest in killing the female he created, and Anna's interest in killing herself, converge and separate, are at one moment indistinguishable, at the next shockingly in conflict. There is however a link between the two imperatives which can once again be retrieved from the now familiar lines from *Life and Death in Psychoanalysis*: 'Seductive and traumatic as it was [Laplanche's underlining], the forced introduction of the death drive could only provoke on the part of Freud's heirs every conceivable variety of defense . . .' (p. 107). They, like most of us, were and are unwilling to grasp the nettle; yet, as we have just seen, it is a 'seductive' nettle. . . . The essay itself creates reactions of such disavowal that they amount to an admission of a sore spot; but one knows how often the tongue seeks out the aching tooth and lovingly caresses it.

Following the account of Andrei's resigned and almost triumphal end in *War and Peace*, Tolstoy was now tending to write about death in increasingly minatory tones. The novella *The Death of Ivan Illych* and the short story 'Three Deaths' both centre on demises of various forms. But these works, in indicating how the organism should die, are really concerned with showing how it should in the first place live.

That a more sombre and personal concern with death existed in Tolstoy's mind is evidenced from Sonya's comments on him in her diary, from the completion of *War and Peace* onwards. On 14 February 1870 she records that her husband often said now that 'it was time for him to die', the thought perhaps precipitated by recurrent memories of a vivid personal experience that had occurred the year before when he was away from home, buying land in the region of the present-day town of Gorky. Tolstoy recreated the event of 1869 in a story entitled 'Notes of a Madman', which he did not actually set down till 1880 (*SS* 12). Given our comments on the erotic initiation of narrative in Chapter 2 (for example, Peter Brooks' remark that narrative desire is an 'arousal that creates the narratable as a condition of tumescence, appetency, ambition quest, and gives narrative a forward-looking intention – p. 103) it is interesting to note that, within a frame of triggering circumstances and reminders of childhood, the main story of 'Notes of a Madman' begins with an allusion to the 'auto-eroticism' (meaning here masturbation) common to young boys. This is followed by the remark, 'I began to know women, and thus, seeking pleasure and finding it, I lived to the age of thirty-five' (*SS* 12, p. 47). Until that age he had exhibited no signs of 'madness', but now, in the tenth year of his marriage, the hero suffers an attack of terror similar to one he had had once before, when a child. He cannot sleep; he gets up from the bed and goes into the corridor, where his servant and the night watchman are sleeping; an icy shudder seizes him; death is at hand. She (death is grammatically feminine in Russian) is coming, although she has no right to. He is not so much frightened as insistent that she should not come; his whole being is suffused with the demand and the right to live, but mixed with that is the sense of death 'happening', accomplishing herself. He is torn in two and the split is dreadful. Life is nothing; death *is*, but should not be. But for death too, everything is dreadful, just as to the dying, life is dreadful. And not only dreadful, but '*zhutko*' – uncanny. . . . 'Somehow life and death have fused into one – ' and it is 'uncanny'! *Unheimlich*! Uncanny indeed that both he and Freud should hit on the same word to describe 'something familiar and old-established in the mind that has been estranged only by the process of repression . . . something which ought to have been kept concealed but which has nevertheless come to light' (*PF* 14, pp. 363–4). We sense, as Neil Hertz claims the reader of 'The Sandman' also does, 'the imminent return of the repressed' (Hertz, 1979, p. 304), for there is another entry in Tolstoy's notebook which goes four years back, to 1865, when after happily welcoming some well-liked guests he went to bed but could not sleep:

> My soul was striving towards something, wanting something. 'What can I want?' I asked myself in surprise. 'My friends are here. Isn't that what I needed to regain my peace of mind . . . ?' Nothing could satisfy this desire in me. And the desire persisted, it still persists and indeed it is the most important and strongest thing in my soul. I desire what does not exist in this world. . . . To be reborn, *to die*. This is the peace I yearn for, we all yearn for . . .          (*Diary*, 4 December 1865)

Anna is not only a projection of Tolstoy's repudiated sexual passion; she also plays out for him that aspiration towards death that Freud, de Rougemont, Bernheimer, Brooks *et cetera* acknowledge as 'seductive and traumatic', but which remains socially unacceptable, not to be said, always to be repressed, and to be returned to only in the form of fantasy. Or fantasies. We recall Vronsky's attempt to shoot himself and Levin's contemplation of suicide when he does not have, at that moment, the means close at hand.

But it is of course Anna who occupies the main stage in the drama of death, and unconsciously enacts attributes associated with the death wish long before she seriously thinks of killing herself. The many conflicts she instigates with Vronsky are a clear

example: 'The death drive . . . is present in Freud's final formulations, not as an element in conflict but as *conflict* itself substantial-
ised, an internal principle of strife and disunion', comments
Laplanche (p. 122). Tolstoy writes, 'She [Anna] did not want strife
and blamed him for wanting to fight, but she involuntarily took up
a fighting attitude' (*SS* 9, p. 315). When the attitude erupts into
open hostility Anna claims she is at such moments 'near catastro-
phe', and 'afraid of herself'. But afterwards, although temporarily
reconciled, she feels that 'side by side with the love that united
them there had grown up some evil spirit of strife, which she could
not drive out of his heart and still less out of her own' (*SS* 9,
p. 317).

Soon after that quarrel another one bursts out, in which Vronsky
calls Anna 'irrational'. The issue, as even Anna realises, is only
indirectly significant – they argue over the question of education
for adolescent girls, specifically Anna's protégée, Hannah. But the
matter of Hannah's education is really only Vronsky's opportunity
to express his revulsion from Anna's increasingly shrewish behaviour. It is all simply 'unnatural'. Perhaps he is also recoiling from
the memory of his own suicide attempt, to which he never refers,
but watches the same seeds growing rampant in his hysterical
wife.

That quarrel and its renewal a little later lead to the classic
rehearsal of the female need for love that we have already noted in
the context of both passion and narcissism. 'I want love and it is
lacking. So everything's finished . . .'. But the fact that she 'understands what is in her soul' – already – now makes a new connection between love and death. The death wish does not come to her
because of the quarrel, it was always already there; it inhabits all
life, its voice heard only the more loudly in those who are also
narcissistically obsessed by sexual passion. Inevitably Anna cannot
face the boldness of this truth; after entertaining a few false
justifications – Vronsky and Seriozha will be saved from disgrace
by her death, Vronsky's love will be reanimated – she quickly
allows Vronsky to pacify her and temporarily reconcile her to life.

In other words, the organism is not yet ready. But at this point it
is not only Vronsky who shrinks from a woman who 'unnaturally'
courts death. It is also Tolstoy, who, courageous enough to explore
his own longing for death through the surrogate of his heroine,
nonetheless recoils from her as from a thing of horror. His revulsion is expressed by the otherwise inexplicable detail already

referred to – the figure Anna cuts when, raising a cup of coffee to her lips, she sticks out her little finger. It is a gesture of purely ignorant *nouveau-riche* vulgarity. But Anna was for so long gracious, elegant, aristocratic that even now the accusation seems gratuitous. But it is this gesture, and the slurp with which she accompanies it, that enable Tolstoy to write, 'Her hand, her movement, and the sound made by her lips were repulsive to him [Vronsky]' (*SS* 9, p. 741). Even more abhorrent are they to her creator, whose disgust, though repressed in most of the text, and apparently transmuted into the pity he originally claimed would animate the book, is crystallised and revealed in this brief, cruel scene.

At this point, the entrance of a third person, Yashvin, forces Anna to take control of the 'storm raging within her'. But it is clear that the abatement is only temporary, and precedes evidence of real mental derangement. [Vronsky] 'hated her because he loved another woman – that was clear'. Anna 'invents' words which Vronsky did not say but 'had wished to say' – and does not forgive him for then 'any more than if he had said them'. She leaves a message with the maid, telling him not to come to her room on his return to the house, then sets a trap he cannot possibly guess at. If he ignores the message conveyed by the maid, he still loves her; if he obeys her instructions, 'it means it is all over . . .'. Add to this the unspecified effects of drug taking (she has had 'her usual dose of opium') and we are ready to accept Tolstoy's intimation that Anna is indeed half-crazed. Her persistent reiteration of the idea that Vronsky loves elsewhere, the supposed cooling of his love, and the assumed birth of a new hatred for her is not designed to persuade us that there is anything but delirium in her wild ravings. But Tolstoy himself was later, as we have seen, to cloak his own closest confrontation with death under the title, 'Notes of a Madman'. As Foucault has shown, society labels as mad what it does not wish to own. Anna's defiance of the law must be madness, since she does not have right to de-fiance, only to af-fiance, to be a fiancée like Kitty. Madness is the only appropriate word to describe a jealousy without grounds, a persecution complex without a persecutor.

By now Tolstoy does not want to acknowledge that he once loved this madwoman, and Vronsky does not wish to 'see or understand the gloomy and solemn look on her face'. Nor does anyone else. The very fact that Dolly and Kitty, both normally kindness personified, shy away from any attempt to reach her in their last scene together, shows how far Anna has gone down the path towards death. Shored up by their attachment to their own lives, both women find Anna's closeness to zero, to Nirvana, incomprehensible, unrealisable to either of them. They perceive her as 'pathetic', even note that she is 'going to cry'. But their defences prevent them from really comprehending what is happening to their sister-in-law, though she herself penetrates to the heart of what goes on in their minds during her brief visit to them. 'How they looked at me, as if at something dreadful, incomprehensible, and curious . . .', she says after leaving them (*SS* 9, p. 379).

In a moment of lucidity she admits that all her imaginings of Vronsky's 'other interests' are pure fantasy on her part; she knows he loves her – but still, inevitably, she foreshadows Lacan: 'What I desire is lacking' – in life, that is. So life itself, with its inscribed lack, is the final obstacle to the satisfaction of lack. How much easier to turn to Western man's other love, the only one to keep its promise.

Death is a convention of closure for many forms of narrative, and audiences are entitled to expect it and 'The End' to appear simultaneously on page or screen.

*Anna Karenina* was presumed by all concerned, except the author, to have finished with the completion of Part 7, that is, with Anna's death. The public were convinced that there was nothing more to be said (unless there should be a miraculous resuscitation of Anna); the management of the *Russkii Vestnik* (*The Russian Herald*) judged Tolstoy's Part 8 to be unacceptable for political reasons (it included his disapproval of Russian involvement in the Serbian uprising against the Turks, which resolved itself into a declaration of war against Turkey on 12 April 1877), and Katkov, the editor, firmly refused to print it. Tolstoy went ahead and published Part 8 separately in booklet form, under the title 'An Epilogue'.

In this last word, he turns seemingly with relief, and perhaps also with some recovery of face, to those problems of Levin's which were more admissible than the *profondeurs* of Anna's case. It is in this Part 8 that Levin at last persuades himself that he has attained the childlike religious faith that appears to come naturally to the peasants. And also in Part 8 Tolstoy's idealised family is created through the birth of Mitya, Kitty's and Levin's son, who in the last pages of the book reaffirms his author's sense of family and of community by beginning to 'recognise his own people'.

It looks like the triumph of life over death, of Continuum over Closure. Yet Part 8 is so full of oppositions which undermine and displace eath other that the apparent victories are Pyrrhic indeed. It opens with an account of the failure of the book entitled *An Attempt to Review the Foundations and Forms of Government in Europe and Russia* which Koznyshev has been writing – a venture no more fruitful than his intention to propose to Varenka. First, there are no reviews at all; then comes a facetious one in a journal called *The Northern Beetle*; finally, a serious magazine gives it space, but 'the article was dreadful' (*SS* 9, p. 391). The review is followed by dead silence, and Koznyshev sees 'that his six years' work, carried out with so much devotion and labour, was entirely thrown away', for the book has been completely misunderstood 'in an impossible way'. It seems that Tolstoy was exhibiting another of the drives elucidated by Freud, and taken up, as we saw earlier, by Lionel Trilling: he is surely living out the hypothesis that fear or apprehension is developed in order to restore control of the stimuli. 'The dream [or the literary representation – compare Norman Holland's "Literature dreams a dream for us"] is the effort to [re]construct the bad situation in order that the failure to meet it may be recouped' (Trilling, 1981, p. 109).

The failure of Koznyshev's book expresses Tolstoy's inevitable fears of misunderstanding and rejection, and, by anticipating that future despair, produces the energy necessary to overcome a present anxiety. That the reading public in fact loved increasingly the successive instalments of the novel is beside the point – for would they continue to do so if they *really* understood what was in it? It is, after all, in that same Chapter I of Part 8 that Tolstoy betrays an extreme of cynicism which seems to denote bitter disillusionment with much that had previously shored him up. Koznyshev's 'displacement activity' after the failure of his book is his enthusiasm for the Serbian War; but Koznyshev's patriotism becomes Tolstoy's vehicle for jeering at 'the soul of the nation' – the very ideal which lay behind much of the philosophy of *War and Peace*. Even more incredibly, a hint of sarcasm appears in Koznyshev's desire to rest from his patriotic activities by going into the depths of the country – now described somewhat mockingly as 'that holy of holies of the people', the sight of which promotes 'that uplift of the national spirit of which he and all town-dwellers were fully convinced' (*SS* 9, p. 393).

Tolstoy's current self-hatred is even more viciously manifested through another of his alter egos – Count Vronsky, who is now a kind of surrogate for the dead Anna. Vronsky also finds a displacement activity in the Serbian War, though he takes it further than Koznyshev, since he is actually going off to fight. But he is accompanied on the first leg of the journey by his mother – a spectral maternal image now become something close to diabolic. (Countess Vronsky vindictively salts the wound of searing guilt felt by Vronsky at Anna's death – and symbolically expressed by an acute nagging toothache which relentlessly hinders him from speaking.) At the railway station Vronsky relives the moment of seeing Anna's dead body, and then tries to recall her beauty and charm; but he finds his memories are poisoned. Not only has the good Anna has been destroyed forever, the negative reverse of the love-object is paralleled by an equally pernicious mother-image. It is not enough that the Countess will not leave her son alone when he most wants to endure his misery in peace and privacy; we become aware that she herself was instrumental in causing Anna's death. For Vronsky was visiting his mother at her insistence when Anna finally gave up hope; Anna died at the railway station serving Countess Vronsky's country estate. Thus the guilt and inanition Tolstoy feels at wreaking vengeance on his own creation, *a part of his own self* (the Countess dredges up Vronsky's earlier attempt at suicide, frowning at the recollection), and the revelation of this lurking hatred for a too-powerful Mother, result in a determination that Anna will not outwit him by living on as an exquisite memory, her beauty effacing her vindictiveness. Yet in this he was unsuccessful. Although he was certainly correct in insisting that the novel was not finished at the end of Part 7, it was no more finished at the end of Part 8, for it is there that Kitty's 'long series of spiritual relations' with her son 'begin'. Lucky little Mitya!

# 7

# Lenin Deconstructs

The *retrécissement* of novel-space that took place at the end of the last chapter as Levin and Kitty bend over their sleeping child has more than psychological significance. When it is contrasted with, for example, the grand movement of dispersion that is the dramatic and didactic highlight of the last act of Chekhov's *Cherry Orchard* (1902–3), it seems to bear the directly opposite political message. The sale of the orchard is a financial necessity; it may also be moral duty; but it is above all a collective release, enabling Trofimov to exclaim with exhilaration that now, 'The whole of Russia is our cherry-orchard!' With all the characters except Firs forced out into the world, many of them, like Gaev, to earn their living for the first time, one can easily say that the play is prophetic of the changes to come to the whole country. While Chekhov never specifically mentions revolution, Trofimov's hailing of a glorious future can be allowably connected to that event, while some specific details that he envisages have been visibly realised. The modern Soviet Union has certainly provided crèches for its children, and Lenin's aim of universal literacy has involved the construction of libraries in every town. All of which seems to form a strange contrast with the inward-looking preoccupations of the Count and Countess Levin. But perhaps such an attitude is unfair; after all, a young husband is entitled to a personal life even when he is the hero of a novel; and Levin is clearly concerned with a great many more matters than the mere joys of fatherhood. So what of the specifically political issues of *Anna Karenina*? Where is the Revolution, however veiled its heralding?

It is appropriately ironic in view of the name of this book that its writer is always conscious of what is being left out. Once intertextuality is admitted, the parameters of any specified discourse can only be arbitrarily drawn, and the choice of where to do so is usually embarrassing. It is not, one hopes, that the inclusion of Freud, Brooks or Miller requires justification, but rather that the omission of all the rest invites a certain kind of negative (carping?) criticism. As we move through the various areas embraced by

142

modern literary criticism we can only note that the availability of theoretical approaches varies from field to field – here a drought, there a glut.

The predicament of a chapter concerned with political approaches to *Anna Karenina* falls into the former category. The paucity of feminist ideological criticism directed specifically to this work was noted in the previous chapter, but whether because it is, after all, a *Russian* novel, embedded in an era leading inexorably to a socialist revolution, or whether because only Marxist theories of literature have systematically foregrounded the relations between the novel and society, it is simply the case that Vladimir Lenin, George Lukács and Pierre Macherey have almost alone provided substantial criticism of Tolstoy's representation of his own epoch, and hence of *Anna Karenina*, and it is with them that this chapter will be concerned.[1] However, this seemingly neat package at once becomes a Pandora's box, for it is the commitment to the awesome concept of totality that primarily unites these three critics; and totality itself, as Martin Jay has shown (Jay, 1984) has all too many shades of meaning. Ferenc Fehér, in a review article of Jay's book (Fehér, 1985) extricates five working definitions for it, of which three are relevant to literary analysis. Summarising these, we can say with Fehér and Jay that totality can mean a methodological principle in which the parts are understood from the whole, i.e. 'where the primary principle, the preconceived explanatory basis, the whole, always has a particular value-laden character'; it can suggest a *promise of the future*, that is, a potentiality rather than an actuality; and lastly it can indicate an *ultimate principle* of societal life 'from which all subsystems, each and every phenomena [sic] of social life can at least be grasped in a *comprehensive understanding*' (Fehér, p. 866; his emphasis). To reduce these definitions to their most basic meanings: every novel must be considered in relation to the society in which it is produced and consumed; that society can only be grasped as an aspect of a larger dimension, which is history; and history must include both its own past and its future goals. In other words, the daunting perspectives of the desire to 'see things whole' (Jay, p. 537) are pitted against the notion of literary works conceived as finished products, as 'givens', complete within their two covers and interrogated only on their own terms.

The second approach, though recently holding considerable sway in the Leavisite and New American traditions of criticism, appears at the moment to be out of fashion; but some of the problems inherent in the larger schema are immediately apparent. For one thing, the picture of the totality available to and expressed by the characters of a novel is obviously smaller than that available to the narrator, just as his is more limited than that of the author; and no matter how prophetic or far-seeing the author's gaze, it will never be able to contain the ever-increasing dimensions of hindsight enjoyed by each generation of successive readers. The ultimate totality is, as Fehér's second category allows, a mere promise.

A second difficulty is elaborated at length by Fredric Jameson in *The Political Unconscious* (Jameson, 1981). This work rests on the idea that every universalising approach can be guaranteed to be concealing its own contradictions. For one thing, it seeks to repress its own historicity 'by strategically framing its perspective to omit the negative, absence, contradiction, repression, the *non-dit*, or the *impensé . . .*' (p. 110). This has been exactly what we have been arguing in relation to Tolstoy's text read through other discourses; Jameson now adds the theory of a specifically *political* unsaid to that underside that has already shown large parts of its vast belly. However, this part of our enquiry will begin with a man who is little associated in the public mind with works of literary criticism or of hidden silences.

Vladimir Ilich Lenin, it is said, believed that 'a careful study' should be made of Tolstoy, and edited versions of his stories, articles and extracts be distributed to peasants and workers. His own contribution to Tolstoy scholarship consists of six articles written between 1908 and 1911, which tend to refer rather generally to the writer and his works, without paying much attention to the necessary differentiation between texts of one period and those of another. Here, therefore, I shall discuss only those remarks of Lenin's which relate directly to *Anna Karenina*, and also those in Pierre Macherey's commentary on Lenin, 'Critic of Tolstoy', which bear the same relevance (Macherey, 1978).

The first article, 'Leo Tolstoy as Mirror of the Russian Revolution', was sparked off by the public reaction to Tolstoy's eightieth birthday; on this day (28 August 1908) there were more than 30 people at table inside the house, hundreds outside, and 1700 messages of congratulation from all over the world. These included many eulogies to the 'Seeker after God', the 'Old Man Inspired by God', *et cetera*, and came from writers, peasants, academics – even a Catholic priest, according to Alexandra Tolstoy's biography of her father (Tolstoy, Alexandra, *1953*, vol. 2, p. 321). Thus Lenin, writing the same year, less than a month later in fact, is under some pressure to deal with the Tolstoy phenomenon in such a way as to bend this recalcitrant and idiosyncratic material to the uses of the next revolution – Tolstoy's attitude to the revolution of 1905 having been predictably individualistic and on the whole negative. Tolstoy was in favour of some reforms, but deeply opposed to the use of violence to achieve them. As far as he was concerned, to try to bring about social or political change without first advocating an inner, spiritual reform on the part of everyone involved was simply a waste of time, and worse if blood were to be shed. He abhorred the Marxist insistence on the relief of material need, although he was equally rejecting of what he saw as Tsarist and governmental hypocrisy and greed. His unequivocal and unfashionable belief, here expressed to his Liberal son Sergei, was that, 'The lives of men in general will not improve until every single man strives to live well for himself and not interfere in the lives of others' (Tolstoy, A, ibid.). One understands then Lenin's difficulty in recruiting the writings of such a reactionary moral individualist to the cause of revolutionary action, and, at the same time, his anxiety to not forego the enormous value of being able to show some compatibility between his and Tolstoy's divergent aims for the future of Russia.

He begins by meeting the problem head on: 'To identify the great artist with the revolution which he has obviously failed to understand, and from which he obviously stands aloof, may at first seem strange and artificial' (Lenin, 1963, vol. 16, p. 202). He then falls back on the rather lame assertion that a really great artist *must*, somehow, reflect at least *some* of the essential aspects of the revolution. Before he goes on to analyse in what way this reflection occurs in the work, however, Lenin vehemently attacks the Liberals for their eulogies of Tolstoy, pointing out, on the whole correctly, that no Russian Liberal of the time either believed in Tolstoy's God or sympathized with his criticism of the social order. To rectify the Liberal failure to confront the glaring 'contradictions' in Tolstoy's work and doctrine is one of the prime responsibilities of the true revolutionary. Embarking himself on the first steps of this important initiative, Lenin lists the following positive attributes that can be assigned to Tolstoy: his artistic genius, his protest against social falsehood and hypocrisy, and his criticism of capitalist exploitation, government outrages, farcical courts, and the growth of wealth; on the negative side are his status as a landlord, his obsession with religion, his hypocritical disciples, and his doctrine of non-resistance to evil. However, these contradictions are historically justified in that they truthfully reflect both an imperfectly realized emancipation from patriarchy, and a protest against the capitalistic dispossession of the peasant owners of the land. 'Tolstoy is great as the spokesman of the ideas and sentiments that emerged among the millions of Russian peasants at the time the bourgeois revolution was approaching in Russia' (p. 206). Lenin associates Tolstoy with 'the striving to sweep away the official church, the landlords and the landlord government', while allowing the peasants, by contrast, the indulgence of retaining their 'very crude, patriarchal, semi-religious idea' of what the new life might be. Thus the ideas in Tolstoy's books accurately reflect the limitations and shortcomings of the peasants, although a more worthy overview is attributed to the writer himself. According to Lenin, Tolstoy reflected 'the desire to get rid of the past'. (Tolstoy himself, at the time of writing *War and Peace*, said in a piece that was omitted from the published version: 'I am an aristocrat because I am not only not ashamed, but positively glad to remember my ancestors . . . I am an aristocrat because I cannot believe in the high intellect, the refined taste or the absolute honesty of a man who picks his nose and whose soul converses with God' [Christian, 1960, pp. 100–3]).

Two years after Lenin's remarks were written Tolstoy was dead, and his universal fame was again marked by global recognition and mourning of his passing. In an article simply called, 'L. N. Tolstoy' (vol. 16, pp. 323–7), Lenin used the occasion to point out his regret that illiteracy itself – the lot of millions of the Russian lower classes – prevented Tolstoy's works being known by more than an 'infinitesimal' few. Once again he reiterates Tolstoy's 'accurate' depiction of the era of peasant–bourgeois revolution, whose combined aim was to overthrow Tsarism – even though the bourgeoisie split off from the peasantry to consolidate their task of 'clearing the ground' for capitalism. Once again he identifies Tolstoy with protest against the official church, and speaks of his 'unending opposition to private property in land', whether this took the form of landed estates or of government allotments; and Tolstoy, as distinct from the peasant masses who knew no better, is portrayed as unremittingly opposed to the coming of capitalism. He disappoints the radicals, however, in not knowing any better than a naive peasant how to escape the crisis threatening Russia. His repudiation of politics, his advocacy of his own form of religion, his apathy towards socialist emancipation of the masses, are regrettable but nevertheless historical, in that these contradictions reflect the confusion of the post-reform, pre-revolutionary period of transition. In a separate article written at the same time ('L. N. Tolstoy and the Modern Labour Movement', November 1910) Lenin refines his encapsulation of Tolstoy's position into the conviction that the writer mirrored the sentiments of the patriarchal, naive peasants so faithfully that he imported into his own doctrine not only that the very *naiveté*, but also the mysticism which produced both alienation from political life and a spirit of non-resistance. (vol. 16, pp. 330–2)

A month later Lenin found it necessary to quell more severely the, to him, misguided adulation which now declared Tolstoy to be a 'universal conscience' and 'teacher of life' (vol. 16, p. 354). By studying the literary works of Tolstoy, he writes, the working class will better understand its enemies, but by examining his *doctrine*, the whole Russian people will understand where their weaknesses lie. In other words, the lesson to be learnt from Tolstoy is an ambivalent one. The novels say more about the entrenched fidelity of the upper classes, but the tracts, pamphlets and essays which followed the two great novels indict the flaws and failures of all levels of society – which, to Lenin, were failures of activism, politicisation, and the will to revolution.

Nevertheless, neither Lenin's qualification of his estimate of Tolstoy, nor the intractable nature of some of the material in the novels, have daunted the efforts of the later Marxists, Lukács and Macherey, who perform operations of interconnecting salvage on the political leader and the illustrious writer. And both join with Jameson in regarding the 'totality' as the only possible framework in which to consider both text and author.

In his early work *The Theory of the Novel* (Lukás, 1971) George Lukács refers to 'Tolstoy's great and truly epic mentality' which 'has little to do with the novel form' (p.145). This 'epic' mentality aspires to a life based on a community of feeling among simple human beings closely bound to nature. Nature is posited as an ideal in opposition to culture, but since the destinies of the characters are worked out within the frame of individual love and marriage and in the public world of society, the essence of Nature is not really present; we catch only glimpses of it, as in the death-bed scenes, before the story passes back into conventional life. 'The glimpsed world of essential nature remains an intimation . . . of the same kind as any other longing for a more adequate reality.' (p.151). For this reason, in Lukács' view, Tolstoy's novels are novels of disillusion, being born of the epic desire for totality and the incapacity of the real world to fulfil this.

In his later, much longer, essay 'Tolstoy and the Development of Realism' (Lukács, 1972), Lukács nods in the direction of Lenin's 'brilliant' analysis of Tolstoy's attitudes to the revolutionary developments in Russia, but concentrates much more attention on the issue of *genre*. Reiterating his claim that 'Tolstoy himself was well aware that his great novels were genuine epics' (p. 149), Lukács advances two principal grounds for maintaining his own insistence on the epic nature of Tolstoy's fiction. First is the fact that the world depicted by Tolstoy is a world 'much less *bourgeois* than the world of the eighteenth-century English novelists'; and second, that the necessary condition, the 'epic presentation of the totality of life' based on the 'totality of objects' (p. 151), is richer and more complete in Tolstoy than any other modern author. Specifically in *Anna Karenina* he cites the 'dances, clubs, parties, social calls, conferences, work in the fields, horse-races and card games'. The horse-race at which Vronsky's horse falls attracts an extended and laudatory commentary: 'Vronsky's accident is . . . not merely an opportunity for the crises to become manifest, it also determines the crises . . .' (p. 154). Tolstoy's superiority is supported by a favourable comparison with the horse-races in Zola's *Nana*, which are demoted to 'a mighty but indifferent background to human destinies with which they have no connection; . . . they are at best . . . more or less accidental scenery' (p. 152).

Nevertheless, Lukács is forced to acknowledge the presence in *Anna Karenina* of less-than-epic traits. The process of capitalistic development is already apparent; the village idyll is threatened; the structure of the novel is more 'European', more closely-knit, the pace less leisurely. Thus two important conclusions emerge: firstly, the epic greatness of Tolstoy's novel is based on the landowners' *illusion* that the problem was capable of solution. Precisely because of the fact that 'a break with the system of private property' was not 'within the range of Levin's social and human possibilities' (p.181), his conversations reveal the true depths of the problem. It is for this reason that Tolstoy can truly be called 'the poet of the peasant revolt that lasted from 1861–1905' (p. 145).

Secondly, despite the epic dimensions of Levin's dilemma, the importance of the strand concerned with the depiction of bourgeois marriage means that '*Anna Karenina* is far more novel-like than *War and Peace*' (p. 151). This second judgement betrays Lukács' somewhat conventional notion of 'the novel' – certainly not one that would stand up to postmodern examples of the *genre*; his first conclusion is best reviewed in the context of other, related accounts of 'the totality', as they are set out by the already nominated writers.

For example, a different tack is taken by the French Marxist Pierre Macherey in his *Theory of Literary Production* (Macherey, 1984), even though he embarks upon a similar rescue operation of the Lenin–Tolstoy double-event. Ascribing a much greater importance to Lenin's articles than does Lukács, Macherey views them as an attempt to allot 'a true role to literary production at the moment of its potency' (p. 107), and devotes a lengthy essay to an almost reverential defence of them. Nevertheless, the density of its arguments does not mean that the essay rises above the essentially historicising strategy essential to any Marxist interpretation. Macherey cites with approval the general principle of Lenin's critical method, that 'the literary work only makes sense if it is considered in relation to a determinate historical period' (ibid.). But since it also throws light on its period, there is a reciprocity of illumination beaming back and forth between the historical moment and the literary work.

The definition of the relevant historical moment must allow for considerable breadth. The Tolstoyan era stretches from 1861 (the year of the Edict of the Emancipation of the Serfs) to 1905, when the first abortive Russian revolution occurred. Macherey establishes four significant social elements influencing the course of history during this period: the landowning rural aristocracy, now disintegrating; the peasant protest against both the relics of feudalism and the growth of capitalism; the bourgeoisie; and the proletariat, which makes its appearance at the end of the epoch. This last term is for Macherey the most important of the four:

Events between 1861 and 1905 in both feudal, bourgeois and peasant Russia, derive their real meaning from the fact that this is the moment of the emergence of the working class and its party, both consequences of the disruption of the rural areas by the development of capitalism. (p. 110)

Macherey defines Tolstoy as spontaneously representing the landed aristocracy, but enjoying a mobile social mentality which enables him to identify and sympathise with the peasant. By contrast he is blind both to the power of the bourgeoisie and to the growth of an urban proletariat, although aware of some of the immediate consequences of the development of capitalism. Hence his work satisfactorily reflects, even though he himself does not fully understand it, the essential turmoil of his age. Here, obviously, the literary philosopher and the political reader are in full agreement with each other. When it comes to professional criticism, however, Macherey believes that this must be concerned neither with the 'straight' historical events, nor with the ideological concepts of the literary work, but only with its 'literariness' – an aspect which, Macherey admits, Lenin was singularly ill-equipped to deal with. His deficiency is nevertheless less harmful than the positive damage perpetrated by bourgeois criticism inexorably grounded in its own shackling ideology. Macherey approvingly qoutes Engels' words:

> A novel of the socialist tendency perfectly fulfils its function when, by faithful picture of real relations, it destroys the conventional illusions about these relations, when it shakes the optimism of the bourgeois world, when it casts doubts on the eternal nature of the existing society, even if the author does not propose answers, even though he might not openly take sides.
>
> (Macherey, p. 119)

If this statement is taken to mean that any novel should cast doubt upon the eternal nature of the existing society, it is a perfectly acceptable definition of one of the many roles of literature, and particularly of the problematic *genre* of the novel. However, the forceful quality of all the verbs in Engels' statement ('Destroys . . . shakes . . . casts doubt') seems to carry implications of a political significance loaded towards revolution – in other words, to be a somewhat partisan view. Macherey underwrites this interpretation when he asserts that if a work of art can in any way be considered as a faithful picture, or a mirroring of society, it does so as a mirror which registers its own partiality. 'It is privileged because it does not have to elaborate the totality in order to display it; it can reveal just the necessity of that totality' (p. 122). He then adds two remarks which are more dubious in their assertions. Firstly, he claims that the necessity of the totality can be deciphered *from the work*, and that it is the task of 'scientific' criticism to achieve such a reading. It seems at least to this writer that while it is undoubtedly the case that *Anna Karenina* poses many problems, including, very explicitly, those facing the agricultural landlord in rural Russia, the 'necessity of that totality' – which, we must remember, includes the absent cause of the resurgent proletariat – *cannot* be deciphered from that text; it must be constructed from 'scientific' addenda which will at least include an objective account of the historical situation, and, if it is to suit a Marxist totality, the interpretive strategy of showing the *future* role of the urban proletariat and the Communist party.

Perhaps this difficulty can be made clearer by considering it in terms of the novel itself. For example, when Levin argues with his brother, or with his friends, none of the various arguments put forward is shown to be more convincing than another; neither resolution nor consensus is attained, and Levin simply resolves not to engage with these debaters, for 'they are clad in impenetrable armour', while he feels naked. The authorial gloss, however, explicitly states that Levin does not see the views advanced *concerning* the Russian people as inherent *in* the Russian people, and that what is best for the general welfare remains a mystery. 'All these were thoughts that could not decide anything.' Levin's only solution is that everyone should be like him, aspiring to the 'strict fulfilment of the law of goodness which is revealed to every man' (*SS* 9, p. 436). Thus it is a logically possible solution, within the grasp of all; it is also, realistically, a highly unlikely one, a surmise which Tolstoy does not hide from us. The answers to the social and political problems set out in the novel will only be found on a spiritual plane which lies so far outside probability than not even Tolstoy offers them as anything more than desirable goods unlikely to be realised. Nevertheless the sources of that answer are locatable *within the text*, i.e. within the aspirations of characters such as Levin. The sources of Lenin's and Macherey's solutions to the problems of the text lie elsewhere: in the history of the Russian revolution, and specifically in the role played in that event by a force entirely absent from the novel, that is, the urban proletariat – which is by contrast vividly present in many of Dostoevsky's novels, particularly *Crime and Punishment*.

Similarly, although the necessity of the future bourgeois revolution may be said to be 'present' embryonically in the novel, in details such as the land-deal between Oblonsky and the *entrepreneur* Ryabinin, the connection between the two revolutions, bourgeois and proletarian, can hardly be said to be predicable on events as slight as this. Symbolic it may be, even symptomatic, but scarcely large enough to infer the totality of which Macherey is so confident.

These two examples show the difference between a *present* cause, that is, something citable in the novel (such as Levin's argument or Oblonsky's land-sale), however it may be interpreted, and the essentially absent cause of the future proletariat revolution which, in order to be made relevant, requires a completely different interpretative step, only relying *wholly* on context, and not, as is the case of the land-buying merchant, on one which pertains both to text *and* context. Another way of putting the issue is simply to note that the introduction of extraneous interpretative material exceeds the normal relation of *siuzhet* to *fabula*; yet another would be to say that it is one thing to match up a text against an explanatory paradigm, but a different and more doubtful exercise to find within that text evidence for a model which depends on some putatively causal-in-reverse process. The most positive way of looking at it would be this: if the Revolution of 1917 was made successful by the action of the proletariat, then the necessity for that Revolution must imply the necessity of the proletariat; and if the necessity for the Revolution is also implied in the conflicts and turmoil of Tolstoy's portrayal of Russia in *Anna Karenina*, then it too must imply the future necessity of the proletariat – just as, according to Lukács, 'Russian literature and Pushkin's significance in it can only be grasped from the perspective of 1917' (Lukács, 1970, p. 227).

Macherey's criticism, however, undermines both this kind of assertive stance and, more importantly, itself. Arguing that indeed the term 'mirror', so beloved of simple reflection theory, takes on new meanings when deployed for the benefit of his more sophisticated theory of literary production, Macherey claims that 'it is not enough to say that the mirror catches a fragmented reality; the very image in the mirror (the work) is itself fragmented' (p. 122). The work, that is, does not itself know the whole story. This of course has been the argument of the whole of the present study, although the evidence has been drawn from other fields; and as we recall that one of those other fields was that of psychoanalysis we read, in Macherey, these words: 'Just as Freud has established that a dream has to be deconstructed into its constitutive elements before it can be interpreted, Lenin states that the literary text must be studied in the same way – not in the pursuit of a factitious totality, but according to its real and necessary discontinuity' (ibid.). Amazingly, we have come by a somewhat circuitous route to one of the favourite assertions of the psychoanalytic and deconstructive approaches, and found it attributed to the mouth of Lenin! (Compare, for example, Frank Kermode's remark: 'Whatever the comforts of sequence, connexity . . . it cannot be argued that the text which exhibits them will do nothing but contribute to them; some of it will be indifferent or even hostile to sequentiality' [*Critical Inquiry*, Summer 1981, p. 83]. Or Christopher Norris' gloss of Derrida: 'Writing is the endless displacement of meaning which both governs language and places it for ever beyond the reach of a stable, self-authenticating knowledge. . . . Language is always inscribed in a network of relays and differential "traces" which can never be grasped by the individual speaker. . . . Writing is that which exceeds – and has the power to dismantle – the whole traditional edifice of Western attitudes to thought and language' [Norris, 1983, p. 29]). We are even told that the *bourgeois* judgement of Tolstoy is a 'significant misreading' – a misprision perhaps? It must be remembered that we are reading Macherey's gloss of Lenin, with its appropriately updated and not innocent vocabulary. Tolstoy's 'bourgeois judgement' is now in Macherey's own words, an 'index of [their] imbalance' – that is, the imbalance between Tolstoy's blind championship of the past, and the wisdom which bade him reject, for example, private property. The literary work is, in the end, 'profoundly dissymetrical. There is more than one mirror . . .' (pp. 123–4).

The point reached which might have the deconstructionists leaping with aporial joy, Macherey suddenly narrows the focus rather severely. 'The problem is, not to interpret this multiplicity as equivocation . . .'. There can be no question of ambiguity, of either/or; it is a matter of both/and, or rather of a two-tier interpretation. We should be very clear that Macherey does not go as far as a Hillis Miller or a Barbara Johnson. He is not in fact advocating a simultaneous 'A and not-A', but rather a middle road between the weak and the strong deconstructive turns, a simultaneous presence of two non-identical but also non-contradictory terms. The 'exact' readings, he claims, are to be found in Lenin's commentaries, one stating that Tolstoy's literary works represent a protest against capitalism which *had to* arise from the patriarchial

Russian countryside, the other (written two years later) claiming that another appraisal must equally be made from the viewpoint of the local democratic proletariat. Macherey sees the former as the point of view 'by which Tolstoy's gaze is defined'; the latter as a viewpoint which, by confrontation, reveals the 'false interiority' of the work – a judgement dependent on a Marxist interpretation which seems every bit as ridden by ideology as the bourgeois criticism he denounced earlier.

While Macherey thus celebrates the notion of 'double reading' and of Lenin's own insistence that Tolstoy's virtues inhere in the very contradictions of the novel, he stresses that it is a *necessary*, non-accidental contradiction, one which gives Tolstoy's work its real meaning – a meaning limited by his incomplete knowledge of the historical processes and defined by the work's relation to something other than itself, that is, ideology. The work reflects 'the ensemble of the contradictions which define the historical situation as an insufficiency'. The work is *both* incomplete, because it does not fully know either the total historical situation or the ideology which alone understands this, *and* complete, because it is adequate to its own meanings. It is simultaneously a reflection and an absence of a reflection; thus it is not a case of A and not-A, but of different mirrors reflecting different pictures.

For deconstructionists such paradoxes are essentially textual, but Macherey does not want to stay locked into a particular story. For him, while the text is itself self-sufficient, it is at the same time insufficient to a total historical viewpoint. But here we come to a more fundamental disagreement with the tactics of deconstruction – for in Macherey's view the gap must be closed, and closed by criticism.

In this writer's opinion, however, the criticism offered by Lenin and quoted by Macherey does not confine itself to merely closing gaps; it actually distorts the given terms of the book. 'The contradictions in Tolstoy's views are indeed a mirror of those contradictory conditions in which the peasantry had to play their historical part in our revolution . . . ' (p. 124). In *Anna Karenina* the peasantry cannot credibly be cited as actants; they play no active part whatsoever; and since they are the only representatives of 'the people', that 'people', cannot be seen in anything but a passive role, simply incapable of any change, let alone of revolution. On the other hand, Levin, an authentic protagonist in the literary sense, strengthens his political position at every turn, shoring up his status as a patriarchal landlord.

Refutation of the baseless notion that Tolstoy, through Levin, displays an innately peasant mentality, is perhaps best summed up in the reminder that for all Olenin's inner conflict, he could not turn himself into a Caucasian tribesman.

Of course, no one would want to deny that there is conflict in Levin's mind, and many contradictory urges; and in this sense one can accept Macherey's assertion that the ideology of the work is established in a relation of difference with the work itself. But to argue that the work is 'defined by its relation to something else' (p. 127) does not in itself establish the nature of what that something else might be. Moreover, if that something else lies *outside* the text, then its definition will be arbitrary until the connection is proven. The leap to close the moral dilemma on behalf of a feudal landlord by assuming that his heart lay with a communist revolution does not seem to me to be justifiable in terms of Tolstoy's text.

It is certainly possible, indeed it is eminently reasonable, to accept the historical totality as not just a backdrop, but as an effective force operating upon the characters of the novel, and to find support for that view in the generic discontinuities of its structure. And this view would also encourage us to accept what Macherey claims regarding Lenin's opinion of literary texts – that they must be 'deconstructed' in order to reveal their contradictions. But all this makes sense enough without the extra, deterministic anxiety to go beyond what Macherey claims Lenin to have said, that 'Tolstoy's silences are eloquent' (Macherey, p. 132; but not found in Lenin's articles on Tolstoy). If ideology is, as Macherey says, a non-systematic *ensemble* of significations, and if a work prepares a reading of these significations by combining them as signs (p. 133), then the possibilities of different readings through different contributions must always remain. It is true that Lenin undertook a 'rigorous scrutiny' of the mirrors – broken, selective, or blind – that a text holds up to history, but where one stands in relation to the mirror will inevitably affect the reflection – and that is an angle Lenin and his disciples have not taken into account.

In sum, there is without doubt a political unconscious beneath the superficial appearances of *Anna Karenina*; but as with the psychological unconscious, one is entitled to choose one's therapist. It is indeed a pity that Macherey did not subject the subject of

Lenin's articles to the same scrutiny as he himself brought to bear on the novels of Jules Verne; for in that more independent exercise Macherey cannot be accused of introducing into the text which he is discussing terms which are external to it, even though his own critical, informing consciousness does. It lies properly within the nature and obligation of criticism, appearing as it does always after the event, to take account of the hindsight knowledge provided by the *post-facto*. Macherey's treatment of Verne's novels retains the integrity of their internal form, logic and meaning; by contrast, his comments on Lenin, critic of Tolstoy, do not confine themselves to the internal levels of the works of Tolstoy, but ride upon a total-izing, external criticism whose relation to the novels is partial and selective.

It should now be evident that as far as *Anna Karenina* is (exclus-ively) concerned, Lukács proves to be a more truly text-centred critic than does Macherey, since he attaches more significance to the posing of the dilemmas within the novel than to the Marxist-approved outcomes offered by the historical process; and, also, it will be remembered, because he understood that the differences between *War and Peace* and *Anna Karenina* are not just those of content (the nation *versus* the family) or of epoch (a historical account of the Napoleonic invasion *versus* a contemporary story of everyday events), but also in some way involve a difference of form. *Anna Karenina is* far more novel-like than *War and Peace*. Lukács chooses to concentrate his efforts on detailing the epic form of the latter, but his relative inattention to *Anna Karenina* can largely be made good with the help of the insights into both the novel and the totality offered by *The Political Unconscious*.

Most readers will no doubt be familiar with the argument, the methodology and the demonstrations that lie behind Jameson's defence and practice of a totalizing hermeneutic (set out in his first chapter 'On Interpretation'). Jameson recognizes at least as many 'shades of meaning' in the notion of totality as does Jay, and takes on a similar array of social theorists. But because of his basic concern with 'the socially symbolic act' that is literature, he never loses sight of the textual connection, arguing that the immanent analysis of any individual or manifest text must be accompanied by the uncovering of its deep structure, apprehensible through the diachronic perspectives of literary form. It is the fact of the inevi-table deviation between the manifest text and these same deep structures that necessitates the positing of another element, the 'absent cause' that he designates History.

To paraphrase his method: in the first instance the 'text' is construed as coinciding with the individual literary work or utterance, though with the rider that the individual work is always an essentially *symbolic* act; in the second instance, the literary text is viewed as a *parole* within the *langue* of other discourses (for Jameson, those of class and the collective); lastly, the 'passions and values' of a particular social formation must be relativised by their placement within 'the ultimate horizon of human history as a whole' (p. 76).

Jameson is quick to point out that this last move must not be seen as a lapse into the evolutionary fallacy of which we have indirectly accused Macherey – that is, of anachronistically designating a term of one system the 'precursor' of that which does not yet exist. To adapt Roussel's anecdote to the matter in hand, the (false) claim would be – not seeing *'le crâne de Voltaire enfant'* under a glass screen – but using the novel *Anna Karenina* as an X-ray machine to discern and display the future Russian Revolution encoded in Tolstoy's pre-revolutionary brain. Which is, of course, what both Lukács and Macherey do.

The evolutionary model, Jameson continues, is not merely a misreading of Marx's perception of diachronicity – it also the wrong constructional model to use. A more appropriate one is provided by the concept of genealogy. We begin with a full-blown system (capitalism in Marx, reification in *The Political Unconscious*, and in *Anna Karenina*, presumably, the socialist system inaugurated in 1917) in terms of which elements of the past can 'artificially be isolated as objective preconditions' (p. 139). Thus Tolstoy's novel can be said to pick up certain elements in the Russian situation which according to Jameson's argument would be conceived as objectively present and independently pregnant with the seeds of revolution. But far from insisting that the revolution thereby becomes one of the terms of the novel, Jameson argues that the text itself deviates from the clear-cut historical path towards that goal, proceeding instead by way of discontinuities and contradictions.

These last differ from Macherey's discontinuities on two major counts: they are semantic and semiotic rather than simply ideological; and they embed their effects so markedly in the text that this latter takes on the form of what Jameson calls the 'omnibus' (p. 143) monuments of nineteenth century novelistic production. In other words, the nineteenth century novel, forced as it is to express complete societal developments, while having to hand a variety of literary sub-*genres*, becomes an enormously complex affair which defies generic categorisation at the same time as it grapples with the conflicting ideologies, changing values, and material upheavals brought about by industrialisation and *embourgeoisement*. On this definition the novel form is no sooner named than it deconstructs itself. For example, Jameson asks whether Manzoni's great novel, *I Promessi Sposi* is a romance, a historical novel, or a late and unexpected avatar of the Byzantine novel, in which the lovers are 'torn asunder by labyrinthine adventures and coincidences which ultimately reunite them . . .' (ibid.). His answer is, all these things at once, the different generic modes intertwined within it allowing ample space for at least two major narrative threads: the Gothic romance of Lucia's story, and the *roman d'aventure* in which Renzo features as the almost picaresque hero. Eminently susceptible to a similar kind of analysis, *Anna Karenina* no longer appears as a powerful but doomed attempt to reinvent the epic (as Lukács described it) but a triumphant triple-header which miraculously conjoins the *troika* of generic sub-forms required to cope with Levin, Anna and Oblonsky.

Nevertheless, Jameson believes that all the great nineteenth-century novels, with their many-layered and multi-stranded components of sub-forms, can be subsumed under the general title of Romance as it has been described by Northrop Frye in his *Anatomy of Criticism* (Frye, 1973). Here Frye adopts the generic categories growing out of the four medieval levels of meaning, and emerges with the literary codes of Tragedy, Comedy, Romance and Satire. Jameson is mainly interested in Frye's concept of Romance, since he believes it best explains the ultimate goal of the nineteenth-century novels he himself collectively discusses:

> Romance is for Frye a wish-fulfilment or Utopian fantasy which aims at the transfiguration of everyday life in such a way as to restore the condition of some lost Eden, or to anticipate a future realm from which the old mortality and imperfections will have been effaced. (p. 110)

In other words, Romance perfectly describes the Marxist belief that the world is, or should be, progressing steadily towards a Communist Utopia. Jameson stresses that in Romance ordinary reality is not replaced, but rather transformed, for the fulfilment of the quest 'will still contain that reality' (p. 103).

It is also curious that in order to specify the physical contours of the Romance space, Jameson makes use of the word 'world' in a sense not entirely dissimilar from the way that we earlier saw Lotman using it:

> A first specification of romance would then be achieved if we could account for the way in which, in contrast to realism, inner-worldly objects such as landscape or village, forest or mansion – were temporary stopping places on the lumbering coach or express-train itinerary of realistic representation – are somehow transformed into folds in space, into discontinuous pockets of homogeneous time and of heightened symbolic closure, such that they become tangible analogic or perceptual vehicles for *world* in its larger phenomenological sense.
>
> (Jameson, p. 112)

In what does Levin's utopia consist if not in *'etot mir'* (*etot* = 'this'; *mir* can mean 'village' or 'world') miraculously stripped of its social inequalities? There is even an echo of Levin's ambivalence towards Kitty and the exclusion of the peasants from the novel in Jameson's declaration of the 'essential marginality of the most characteristic protagonists of romance, slaves or women' (p. 113). It is equally inviting to confirm Romance's assignation of good and evil to positional concepts coinciding with 'us and them', by lumping together all the characters whom Levin finds alien and hence 'bad': the academics, the priests, the bureaucrats and the *mondains*.

By contrast Anna remains outside this 'world', her Otherness already established at several levels, but, on Jameson's grounds, constituted by her participation in her own tragedy. Tragedy, he says, transcends the normal understanding of individual virtue and vice. The ethical opposition is 'wholly absent from tragedy . . . which is beyond good and evil' (p. 116).

The categories of Comedy are also different from those of Romance, being more concerned with the regeneration and continuation of the social order. Thus the Comic third strand of the novel is represented by Stiva and Dolly, whose role is to affirm the continuance of the family and thus ensure the future of the dynasty, the class and the nation. Stiva, like Anna, also falls outside the good-evil category of Romance actants, not being a part of Levin's world, though not entirely alien to it. He is rather its most welcome guest. When visiting Levin's domain (and thus assuming temporarily the guise of one of the Romance *dramatis personae*) Stiva acts as a Donor, facilitating, for example, the marriage between Levin and Kitty. (When he fails to bring about Anna's divorce, however, he is a helper without enough magic.)

It is also the case that Stiva, unlike Levin, is an enabler of the incipient practices of capitalism in feudal Russia. The sale of his forests (or rather, of Dolly's) dislocates the conjunction of land and money previously held by a single person, putting property in the possession of the middle-class *entrepreneur*, and money in the pocket of the impoverished aristocrat. These economic aspects of *Anna Karenina* support Jameson's claim that 'the play of structural norm and textual deviation' is predicated upon a third term, the absent non-representable effects of a historical situation, which he insists should not be understood as determinate, but as limiting. In other words, the historical situation does not 'cause' a given text; it simply 'maps out its condition of possibility' (p. 148).

Jameson's magisterial thesis, to which only brief reference has been made here, is sophisticated, dense, and very fruitful in regard to English and French novels of the nineteenth century. His reversal of the evolutionary or Hegelian model of the relation between fiction and history seems to be a far more satisfactory account than anything assumed by Lukács or elaborated by Macherey. Yet even his powerful combination of 'sedimented forms' and Utopian goals seems to be an inadequate basis on which to discuss the politics of *Anna Karenina*. And this is not just because Jameson's study can only be suggestive, given that the Russian novel falls outside the ground covered in *The Political Unconscious*. In regard to Tolstoy himself, Jameson's parameters seem to lack a dimension, which we shall try to make good in the next and final chapter.

# 8

# The Rhetoric of Morality

Despite many of the issues that have come up for discussion – the innocence of the unconscious, the ambivalence of the text, even the vindication of 'our hero' – there remains little doubt that *Anna Karenina* is still a *'conte moral'*. Nor can there be much hesitation in the reader's mind as to what the author thinks of as 'good' and 'bad'. But the question arises of *how* such value judgements are communicated without the wearying and counter-productive effects of sermonizing; and, further, whether they bear any relation to the political issues of the novel. To answer these enquiries is to reveal a number of things besides the mere contents of Tolstoy's box of black and white balls.

Part of what constitutes the morally loaded backdrop of the novel, against which the more specifically individualised moral events take place, is fed into it direct from what we may still dare to call history in the old-fashioned sense. Not Jameson's invisible Absent Cause, discussed in Chapter 7, but simply the generally corroborated view of what happened in the public arena during the epoch contemporary with the novel. Certain formative temporal events in 'history' may be supposed to have a bearing on the events of the novel, and are indeed shown to be assimilated into the minds of the characters. Amongst these are such landmarks as the edict of the Emancipation of the Serfs (1861), the setting up of the *zemstva* (the organs of local government authorised by Alexander II), and the translation into Russian of Darwin's treatise on the Evolution of the Species (1864). These 'factual' events can also be counted among the pointers to the moral values inscribed in the novel because their presence enables us to shuttle back and forth between the 'history' and the 'fiction' of the total *Gestalt*. Levin's rejection of Darwinism, for example, can be situated within a debate external to the novel and hence judged against 'objective' criteria which may, *en revanche*, question the assumptions behind Levin's position.

One of Mikhail Bakhtin's articles, however, reminds us that there are two chronotopes to be considered in a full overview of any novel (Bakhtin, 1981). In *Anna Karenina* (by contrast with *War and Peace*) the axis of space is more significant than that of time, at least when it comes to considering how each contributes to the semiotics of morality. The geographical *topoi* of *Anna Karenina* consist of four specific points or areas on the map – Moscow, St Petersburg, the country estates belonging to the characters, and Europe. Their historicity is for us factual: we do not doubt either the history-books or Tolstoy's fiction, and readily believe that these places existed in the real world as well as in Tolstoy's mind – even though the St Petersburg of the 1870s is hardly the Leningrad of today, any more than Levin's estate can be completely identifiable with the national monument that is now Yasnaya Polyana. But more importantly, it is also true that the spaces designated by these names in the novel are less objectively constructed than their history-book counterparts. Despite their referents in the real world they also have a *metaphorical* value, standing for certain moral concepts in Tolstoy's mind. This metaphorical value-system is expressed for the most part *metonymically*, built up through the conglomerative detail of associated activities and characters located in each of the *foci*. Thus the first two requirements of the 'archetypal plot of discursive formations' discussed by Hayden White in the Introduction to his book *The Tropics of Discourse* (White, 1978) are fulfilled (the moral gloss remaining Tolstoy's).

In White's concept of 'plot' the narrative 'I' of any discourse moves through the four main or 'master' tropes identified in post-Renaissance rhetorical theory – metaphor, metonymy, synechdoche and irony – in a process whose ultimate goal is the understanding of an unfamiliar field of experience. The initial metaphorical apprehension of a foreign aspect of reality (in this case a value-system imaged through certain places) gives way to a 'metonymic dispersion of its elements across a time series or a spatial field' (White, p. 6). Levin's estate, for example, is a metaphor for a certain kind of lifestyle; the mowing is an associated activity. White allows that this second move *may* be sufficient for the purposes of an analysis; but he provides a further procedure, that of integrating the elements by 'assigning them to different orders, classes, genera, species, and so on . . .', (the synechdochic move); and again a final stage in which the ironic gaze of the narrative 'I' reviews the operation first undertaken, and assesses its successes (the achievement of retrospective understanding) and failures (perhaps the presence of an inherent distorting subjectivity).

Allowing for what I hope has now been sufficiently demonstrated, that is, the unconscious splitting of the narrative 'I' in *Anna Karenina*, a consideration of the major protagonists in the light of both rhetoric and morality does indeed find that each constitutes the 'metaphorical characterization' of an almost literal 'domain of existence' which is immediately endowed with moral overtones. Levin inhabits the country, and lives an 'authentic' life close to nature – the basis of a Tolstoy-approved ethic; Anna moves between two cities, one of which (Moscow) is only slightly less corrupt than the other (Petersburg) because the latter is in every way more Westernized. Kitty and her family in one instance, and Anna and Vronsky in another, move out of the country-city, Petersburg-Moscow axes in order to test themselves by a growth experience (Kitty), or by isolation (Anna and Vronsky) – in both cases in Europe.

For Kitty Carlsbad provides the site of an important moral rite of passage, in which she clarifies her personal values and in so doing unconsciously prepares herself to become a fit mate for Levin; Anna and Vronsky's period in Italy on the other hand induces both a deterioration in their relationship, and an acknowledgement of other ties conceivably more fundamental than their mutual love. Anna needs to see her son, Vronsky has business concerning his property, his land. It is clear that the notion of a life lived in permanent severance from these basic connections is not a real possibility for Tolstoy's characters. Europe is, except for visits, off the board. It is outside Bakhtin's *topoi*, beyond Lotman's semantic field – precisely because it lacks the moral reverberations to which Tolstoy was attuned in his native landscape. (In this he stands in clear contrast to Dostoevsky, in several of whose novels Europe plays a vital, if negative, role. Geneva for example – anathema because of its early associations with socialism – taints half-a-dozen of the characters in *The Devils*, and thus bears a responsibility for their downfalls.) Levin's estate, the enabling site of idealised family life; the Shcherbatskys' residence in Moscow where the old Prince gently but incontestably voices Tolstoy's moral beliefs; and St Petersburg, with its various forms of 'unnatural' life (Society; the bureaucracy; the military) – these are essentially the geographical *topoi* of Tolstoy's universe. While they remain historically recognizable, their metaphoricity consists in the fact that they are not morally neutral.

The metonymic shakedown of the elements of these domains of experience corresponds to the quantitative detail for which Tolstoy's writing is so famous. The depiction of Levin's life-style, for example, centred on his house and estate, ranges from the production and consumption of cabbage soup to the veneration of the religious faith of the peasants; it includes other forms of simple food, homely dress, and shabby but comfortable furnishings, care and concern for animals, harmony with the seasons, serious interest in agricultural practices and improvements, the pleasures of shooting and fishing expeditions, concern over peasant illiteracy, and the championing of the Russian language (as opposed to French). It rejects sophisticated education for the peasants, delegated local government, railways, industrialization, modern medical practices, and everything associated with Western Europe. It would be tedious to elaborate the details of the metonymic *topoi* for the other strands of the novel; this example should suffice to indicate that the metonymic axis lies between negative and positive poles which define, by their position on it, the moral status of all the apparatus of individual life style.

Synechdoche comes into operation when either Levin (to keep, for simplicity, to the same example) or the reader sees each of these distinct elements as part of a whole. In Levin's case the whole is the centuries-old Slavophilic tradition of the Russian landowner whose essentially close ties with the soil link him inexorably to the great Mother Earth and her surrounding mystique. When Raskolnikov, for example, (to cite another Dostoevskian case in point), is ordered by the spiritually immaculate Sonya to kiss the ground of the Haymarket, this is less to demonstrate a repentance he does not yet feel than to acquire from the contact the grace he needs to achieve it. Russia is in fact the only morally valid space in which true Russians can operate, and their happiness and goodness are both, for Tolstoy, in direct proportion to the closeness and harmony with which they are inserted within her physical manifestation.

Significantly, however, White's fourth term – irony – is noticeably missing from this strand of the novel; the final trope is scarcely to be found, for the very good reason that Tolstoy is incapable or ironizing country life and all it signifies. He occasionally mocks Levin's earnestness; he sometimes even makes fun of his hero's gaucheries; but basically all that Levin is and stands for receives its status from the absence of overt authorial criticism or questioning. As we have already shown at some length, this is not to say that the rest of the characters also support what Levin represents and Tolstoy approves; to the contrary, nearly every principle to which Levin assents is overtly or implicitly opposed by one or more secondary characters. This is in fact one of Tolstoy's deliberate principles of writing: when a visitor, A. D. Obolensky, asked him in the mid-seventies whether he was on the priest's side or Levin's in the matter of the pre-nuptial confession, Tolstoy replied, according to Obolensky's written record:

> I myself am, of course, on the priest's side, and not at all on Levin's. But I rewrote that account four times, and still it seemed to me that it was apparent on whose side I was myself. And I have noticed any work, any story, makes an impression only when it is impossible to make out with whom the author sympathises. And so I tried to write everything in such a way that it was not noticeable. (Quoted by Eikhenbaum, p. 134)

But neither dissimulation of the authorial point of view nor opposition from other characters within the novel succeed in hiding the approval bestowed on Levin's values, and the privileged treatment he receives in not being ironised. Showing all sides to a question is not at all the same thing as irony. The latter has been usefully defined by the rhetoricians Donald Rice and Peter Schofer as a 'semantic and referential relationship of opposition made possible by the possession of one or more contrary semantic features' (Rice and Schofer, 1983, p. 31). In their example taken from Voltaire's *Candide*,

> Cunégonde dropped her handkerchief, Candide picked it up; she innocently took his hand; the young man innocently kissed the young lady's hand . . . their mouths met, their eyes flashed, their knees shook . . . (p. 133)

the irony is attached to the word 'innocently'. The reader understands that the word is incompatible with the complete macrocontent of the passage (the established behaviour patterns of the two young people). There is no violation of the semantic code, for the sentence makes grammatical sense even when not read ironically, but the reader knows that for 'innocently' he is supposed to substitute a contradictory signified such as 'meaningfully'.

In most cases, of course, the use of irony involves longer textual segments than this brief sentence; certainly it is not at all difficult to find examples of its extensive exploitation in Tolstoy's writings. One of the most famous is his celebrated account of war in the pamphlet 'Christianity and Patriotism' (1894) which starts:

> The bells will begin ringing, men with long hair will dress up in gold-embroidered sacks and begin praying for murder . . .
>
> (Quoted by Janko Lavrin, 1948, p. 148)

It is precisely this tone which is absent from all the accounts of Levin's activities. In the mowing scene, for example, the old man uses irony in the form of a joke, when he dips his whetstone box in the stream and offers it to Levin with the words, 'A little of my *kvas*?' His implied meaning is that the stream-water is not quite as interesting a drink as *kvas*; but Tolstoy actually corrects this irony by asserting that the stream-water is better than *kvas*: 'Really, Levin thought he had never tasted any drink nicer than this lukewarm water with green stuff floating in it and a flavour of the rusty tin box'. The complex message of this 'innocent' statement is that the reader, like the old man, would be likely to taste only tin and green stuff, and his sophistication would find objections to such a beverage. Levin, however, because of his spiritual affinities with nature, is uniquely able to appreciate the innate attraction of a truly natural drink. In sum, since irony is normally invoked in order to distinguish, ridicule, or castigate that which is not approved, Levin is, by definition, no target. In a circle which can hardly be called vicious, Levin's virtue is expressed by the absence of the fourth trope; but the fourth trope is missing because Tolstoy offers no fundamental criticism of Levin. (Similarly, it has been said that the only nineteenth century writer never to have been satirized in the Soviet Union is Pushkin.[1])

If Levin is the principal, virtually the only, character to be identified so totally with the rural field of experience, the *topos* of the city on the other hand spawns a cluster of negative figures who represent various strata within the sub-divisions of Moscow and St Petersburg. The three men close to Anna – her brother, husband, and lover – are all city dwellers, but of different kinds, and beyond them perambulates the whole spectrum of city society, glimpsed fleetingly but in sharply defined silhouette. It would again be tedious to labour the progression of the four tropes for all of these characters, but it is worthwhile to think very briefly of Vronsky and Karenin in their light. While both men stand, metaphorically, for an aspect of 'citiness' and all it implies, and share in the rootlessness of urban disjunction from the earth symbolised by their common lack of a proper family upbringing, the immediate metonymic breakdowns diverge widely. Vronsky is a soldier, and his appearance betokens, apart from military smartness and pre-cision, elegant simplicity. His want of sensitivity and subtlety are symbolized by the sharp contrasts of his natural colouring – his black, close-cropped hair, and white teeth. The activities he crams into his busy and varied life are indeed a microcosm of those of the city at large, composed as both are of necessary duties and venal pleasures. Irony comes into its own – and surely not even Tolstoy could claim impartiality here – when Vronsky's moral system is described:

> In his Petersburg world people were divided into two quite opposite sorts. One – the inferior sort: the small-minded, stupid, and above all, laughable people who believed that a husband should live with the wife he married, that a maiden should be pure, a woman modest, and a man manly, self-controlled and firm; that one should bring up one's children to earn their living, pay one's debts, and other such nonsense of this kind. These sort of people were old-fashioned and laughable . . .
>
> (*SS* 8, p. 113)

It is clear that the authorial macro-content requires the reversal of one set of the adjectives in this passage: 'superior' for 'inferior', 'admirable' for 'laughable'. Words such as 'pure', 'modest', and 'self-controlled' retain their truth-value and thus signal the correct moral message. The clash of the 'referential relationship of oppo-sition' certainly forces a choice – but scarcely a free one.

Karenin, on the other hand, is given a more complex *Gestalt*. In the first place, he is used as a metaphor for the bureaucratic stratum of Petersburg society, which prompts the informed reader immediately to bring to mind all that long and bitter controversy that was associated with the building of Peter the Great's 'window onto the West'; the toll its construction took in human lives and misery; its association with secularisation (Peter made the Orthodox

Church just another 'department' of the State); its repudiation of Russian architecture in favour of Italian; its deliberate severance from the Slavophile tradition. It was the view of many conservative Russians, including Tolstoy, that St Petersburg was spiritually sterile, and thus Karenin is characterised by synechdochic attributes of lifelessness. His grisly flesh is summed up by his gristly ears which stand out like the obstruction he is to Anna's happiness; his coldness is at one with Petersburg's icy climate and unwelcoming *snobisme*; his indifference to the psyches of those around him repeats the hostility of the city's inimical hinterland. Inevitably there is a fusion between metonymy and synechdoche in the descriptions of his work, which is both an extension of his personality and a microcosm of the stultifying bureaucracy that he inhabits.

But both tropes are then subsumed under an overarching irony in the long paragraph in Part 3, Chapter 14 that follows the letter to Anna in which he refuses her plea for a divorce, and expresses instead confidence in her 'repentance' and the anticipation of a later 'personal interview'. The dryness of the letter is contrasted with the flush of animation that suffuses his cheeks once he turns to more 'engrossing' business-matters such as irrigation, and the subject-races of the Zaraysk Province.

The parody involved in the notion of Karenin's dealing firstly with irrigation, when he is so essentially arid himself, and secondly with subjected people, which is how he thinks of his wife, is one aspect of the irony running viciously throughout the passage; another is the pedantic, laborious and futile attention he patently devotes to the problem, when he in theory prides himself on his ability to cut through red tape and relate directly to the 'real facts'. If he feels, as the text tells us he does, that he is now seeing more 'deeply' into the issue, and that his action merits a 'barely perceptible smile of self-satisfaction', then such language is but an open invitation to substitute 'shallow' for 'deep' and to deplore rather than commend the attitude he brings indiscriminately to both his work and his wife. Although many readers experience sympathy for his plight and pity for his initial loss, these reactions no longer seem appropriate to the man who, under the influence of the Countess Lydia Ivanovna (who is not divorced, but who has lived separately from her husband for thirteen years, and has fallen in love with Karenin) will not let Anna see her son Seriozha, and later refuses to grant her a divorce.

Tolstoy ironizes this last decision in a very elaborate fashion. Karenin, grateful to Lydia Ivanovna for the attention that soothes his vanity after Anna's betrayal, allows himself to share in her infatuation for a French ex-shop assistant who has learnt how to gull the aristocratic circles of St Petersburg into believing that he is a *clairvoyant*. Nothing is settled by either her or Karenin without consultation with this charlatan, and, as a result, Karenin communicates to the go-between, Oblonsky, a definite refusal of divorce based on 'what the Frenchman had said the evening before, in his real or pretended sleep'. The ludicrous manner in which this crucial decision is taken, involving as it does Lydia Ivanovna's hypocrisy (she does not admit her proprietorial interest in Karenin), as well as the spiritualism abhorrent to Tolstoy, are the author's way of signalling to the reader his condemnation of the whole episode.

However the fact that Tolstoy sets up a ridiculous event in order to avoid the divorce issue suggests that there is a double irony at work here. The irony that Tolstoy is *not* aware of is that to discredit divorce by associating it with spiritualism is not an adequate dismissal of its claim to offer a rational solution. Perhaps all we can say is that Tolstoy-the-fox was a ready ironist of the details he did not approve; but when it came to the 'one big thing' he so longed to believe in, any form of scepticism was inadmissible.

In other words, this application of the use and non-use of the four tropes throws new light on old criticism. If Tolstoy is concerned to apprehend, convey and consolidate a certain set of moral values, we can certainly agree that his chosen metaphors of character and *milieu* instantly communicate what they stand for; further, their synechdochic insertion into the Russian *mythos* is almost predictable. But the metonymic devolution of the detail of daily life – what all critics have traditionally celebrated in Tolstoy's writing – suddenly shows itself to have a new significance. The variety, vividness and veracity of these minutiae take up the greatest space and make the most noise. Through this they do good work in persuading us of the message Tolstoy was also trying to persuade himself of. But it is the silence of the empty space *not* filled by the fourth trope that tells us that where irony is suppressed, so also is much more.

In the second essay in *Tropics of Discourse*, entitled 'Interpretation in History', White situates the fourfold table of tropes amongst other typologies which all devolve on the notion of quarternarism in historical interpretation. But moving on from his interest in historiography White also considers concepts used in other, related, kinds of writing, specifically those of myth, as defined by Lévi-Strauss, and 'poetry', as discussed by Northrop Frye. The former, according to White, offers his opinion that history is unable completely to escape mythological explanations, which are naturally couched in narrative form; but Frye is said to go still further in associating history and fiction, arguing that historical writing not only becomes mythical in shape when it 'gets to a certain point of comprehensiveness', it even 'approaches the poetic in its structure' (p. 57). 'The difference between a historical and a fictional account of the world is formal, not substantive; it resides in the relative weights given to the constructive elements in them', writes White (p. 58), paraphrasing Frye. Because of the shared reliance of both history and fiction on narrative (though it should be made clear that not all historiographers subscribe to the narrativist view), White believes it appropriate to discuss historical writing in terms of the same classifications of emplotment as those which Frye, and after him Jameson, used to categorise fiction: Romance, Tragedy, Comedy and Satire.

However, White notes the affinity between Frye's quartet of categories and the four modes of explanation or procedure elaborated and practised by various individual historians. These are the Idiographic, which tries simply to render a field more visible and more vivid to the mind's eye; the Contextual, which seeks to offer that picture or set of data some kind of significance through generalization; a stronger, more expressly integrative approach, which he labels Organicist; and lastly a technique which explains events by the laws of cause and effect, and can thus prefigure future events as well as account for what happened in the past. This is the Mechanistic approach.

The connection between the modes of emplotment and the modes of explanation is, White stresses, 'elective'. But he pursues these elective affinities through one further typology: the mode of ideological implication whose categories (as discussed by the sociologist of knowledge, Karl Mannheim) are: the Anarchistic, the Conservative, the Radical and the Liberal.

All these, and the four terms of the category of rhetoric already introduced here, are, White suggests, structurally homologous with one another, as can be seen from the grid or table of correlations he draws up. (In the reproduction below I have added in the column of tropes, for the sake of clarity.)

| Trope | Emplotment | Ideological implication | Explanation |
|-------|-----------|------------------------|-------------|
| Metaphor | Romance | Anarchistic | Ideographic |
| Synechdoche | Comedy | Conservative | Organicist |
| Metonymy | Tragedy | Radical | Mechanistic |
| Irony | Satire | Liberal | Contextualist |

Inevitably, this grid has been interpreted by some critics as a rigid structure which White's readers must be warned against. Dominick Lacapra, for example, writes of *Metahistory* (White, 1973), the book in which White first applied the tropes of rhetoric to historiography:

> There was a Procrustean tendency to see texts as embodiments of patterned variables on modal sets of tropes, emplotments, arguments and ideologies.                    (Lacapra, 1983, p. 81)

But he recognises in *The Tropics of Discourse* an effort to pre-empt criticism of this sort. Thus when White writes:

> In my view, any historian who simply described a set of facts in, let us say, metonymic terms and then went on to employ its processes in the mode of tragedy and proceeded to explain those processes mechanistically, and finally drew explicit ideological implications from it – as most vulgar Marxists and materialistic determinists do – would not only be very uninteresting but could legitimately be labelled a doctrinaire thinker who 'bent the facts' to fit a preconceived theory.                    (p. 129)

Lacapra concludes, 'I think that White is right in believing that formalized schemata are necessary for interpretation. The problem is how to understand them and their relation to actual discourses and texts . . .' (p. 82)

And Fredric Jameson, also reviewing White's *Metahistory*, writes:

> As a matter of empirical critical practice, a model which distinguishes different *levels* in a text only yields interesting results

when these levels are understood as *contradicting* each other:
. . . if the levels are really structurally homologous, then they
tend to fold back into each other and not much has been gained
by the initial analytical distinction.          (Jameson, 1976, p. 7)

In fact, White had already foreshadowed this kind of admonition
in both *Metahistory* and *The Tropics of Discourse*. Perhaps he should
be allowed a last word before we test the relevance of his hypothesis to *Anna Karenina*:

The tension at the heart of every historical masterpiece is created
in part by a conflict between a given modality of emplotment or
explanation and the specific ideological commitment of its author.
                                                                              (*Tropics*, p. 70)

In illustration he points to historians such as de Tocqueville who
changed their previously favoured modes of emplotment and
explanation (in this latter's case from tragedy to satire and from the
mechanistic to the contextualist) as their true natures came to the
fore in their later years.

White himself is less concerned with fictional writers than with
theoreticians of history. But he has written one essay, 'The Problem of Style in Realistic Presentation: Marx and Flaubert', in which
*The Eighteenth Brumaire of Louis Bonaparte* is compared to *L'éducation
sentimentale* (White, 1979). Despite obvious differences of style
between the two works, White argues that the form is similar in
both, each being a *Bildungsroman* whose hero is either personal – a
young French provincial seeking self-realization – or a whole class
– the French bourgeoisie itself. In both cases the story ends with
the cynical acceptance of comfort at the expense of ideals; and
White insists that the final condition was implicit in the structure of
consciousness articulated at the start of each work. Both works
follow the sequence of modes he has established as 'normal', that
is: metaphoric, in which both Mme Arnoux and a 'socialist republic' are established as images of desire; metonymic, in which
there is a dispersion of unfulfilled desire onto a series of objects
(e.g. Rosanette; a constitutional republic); synechdochic (desire
universalised by the equation of every object with its value as a
commodity, the interests of a particular segment of society identified with the interests of society as a whole); and ironic, a melan-
choly recognition of the gap between the reality and the ideal,

whether in relation to love or revolution. The interest of White's
exercise lies in the demonstration that 'his' tropes can be used to
prove Frye's point about the purely formal differences between
fiction and history; but it is also interesting to lay *Anna Karenina*
over the same four-tiered grid – much as the corpse of the governess Pirogov was laid out on the table in the railway-station waiting-
room. Such an exercise may well lay *itself* open to accusations of
morbidity and/or reductivism; but since it actually says more about
tension and complexity, such a criticism would be short-sighted.
However, while the grid is valuable for plotting the larger conceptual schemata of Trope, Emplotment, Ideology and Explanation,
each component of these modes must obviously be susceptible to
further sub-division, such as the phases into which Frye breaks
down each of the modes of emplotment. And at the same time,
there are those geographical *topoi* suggested by Bakhtin, which can
also be said to inhabit the 'worlds' (*this* one and *that* one) elaborated by Lotman. Far from being constrained by a Procrustean bed,
we rather seem to be juggling with square-cornered concepts –
whose interplay is nevertheless rewarding.

As we noted earlier, Fredric Jameson's enterprise in *The Political
Unconscious* was to read nineteenth century novels in terms of a
Marxist vision of history whose Utopian ideals subsume them
under the paradigm of romance. But, 'In *Anna Karenina* I loved the
idea of the family . . .' wrote Tolstoy. In the first analysis it would
seem that the Levin story conforms not to the quest of Romance (or
at least not after Kitty's hand has been gained) but to Frye's
simplest version of Comedy: 'A young man wants a young
woman . . . his desire is resisted by some opposition, usually
paternal, and . . . near the end of the play some twist in the plot
enables the hero to have his will' (p. 163). In Levin's case the
opposition is maternal, and complicated by the young woman's
critical involvement elsewhere; but his final triumph seems to
proclaim the essentially comic structure of his trajectory. Any
deviations from the elements commonly surrounding this simple
pattern can be explained by reference to specific features of the
Russian historical situation – a move which, despite a transposition
of *genre*, conforms to what Jameson requires of a methodology, 'if
archetypal paradigms are to have any more than typographical
significance'.

So when Frye continues,

The movement of comedy is usually a movement from one kind
of society to another. At the beginning of the play the obstructing characters are in charge of the play's society. . . . At the end
of the play the device in the plot that brings hero and heroine
together causes a new society to crystallize around the hero, and
the moment when this crystallization occurs is the point of
resolution in the action,

points of similarity between this paradigm and the marriage of
Kitty and Levin can certainly be glimpsed. But, as Jameson has
foreshadowed, the Absent Cause of history makes its mark also.
Since Frye bases his notion of Comedy on its dramatic form, the
action he discusses is confined to the single *topos* of the stage. But
in *Anna Karenina* this is replaced by the greater mobility and
varying *loci* of the novel-form. The practicality of the coach and the
railway as means of travel in nineteenth-century Russia configures
a world of connected outposts; but the map on which these are
located can also be conceptualised as a series of rings in which the
estate constitutes the inmost circle situated within the encompassing
countryside. Beyond these there is a much larger circle which is
Society, and within it, the City, or Cities. In the outer limits of
non-Russia lie Italy and Carlsbad. *Only within the circle of the estate
does Comedy obtain*: Kitty instinctively rejects a honeymoon elsewhere in favour of an immediate post-nuptial wedding-trip back to
Pokrovsk, and several months later she is joined there, in the
penultimate chapter, by her sister, her parents, and various
friends, thus playing out 'the tendency of comedy [ . . .] to include
as many people as possible in its final society' (Frye, p. 165). But
the certainty that everyone will henceforth live happily ever after is
subject to the doubts already raised; and this shadow can arguably
be said to inhabit the text itself, as well as being deducible from the
extratextual evidence (the diaries, letters and subsequent works)
undermining the supposedly stable edifice of the comic paradigm.
In other words the comic archetype can be traced in *Anna Karenina*,
but it exists only at risk. Thereafter it crumbles altogether, suc-
cumbing to the erosion of the long-term changes of attitude visible
in the total corpus of Tolstoy's life and works.

Similarly, one could argue that if Comedy is at least in part the
mode of emplotment of Levin's story, then the corresponding
mode of ideological implication, the Conservative, fits equally
neatly. Who could be more conservative than Levin, who rejects

the *zemstva* in favour of the *mir*, who prefers to play the patriarchal benefactor himself rather than allow schools and medical centres to be set up by the state – who, in short, deliberately clings to the role of enlightened feudal despot rather than embrace the Liberalism of his friend Stiva, or, worse, the Radicalism of the political avant-garde? Yet we have the same sense of unease with Levin's political stance as we do with his marriage. Both common sense and history tell us that he could not play a land-locked Canute holding back the future for more than a few decades. The disintegration of the world of *The Cherry Orchard* was looming, and Levin's chosen self-image and vocation are simply anachronistic. Thus, while he can never not be described as Conservative, his ideological position is also subverted by a kind of negative Anarchism, which is in fact the category most appropriate to his extreme individualism. Although he is conservative, indeed reactionary, in his determination to cling to and uphold the traditional system, that system was already dissolving. While most of the country, represented in the novel by characters such as Koznyshev and Sviazhky, was genuinely concerned to find alternatives to feudalism, those who clung to Levin's views were becoming increasingly isolated. The result is that Levin can, and does, continue to run his own estate as he wishes, while his life-style provides neither example nor persuasion *vis-à-vis* his fellow land-owners; he simply 'does his own thing' and withdraws ostentatiously from all participation in public life.

This position is of course his own idiosyncratic choice, but it is also one that is forced upon him by what is going on outside his magic circle, as is evidenced by the visit to his neighbour Sviazhky. The latter is the essential pragmatist, who entertains progressive and advanced ideas on politics, agriculture, and 'the woman question', while continuing to engage in old-fashioned farming and familial practices. As we and Levin observe, he lives 'instinctively', while believing himself to be guided by reason. He is of course a proclaimed Liberal; but his Liberalism is mediated by his Conservatism, just as Levin's Conservatism is paradoxically close to Anarchism. Thus, in that era of hopeless confusion and frequent despair, when the Emancipation had already begun to yield its many disappointments, and the next major event on the domestic front would be the futile assassination of the Tsar Alexander II, author of so many supposedly salvational reforms, no fail-safe ideology was at hand to provide a unique and total remedy. In this situation Levin's highly personal solution is understandable but totally inadequate, despite his status as hero of the novel and frequent spokesman for his author.

The tension between the national need and the personal imperative, which constitutes much of the interest of Levin's non-domestic story, can be taken further in relation to White's models of explanation and tropic categorisations. If Levin operates, on the whole, within the Comic mode of emplotment, and retreats to some fierce Individualistic stance under a Conservative umbrella, the related mode of 'explanation' for his view of history should be Organicist. The Organicist, says White, 'insists on the necessity of relating the various "contexts" that can be perceived to exist in the historical record as parts to the whole which is history-in-general'. Under this rubric explanation 'must take the form of a synthesis in which each of the parts of the whole must be shown either to mirror the structure of the totality or to prefigure the form of either the end of the whole process or at least the latest phase of the process' (p. 65). He adds that the Organicist Hegel 'explicitly prohibits the historian from speculating on the future'. The historian's own present is conceived as 'the *culmination* of a millennial sequence of phases in a process that is to be regarded as *universally* human' (p. 66).

This is of course exactly how Levin would wish things to be – that is, as they were, are now, and ever shall be, as long as he is the central, patriarchal priest-figure at the centre. But the solipsism of his position is sufficiently patent for it to lack persuasion when viewed from the vantage-point of subsequent history, while within the novel it derives authority only from his status as *roi-soleil* at his own court. Even most of his own retinue, not to mention the populace at large, remain sceptical. Another way of putting this is to say that while the issue of Levin and his views can be found in the categories associated with Comedy (Conservatism and Organicism), the embattled retreat from the political issues of the day slides over into a position of Romantic Anarchism. While the synechdochic principle of representation appears to operate, in that Levin is but one pea in the aristocratic pod, it is his very unrepresentativeness, his individuality, which defines his real self, and the personal position from which he categorically refuses to engage in any kind of dialectic. He works out a new plan for the management of his estate while lying in bed at night, a scheme involving shareholding, which he has come to by rethinking the ideas of an elderly landowner still committed to serfdom. But Levin communicates his idea – which can only be called a rehash of the existing system – to no one except his steward. Even if it works, it will be contained by its local and temporal limits; it will be *unrepresentative*, because Levin is wilfully determined to ignore what the rest of society deems to be necessary.

There are, then, fissures in what I have labelled 'the country-side'; and because of these fissures there are shifts of movement, which occur over both the grid and the terrain. The enclosed domains of Levin's and Sviazhky's estates, while self-contained, are not impermeable; they crumble at the edges where progress taps. And outside these circular entities there exists a larger world, with which Levin must engage in some dialectic, since it so persistently challenges his inner sanctum. This is the world of Society, inhabited and largely represented by the Liberal Stiva, who looks at and is looked at by his friend Levin with mutual affection and irony. But he is somewhat sharply satirized by Tolstoy:

> Stiva did not choose either his inclinations or his views; he came by them in much the same way as his hat or coat, which he also did not choose, simply taking what was being worn. If he had a reason for preferring the Liberal position to the Conservatism of many of his circle, it was not that he considered Liberalism more reasonable but because it was better suited to his life-style. . . . Liberalism had become habitual to Oblonsky, and he loved his news-paper as he loved his after-dinner cigar, for the slight haze it produced in his head. (*SS* 1, pp. 13–14)

However, Stiva is always at home in whichever social group he finds himself, and regularly puts its disparate members at their ease. We have seen him 'kneading the society dough' at the Ministry, at the wedding, at his own dinner-party to which he arrives late. Everything he does in society leads toward what White calls a provisional integration of dispersed entities, 'who come to share a context and bathe in a common atmosphere' (p. 65). It is a procedure which gives the reader an excellent 'feel' for the social life of a distant epoch and locale, but which does not seek to hypothesize generalisations that can be made into theories of historical causation. This is how it was, that is all. It is the Contextualist mode of explanation, corresponding, correctly, to the ideological category of Liberalism.

Like an annulus around the inner circle of the countryside, Stiva's world is dialectical at both peripheries. He is at home in the country, and frequently invades Levin's retreat, making *him* look more at the outside world. But it is really the circle of Society that is Stiva's natural habitat; and from there he negotiates with that last and final outer circle that lies at the extreme periphery of the social world, that limbo of ostracisation into which his sister finds herself cast by her former friends and associates. Beyond that outer edge lies only Italy, remote from both country and city, unrelated to those locales recognized by history, situated indeed in the mythos of Tragedy.

Italy thus becomes a spatial metaphor for Anna's isolation. But once again, the notion of 'world' can be laid over that of the grid, and progress through it broken down into various phases. Thus Anna's trajectory from the world of Society that she inhabited with her brother to '*tot mir*' where she becomes an alien, is but a simpler version of Frye's account of any tragic career, in the first phase of which the central character enjoys 'the greatest possible dignity in contrast to the other characters' (p. 219), and then passes through a stage of *hubris* to the point where the heroic begins to falter. By the time she has reached Frye's fifth stage of tragic action she has indeed, as he prescribes, lost her directions and her understanding of how to act correctly in the world. Beyond this there is only the sixth stage of 'shock and horror' (p. 222) – the shock of society's cruel rejection, the horror of her path of unfounded jealousy and unjustified despair. Now her agony is too great to qualify for heroic status; she becomes demonic, giving us glimpses of her mental torture, her madness, and the 'huge and relentless' compulsion to kill herself. The inevitability appears Mechanistic – the mode corresponding to Tragedy.

Thus while Anna's categorisation is consistent, though not static, in that she conforms perfectly to the inner progress of Tragedy and to its affiliated categories, that of Levin is ambivalent. He hovers between Romance (as in the battles he joins for the sake of his Slavophile Utopia) and Comedy (in the emphasis he places on the society of the family and its increase). But Stiva represents a truer, though tarnished, form of Comedy, in that his pragmatic life-style will result in the perpetuation of the society, and the assurance that *this* world and its values will obtain in their appropriate *topoi*.

Thus a suitable mixture of fit and non-fit has been demonstrated, and we can remind ourselves that the grid itself is only a means to an end – to an understanding that is somehow contained in, but also beyond, its own fourth term. White defines the whole process as one of rendering the unfamiliar familiar (p. 5); and of course this terminology echoes, as he himself points out, Freud's essay on the significance of rendering familiar what can also be called the uncanny. The product of 'understanding' is to turn 'exotic' or '*unheimlich*' experience into something 'humanly useful, non-threatening' (ibid.). But it is precisely the confident progress of the tropes towards the comfortable asylum of the 'canny' that is in question, for the 'usefulness' of Levin's solution to Russia's political future is non-existent. And it is equally arguable that while Tolstoy has brilliantly and graphically portrayed the degeneration of Anna's passion into despair and madness, he has neither domesticated it nor made it any the less threatening.

Examination of the eschatological bafflement that has always surrounded the 'meaning' of the novel indicates that this meaning is found not so much in what is familiar as in what is unfamiliar – in the novel's *unreasonable* elements. In the Epilogue, for example, Levin has apparently matured into an adult male capable of founding a new mini-society in a Utopian setting which shuts out the crises of the nation. Yet – 'though he was a happy and a healthy family man Levin was several times so near suicide that he hid the rope lest he should hang himself and feared to carry a gun lest he shoot himself' (*SS* 9, p. 413).

The very unreasonableness of Levin's contradictory urge to kill himself when everything about his life is so 'positive' is both symptom and malady. It is Reason itself which claims that all is well, when Levin knows in the depths of his heart how superficial such a contention is; and therefore Reason, and all its spurious pretentions now exploded by the divulgences of the Anna story, must be exposed before Levin's story can be given the final seal. But it must of course be removed into an arena separate from the bulwarks of happy, healthy family life. The conflict is displaced onto the secular beliefs of the age – liberalism, scientism and above all the Darwinian theory of evolution – all of which Levin simply rejects in favour of an intuitive trust in the existence and goodness of a God who cannot be either conjured up or justified by Reason. In adopting this position, Levin believes he has liberated himself from the rigid and restricting chains of cause and effect. He is not unlike William in *The Name of the Rose* (Eco, 1984) who similarly challenges the acquisition of truth through reason alone – 'The only truth lies in learning to free ourselves from the insane passion for truth' (Eco, p. 491) – but who continues to search precisely for that truth which will solve the mystery of the deaths in the monastery, by methods which at least include Reason. Similarly, Levin uses exactly the rejected mode of rational argument to refute it: 'If goodness has a cause, it is no longer goodness; if it has a consequence – a reward, it is also not goodness. Therefore goodness is beyond the chain of cause and effect'. If, then, therefore . . .

Nor can he demolish analogy, another method of logical think-ing – ('ways of thought strange and unnatural to man [which] lead him to a knowledge of what he knew long ago', as he puts it) – without having recourse to that very method. He is prompted to his conclusion by meditating on the significance he can attribute to Dolly's children's game of pouring jets of milk into their mouths:

> What if the children were left alone and had to get their own cups, or make them, and milk the cows and so on. Would they just play, then? No, for they would die of hunger. What if we, with our passions and thoughts, were left without any concept of the one God, the Creator. Or without any concept of what is good, and without an explanation of moral evil. Try to build up anything without these concepts! (*SS* 9, pp. 422–3)

and reverts to simile to explain, rationally, his act of so-called irrational belief. His argument that,

> The sky looks like a vault but is in fact space. But since I see it as a vault I should not therefore think of it as space . . .

is paralleled by the syllogism:

> Faith is experienced as human but is in fact supernatural. But since I choose to experience it as human, I should not therefore concern myself with what it means supernaturally.

Levin's determination to make clear to himself *how* and *why* he has suddenly attained the gift of faith is as dependent on rational thought as is Jorge's realisation that William has shown him he arrived at the truth 'by following a false reasoning' (Eco, p. 471).

In fact, every tenet of Levin's so-called intuitive faith is susceptible to a rational explanation which he simply chooses to ignore. 'The law of loving others could not be discovered by reason because it is unreasonable', he claims (SS 9, p. 422). But utilitarianism and the demands of the common good can readily be invoked in support of 'brotherly love', just as his choice of Russian Orthodoxy over other religions such as Hinduism can be explained by the effects of socialisation. Thus Levin's claims for Unreason are undermined from within and without by his reliance on the inherent strengths of Reason, while, simultaneously, Reason is shown to be inadequate to his felt needs. 'Whether he was acting well or ill he did not know, and far from trying to demonstrate it, he now avoided talking or thinking about it. Thinking about it led him into doubts and prevented him from seeing what was required and what was not . . .' (SS 9, p. 416). His position again might well have been addressed by another character in *The Name of the Rose*, Adso, who says to William, 'You act, and you know why you act, but you don't know why you know that you know what you do . . .' (Eco, p. 207).

Levin's oscillations between Reason and Unreason, between causality and the rejection of it, and his sudden new reliance on analogy/metaphor (out in the cold without the cloak of religion) make clear how frail is his new found faith, whose very process of establishment has cast into doubt the possibility of an Ultimate Cause, and whose metaphors never seem to stem with any certainty from a Universal Signifier. He has conceived a fantasy of faith of which he is both the author and the authorisation; despite his claims for its 'senselessness', it makes sense to him, but he avoids – casually with Koznyshev, but strenuously with Kitty – the impulse to communicate it.

It is this position of extreme individualism (or Anarchism) which (logically) prevents Levin from taking the Nationalist line in the debate over the war with the Turks, for he is unable to give any meaning to the notion of 'the will of the people'. It is only through an impasse such as this that we can see through Levin's blind, triumphal belief that has been the object of a miracle of faith, for at first his certainty appears tempting. It really has looked as though there is a choice to be made between evangelistic belief, a faith willing to 'stand convicted of foolishness in the court of the intellect', and adherence to the powers of reason, and logocentrism.

But the text has shown, no doubt against the conscious intentions of its author, that the choice is not a real one. Faith and Reason are not polarities, one of which must inevitably exclude the other; Levin's lucubrations show as well as any theoretical essay the essential role of the notion of play between such supposed contradictions, and the contamination each insinuates into the other.

Nor can his reliance on, and flight from, Reason amount to a position of greater understanding, either for him or the reader. Its political usefulness, as we have said, is non-existent; its only claim must rest on its appeal to familiarity. But when the familiar is anachronistic, can this appeal be justified? In the end Levin's stance is for everyone except himself and his author distinctly *unheimlich*; and it thus undermines its own power to persuade. Unreason has triumphed after all.

Similarly with Anna. In his almost contemporaneous *Diary of a Writer* Dostoevsky emphasised the element of divine mystery pertaining to her death. Refuting all psychological 'explanations', he ascribed to God alone the right to judge Anna's suicide, on the grounds that He alone comprehends all. 'Finally . . . the laws of the human soul are still so unknown, so unfamiliar to science, so indefinite and so mysterious, that as yet there can neither be any medics, nor any judges, but . . . there is only the One who says, "Vengeance is mind, I will repay"', (quoted by Eikhenbaum, p. 138). Eikhenbaum regards Dostoevsky's view as subjective, relating how, decades after the event, Tolstoy reputedly approved an article by M. S. Gromeka which aimed to demystify the role of passion in the novel while stressing its destructive and pernicious qualities. Tolstoy even went so far as to say that in Gromeka's 'excellent' article, *Anna Karenina* was 'explained'. The article states in part:

> Marriage is nevertheless the only form of love in which a feeling calmly, naturally, and without hindrance forms durable bonds between people and society, preserving freedom for action, giving it strength and incentive, creating a pure children's world, creating the soil, source, and implement of life. But this pure family principle can be created only on a stable foundation of true feeling. It cannot be built on external calculation. And a later infatuation with passion will not correct anything and will only lead to a final destruction because . . . Vengeance is mine; I will repay. . . .        (Quoted by Eikhenbaum, p. 139)

But Eikhenbaum also rejects Gromeka's simplified view of the 'meaning' of Anna's death, commenting, 'One is forced to admit as doubtful Tolstoy's approval in regard to Gromeka's article, or to look at it as a kind of temporary, short-lived enthusiasm for someone else's idea when his own had sunk into the past and was somewhat forgotten' (p. 139). He is more sympathetic to the opinion of M. Aldanov, whom he quotes at length, but whose relevance can be summed up in the lines: 'It may be that some scenes of *Anna Karenina* so move us, tug so hard at out heart strings, because we sense the impotence of the great writer . . . to subordinate the enchanting little world evoked by him to a moral concept . . .' (p. 141). This judgement comes closer to Eikhenbaum's own, which consists finally in the view that the epigraph does not and cannot 'sum up' the novel; that it merely addresses one aspect of it – the relation between 'evil' and 'bitterness' – which he corroborates from some words addressed by Tolstoy to M. S. Sukhotin (Tolstoy's son-in-law), who repeated them in a letter to V. V. Veresaev: 'I chose this epigraph, as I already explained, simply to convey the idea that the evil [*durnoe*] that man does has as its consequence only bitterness, which comes not from man, but from God, and which Anna Karenina, too, experienced' (p. 143). This statement, again made long after the novel was written (the conversation between Sukhotin and Tolstoy was reported in a letter of 23 May 1907) should be treated with as much suspicion as the first; but Eikhenbaum is right, in my opinion, to underscore the narrowness of the epigraph's field of interest compared with that of the whole novel. Tolstoy was grappling during this period with the philosophy of Schopenhauer, including his views on sexuality. It was here, claims Eikhenbaum, that Tolstoy found ample support for his marvellous encapsulation of the perennial double standard that he enscribed in a letter to Strakhov:

> Conjugal fidelity for the man is artificial, for the woman natural; and so adultery by the wife, both objectively because of its consequences and also subjectively because of its unnaturalness, is far more unpardonable than adultery by the man.
>
> (Quoted by Eikhenbaum, pp. 99–100)

But it is also true, as Eikhenbaum concludes, that 'Theories retreat to the second order of things before the pressure of the artistic material'. After all, was it not Tolstoy himself who remarked in an often-quoted letter, 'If I wanted to say in words all that I had in mind to express in the novel, then I would have to write the very same novel which I have written all over again . . .' (*SS* 17, p. 433).

This controversy, confusion and division of opinion, then, over the 'meaning' of Anna's death only serves to show that it confounds meaning in terms of anything but itself (and even then 'the very same novel all over again' would not mean quite the same thing, as Borges humorously demonstrated in his story about another writing of *Don Quixote*). But it also shows that such a reversal of the norms of discourse – the very failure to arrive at a safe harbour of ironic understanding – supports in an argument from rhetoric what has already been suggested by both psychoanalysis and feminist deconstruction.

For whatever the understanding acquired by the readerly eye at the end of Anna's story, the narratorial subject (Anna) can only be said to have *lost* understanding of herself and her situation, so distorted is her mind. Not even her friends grasp what is happening to her. That most poignant moment when she visits Dolly on the afternoon of her suicide in a distraught attempt to make some contact with another human being we have already discussed in relation to her madness. We now see the same scene in a slightly different light; it is no longer a matter of sanity, but of epistemology. Dolly's use of the word 'peculiar' means now that Anna's regress has reversed the norm; she has become totally *unheimlich*. We realise, then, that one of the greatest moments of irony in the book occurs not at the end but at the *beginning* of the novel, when Anna settles herself in the train going back from Moscow to St Petersburg and declares, 'Thank Heaven, tomorrow I shall see Seriozha and Alexei again, and my pleasant, ordinary life will go on as before' (*SS* 8, p. 121). Similarly the most powerful metaphor is the one that closes her story: 'The candle, by the light of which she had been reading that book filled with anxieties, deceptions, griefs, and evil, suddenly illuminated for her more brightly than ever before all that had hitherto been dark; it crackled, began to flicker, and went out forever' (*SS* 9, p. 389).

Thus the reversal of the proper tropic order in Anna's strand corroborates what the absence of the fourth trope and the Unreason of the Epilogue suggested in Levin's: that the subterranean forces at work in Tolstoy's novel affect every level of its operation, subverting the norms of rhetoric and discourse as well as those of morality, sexuality, and identity.

And if we dare bring into play our own irony we can derive one last reward from an analysis of this kind. While I suggested earlier that Stiva's role in the novel is pivotal and frequently underestimated, application of the grid and the schema of what Jameson calls simply 'world' takes this conviction considerably further. Levin's inner circle and the outermost periphery to which Anna is banned are mutually exclusive except when both are mediated by, and meet in, the middle ring occupied by a hypocritically Liberal Society. The inhabitants of this middle ground gaze ironically at the extremes on either side of it. Stiva calls Levin a 'savage', but it is he who tries to alleviate Anna's isolation by bringing Levin to meet her.

It is the fact that this Society, both hypocritical and self-assured, exerts enough power to make Levin withdraw from it into a feudal retreat of rural unworldliness, and to cause Anna to seek in vain for a place of escape from it, that brings us back to the initial concerns of 'the rhetoric of morality'. For Stiva's middle ground teaches a lesson that is antithetical to all his author intended to preach – the message that survival depends on pragmatism, double standards and compromise. In the end, a large part of the moral system to which Tolstoy was committed, and which so inextricably fleshes out the skeletal *topoi* of the story, was defeated by the inevitabilities of that Absent Cause whose invisible effects were as eloquently powerful as the silences of Tolstoy's text.

# Afterword

This study of *Anna Karenina* set out in the first instance to test the novel against 'theory', and theories against each other. With the major categories of theory (those dealing with the subsconscious, the 'social intention' and the 'formal control') suggested by a paragraph from Lionel Trilling, it was assumed, and consequently shown, that within these broad sectors there would be both subdivision and overlap. There could be Freudian, Lacanian, and feminist lines of psychoanalytic argument; feminist and Marxist ideological stances; and semiotic, rhetorical, generic aspects of form, even in a list that is far from exhaustive.

Nor did the subject matter fit equally or evenly amongst the various sub-categories. The dark cave of psychoanalytic application was vaster, had denser airs, and was more difficult to emerge from than I anticipated; the feminist issue became ambivalent, and took an unexpected turn in its vindication of the hero-ine; and the role of form seemed to run like an underground current throughout the whole exercise, mocking the original notion of confining it to a single chapter – let alone a grid! And – something that remains discomforting but unrectifiable – even before publication I was accused of making the Marxist critics into straw men, of minimising their relevance.

The unsettling effects of such attacks and surprises would have been much greater had it not been for the wisdom of one critic, Isaiah Berlin, and for the self-contradictions of another, Mikhail Bakhtin. For these two commentators of Tolstoy seemed to be more aware than any others of the complexities that lie beneath the apparently 'monologistic' text.

Even Chekhov, despite, or perhaps because of, his own superb tact, was sensitive to the overwhelming effects of its rhetoric. 'Have you noticed Tolstoy's language?' he asked. 'Enormous periods, sentences piled on top of each other. These periods create the impression of power!' (Schulze, p. 57, quoting S. Shchukin, in *Russkaia mysl*, no. 10, p. 45) And power, by definition, is unilateral.

Schultze in fact takes up this theme, analysing what she con-

186

siders to be the main instrument of Tolstoy's textual power – his verbal repetition. As with Lewis Caroll's Boatman and J. Hillis Miller, what Tolstoy says three times does tend to sound pretty convincing. Schulze provides a clear and concise account of three-, four-, five-, six- and even eight-fold repetitions in *Anna Karenina*, which it would be redundant to transcribe – particularly as she treats them as elements of style rather than of moral persuasion. But their effect, as Chekhov perceived, is enormously potent, often undermining more superficial impressions of apparent ambivalence.

For example, in the pre-wedding scene, the confession episode begins with several subtle observations, all designed to discredit the ritual of the morning service that Levin feels obliged to attend. The church is practically empty, the young deacon is somehow ridiculous because the two halves of his long back are visible through his thin under-cassock, the readings are mechanical and mumbled, and the money Levin proffers is received stealthily into the deacon's hand, which stretches from beneath a velvet cuff. The old priest from whom Levin seeks confession also offends, but in a different way. His accent is provincial; his eyes, though kind, are weary. Levin, who has been concerned that he will have to either lie or blaspheme, in fact puts up a sincere and sympathetic front, emerging as an honest agnostic – a position so genuine it seems almost noble. His authenticity corroborates Tolstoy's stated claim that he tried to make Levin seem more right than the priest. But, at the same time, the language belies this impression; although the priest is mild, puzzled, thoughtful, that is, not at all dictatorial, his words repeat one proposition so consistently that it becomes it itself persuasive of some higher belief, standing outside the text.

- doubts are natural
- doubt is natural
- what doubt can there be of the existence of God?
- what doubt can you have of the Creator . . .?
- how can you doubt that God . . .?
- even the Holy Fathers doubted . . .

To doubt is thus indubitably natural – but these questions presuppose the existence of a supernatural object *of* doubt; so, paradoxically, man's doubt affirms God's existence – the point Tolstoy wants to make. In later years, as we have remarked, he claimed that he was on the priest's side, but did not want to show it. However, since anything Tolstoy says must always be related to the period in which he said it, these subsequent claims to his own earlier intentions are actually less final than the driving power of those persistently repeated phrases, which so insidiously achieve their goal of casting doubt itself into doubt, and so affirming that which is doubted.

Thus it becomes evident that many of the principles already discussed in this study have been saying the same thing in a variety of different ways. If 'Tolstoy was a fox who thought he was a hedgehog', then this wish for a unifying, central vision corresponds to the monologic voice with which such a desire would naturally be expressed. Tolstoy's glimpses of such a world, and his profound and powerful desire that it should come to pass upon this earth, remain an overriding force throughout the novel, even, as was also mentioned earlier, fooling Bakhtin. To elaborate further this curiosity: in 1919, and again in the final edition of his book on Dostoevsky's poetics, Bakhtin writes:

> Tolstoy's universe is monolithically monological. . . . in his universe, there is no second voice alongside that of the author, hence, no problem of the combination of voices, or of a special status of the author's viewpoint. (Todorov, p. 63)

But in 1934–5, and again in 1945, Bakhtin states the opposite:

> Thus discourse in Tolstoy is characterised by a sharp internal dialogism, and this discourse is moreover dialogical in the belief system of the reader – whose peculiar semantic and expressive characteristics Tolstoy acutely senses – as well as in the object.
> (Holquist, p. 283)

It is of course the second characterisation which is the true one, for what Bakhtin's writings on dialogisation make us see most clearly is not simply the heteroglossic manner in which two, or a number of, disparate views is expressed (such as the conflict between Levin and the priest, or the range of opinions over Russia's entry into the Turkish War), although Tolstoy was always immensely concerned to make each viewpoint sound authentic and convincing, whatever he himself may have thought. (Tolstoy consciously believed that each character's speech should be recognisably individual, and he actually reproached Dostoevsky for making his characters all speak with his, Dostoevsky's voice!) But overriding the variety of opinions, even when each is given its proper weight and most persuasive presentation (and there are of course exceptions to this tactic, such as when Tolstoy loads his account of Vronsky's bachelor views with biting sarcasm), is the fact that Tolstoy himself always appears to be certain about what is right, and apparently wants to persuade his reader of the same. The dialogic quality then appears to occur only because the reader is presumed to hold other views, to come, most probably, from that very worldly society of the city with which Tolstoy/Levin polemicises; thus there runs throughout the discourse of the novel the Tolstoyan equivalent of what, in Dostoevsky, Bakhtin has called the sideways glance. In Tolstoy it is not a lateral, furtive look, but a flash from underneath the shaggy eyebrows, a fierce but measuring assessment of whether the reader has got the right message, which may be quite the opposite of what the character, or even the authorial description, seems to be saying. So, when Vronsky interrupts Dolly with the correction that he is building a hospital, not a maternity home, the exchange *between the characters* is apparently naïve; each assesses the other quite positively. Yet most readers realise that Tolstoy is inviting them to regard Vronsky's lack of interest in a maternity ward as an issue by which Vronsky all unawares condemns himself out of his own mouth, speaking 'without his usual courtesy', cutting through Dolly's hesitant suggestion, peremptorily making his case for the medical services that have already been blackened by the occasion when the young male doctor makes Kitty take her clothes off.

Tolstoy is indeed monolithic in the impression he gives about what is right and wrong; but he is also adamant that *every* reader should also take to heart the questions he is posing; so it is for this reason that Bakhtin later writes that Tolstoy's 'discourse is everywhere determined by the heteroglossia (literary *and* real-life) that dialogically – polemically or pedagogically – permeates discourse' (Bakhtin, 1981, p. 398). In this sense, representations that appear direct and unmediated turn out to be at heart inordinately concerned not just with the words on the page, but with their effect, in dialogism, on the almost defenceless reader.

In other words, what Bakhtin is saying is that Tolstoy's own voice is monologic, but that it *becomes* dialogic when it enters into persuasion or argument with a reader, whose silent rejoinders are somehow incorporated into the one-sided conversation. (Perhaps this is what is meant by the sound of one hand clapping.) It is certainly an important point, and one which does much to explain the extraordinary sense of involvement that the huge reading public of *Anna Karenina* seems to feel with this novel. Whatever else, readers believe that Tolstoy is definitely addressing *them*, individually and personally.

But Bakhtin's preoccupation with the social context of language precludes a full account of his own term, heteroglossia. Despite his detailed typology of the various 'languages' employed in the novel in general (generic, professional, class, generational, etc.) his vision of the internal relationship each individual has with the world about him means that the gaze is always directed to the other. And hence, of course, the characterisation of his imagination as 'dialogic'. But this is not to say that Tolstoy's equally intense interrogation of his own self does not, also, produce a chorus of many voices, even if the result is not an Underground Man wearing his spleen on his sleeve, but rather a Patriarch magnificently unaware of what his preaching constantly betrays.

Even the younger characters Nikolai and Olenin, whom Tolstoy holds up in front of himself, happy to pretend that they are him in fictional disguise, reveal more than he bargains for about the effect of his mother's death and the sacrilisation of Nature, while Koznyshev and Oblonsky constitute a courageous attempt to allow publically that there are other aspects of his character besides the one designated by Levin. Through these two, very different personalities Tolstoy interrogates his residual nostalgia for a mother–son relationship that was never replaced by pair-bonding; and for a life not constrained by his own ideals of marital fidelity.

With the integrity of the authorial 'I' of *Anna Karenina* already broken down into three sub-personae, it becomes easier to grasp that this exercise is both essential in itself, and a necessary part of Tolstoy's devastating confrontation with his total sexuality, including passion (as distinct from both lust and conjugal love) and the related terror of death (since passion and death are intimately bound up). The creation and destruction of Anna, however, who dies both because of her subordination to passion and because her creator wants to kill part of himself, requires yet another character to express a further projection of the composite we once thought of as a united whole. For Anna is also socially and psychologically destroyed by her lover, who, failing to kill himself, is in the end despatched by an author who despises him to the annihilation of war.

Thus Bakhtin has got it half-right; but more and more does Berlin seem completely right to point to Tolstoy's *desire* for unity, while less and less does it seem that any *one* answer could satisfy the conflicts and contradictions that beset such a complex character. Only by adopting and exploring the diverse personae that pulled him in different directions could Tolstoy begin to put the clamorous voices to rest; and then only by wishfully asserting that what he wanted to be the case actually was, could he find anything at all to cling to.

Yet the internal polyphony constituted by Tolstoy's various projected selves is still only a part of the heteroglossia of this novel. There is also a series of dialogues with the world outside, both present and future. Tolstoy takes issue with the voices of his own age – all those speaking for industrialisation, secularisation, Westernisation, democratisation – and particularly with those who would emancipate, in the wake of the serfs, the women of Russia. In turn, of course, he is himself attacked by modern feminists and recouped by twentieth-century Marxists, although it turns out, at least in this study, that both of these enterprises get the wrong end of the green stick.

However, the point is made that for Tolstoy not just two voices, as Bakhtin claimed, are the 'minimum for life, the minimum for survival' (Bakhtin, 1973, p. 213), but the two-times-two-times-two which are required to express his profound complexity. It is precisely to counter this fragmentation that there are also the eight-fold repetitions which in the end denote not moral certitude itself, but an anguished yearning for it.

But what this study has also shown is that the kind of certitude that Tolstoy longed for is unobtainable, for there are no clear-cut polarities. Life is contaminated by death; function-love by narcissism; and Plato's form of repetition by Nietzsche's. Similarly, happily married husbands contemplate suicide, real heroines behave as heroes, and the family survives best through those who pay it least respect. In the end only the collective is monologic, ignoring the fact that faith and reason infect each other.

To make use yet again of Berlin's parable, the hedgehog cannot prevail against the fox's introduction of dialogism, heteroglossia, actions which willy-nilly disrupt the moral vision, and ironies which subvert by their absence as much as by their presence. Both

A and not-A must be retained, as must the work of remembering and that of forgetting, and the spontaneous leaps which defy the grid. And between text and theory there can only, ever, be a mutual contamination.

If, as Shklovsky claimed, *Tristram Shandy* is 'the most typical novel in world literature', then *Anna Karenina* is the one that leaves the most to be said – still.

# Notes

## CHAPTER 1: TOLSTOY'S DEAD MOTHER

*This chapter appeared, in slightly different form, in *AUMLA*, 1986.

1. Appeared first as an article in *Yale French Studies*, nos 55–6, 1977, pp. 280–300; later incorporated with some changes in the monograph, *Reading for the Plot*.
2. The poem in translation reads:
   An angel flew through the midnight sky/ And sang a quiet song;/ And the moon and the stars and the piled clouds/ Listened to that sacred song./ He sang of the bliss of the sinless souls/ In the shade of the heavenly gardens./ He sang of the great God – and his praise/ Was unfeigned.
   He carried a young soul in his embrace/ For the world of sorrow and tears./ And the sound of his song remained in the young soul/ Wordless but vivid./ And for a long time it suffered in the world,/ Full of a wondrous desire,/ And the dreary songs of earth/ Could not replace the sounds of heaven.

## CHAPTER 5: EXECUTING A FIGURE

1. For a fuller account see my *The Novel of Adultery*, 1982, Macmillan.
2. *Poor Liza* (1792), a novel by Nikolai Karamzin, describes the fate of a peasant girl who throws herself into a lake because of an unhappy love-affair with a nobleman.
3. There are two newspapers in Moscow, one called *Pravda* (Truth) and the other called *Izvestia* (News). The saying is that there is no news in the Truth and no truth in the News.

## CHAPTER 6: THE DAUGHTER'S REDUCTION

1. Gallop has recently published a further book on Lacan, *Reading Lacan*, 1985, Cornell University Press.

## CHAPTER 7: LENIN DECONSTRUCTS

1. It is surprising that there seem to be no prominent Soviet critics writing on this aspect of Tolstoy. But of the three main ones, Gudzy is concerned

with the history of the writing of *Anna Karenina*, and Gusev and Zhdanov with the moral positions found in the novel.

## CHAPTER 8: THE RHETORIC OF MORALITY

1. Peter Henry, in the Introduction to his book, *Classics of Soviet Satire*, 1972, Colletts, writes, 'While most writers, including the great Tolstoy, have been parodied, Pushkin, Gorky and Sholokhov . . . never are; nor is Mayakovsky, ever since his canonisation by Stalin in 1933.'

# References

All quotations from the works of Lev Tolstoy have been translated by myself and taken from the *Collected Works in Twenty Volumes* (*Sobranie Sochinenii v dvadtsati tomakh*) 1968, Moscow, abbreviated in the text to *SS*; the volume number is given first, followed by the page number. Most of the other Russian writings have been quoted from English translations, since these are more accessible to the majority of readers.

Quotations from the writings of Sigmund Freud have been taken from the *Pelican Freud Library*, General Editor, Angela Richards, referred to in the text as *PF*, followed by the volume and page numbers.

Armstrong, Judith (1978), *The Novel of Adultery*, Macmillan, London.

Bakhtin, M. M. (1981) *The Dialogic Imagination: Four Essays*, ed. Michael Holquist, trans. Caryl Emerson and Michael Holquist, University of Texas Press, Austin.

Bayley, John (1966), *Tolstoy and the Novel*, Chatto & Windus, London.

Balint, Michael (1968), *The Basic Fault: Aspects of Aggression*, Tavistock Publications, London.

Benjamin, Walter (1969), *Illuminations*, trans. Harry Zohn, Schocken, New York.

Berlin, Isaiah (1978), *Russian Thinkers*, Hogarth Press, London.

Bernheimer, Charles (1982), *Flaubert and Kafka: A Psychopoetic Study*, Yale University Press.

Binion, Rudolph (1981) *Soundings Psychohistorical and Psycholiterary*, Psychohistory Press, New York.

Bloom, Harold (1980), *A Map of Misreading*, Oxford University Press.

Bloom, Harold (1981), 'Freud and the Poetic Sublime', in Perry Meisel (ed.), *Freud: a Collection of Critical Essays*, Prentice Hall, pp. 211–31.

Bollas, Christopher (1978), 'The Aesthetic Moment and the Search for Transformation', *The Annual of Psychoanalysis*, vol. 6, p. 388.

Bollas, Christopher (1979), 'The Transformational Object', *International Journal of Psychoanalysis*, vol. 60, pp. 97–107.

Brooks, Peter (1984), *Reading for the Plot*, Clarendon Press, Oxford.

Christian, R. F. (1960), *War and Peace: a Study*, Oxford University Press.

Christian, R. F. (1969), *Tolstoy: a Critical Introduction*, Cambridge University Press.

Davie, Donald (1965) (ed.), *Russian Literature and Modern English Fiction*, University of Chicago Press.

Deleuze, Gilles (1969), *Logique du Sens*, Editions de Minuit, Paris.

Eagleton, Terry (1982), *The Rape of Clarissa*, Basil Blackwell, Oxford.

Eco, Umberto (1984), *The Name of the Rose*, Warner Books, New York.

Eikhenbaum, Boris (1928), *Lev Tolstoi, Kniga Pervaia, 50-ye godi*, Moscow.

Eikhenbaum, Boris (1982), *Tolstoi in the Seventies*, trans. Albert Kaspin, Ardis Press, Ann Arbor.

Fedotov, G. P. (1946), *The Russian Religious Mind*, Harper & Row, New York.

Fehér, Ferenc (1985), 'Grandeur and Decline of a Holistic Philosophy', *Theory and Society*, vol. 14, pp. 863–76.

Felman, Shoshana (1977) (ed.), *Literature and Psychoanalysis*, Johns Hopkins Press, Baltimore.

Frye, Northrop (1973), *Anatomy of Criticism: Four Essays*, Princeton University Press.

Gallop, Jane (1982), *The Daughter's Seduction: Feminism and Psychoanalysis*, Macmillan, London.

Green, André (1978), 'The Double and the Absent', in Alan Roland (ed.), *Psychoanalysis, Creativity and Literature: a French-American Inquiry*, Colombia University Press.

Grunberger, Béla (1970), 'Outline for a Study of Narcissism in Female Sexuality', in Janine Chasseguet-Smirgel (ed.), *Female Sexuality: New Psychoanalytic Views*, Maresfield Library, London.

Henry, Peter (1972), *Classics of Soviet Satire*, vol. 1, Colletts.

Jakobson, Roman and Halle, Morris (1956), *Fundamentals of Language*, Mouton, The Hague, pp. 76–82.

Jameson, Fredric (1976), 'Figural Relativism, or the Poetics of Historiography, *Diacritics*, spring, pp. 2–9.

Jameson, Fredric (1981), *The Political Unconscious*, Cornell University Press.

Jay, Martin (1984), *Marxism and Totality: The Adventures of a Concept from Lukacs to Habermas*, University of California, Berkeley.

Hertz, Neil (1979), 'Freud and the Sandman', in Josué U. Harari (ed.), *Textual Strategies*, Cornell University Press.

Holquist, J. M. (1974), 'Disease as Dialectic in *Crime and Punishment*' in Robert Louis Jackson (ed.), *Twentieth Century Interpretations of Crime and Punishment*, Prentice Hall, pp. 109–18.

Irigaray, Luce (1974), *Speculum de l'autre femme*, Editions de Minuit, Paris.

Irigaray, Luce (1977), *Ce Sexe qui n'en est pas un*, Editions de Minuit, Paris.

Karpman, Ben (1938–39), *Psychoanalytic Review*, vols 25–6, 1938–39.

Lacan, Jacques (1977), *Ecrits: a Selection*, trans. Alan Sheridan, Tavistock Publications, London.

Lacapra, Dominick (1983), *Rethinking Intellectual History: Texts, Contexts, Language*, Cornell University Press.

Laplanche, Jean (1976), *Life and Death in Psychoanalysis*, trans. Geoffrey Mehlman, John Hopkins Press, Baltimore.

de Lauretis, Teresa (1984), *Alice Doesn't: Feminism, Semiotics, Cinema*, Indiana University Press, Bloomington.

Lavrin, Janko (1948), *Tolstoy: an Approach*, Methuen, London.

Lenin, V. I. (1963), *Collected Works*, Foreign Languages Publishing House, Moscow.

Lotman, Iuri (1973), 'The Origin of Plot in the Light of Typology', trans. Julian Draffy, in *Poetics Today*, vols. 1–2, 1979.

Lotman, Iuri (1977), *The Structure of the Artistic Text*, trans. Gail Lenhoff and Ronald Vroon, University of Michigan Press, Ann Arbor.

Lukács, Georg (1970), *Writer and Critic and other Essays*, ed. and trans. Arthur Kahn, Merlin Press, London.

Lukács, Georg (1971), *The Theory of the Novel*, trans. Anna Bostock, Merlin Press, London.

Lukács, Georg (1972), *Studies in European Realism*, Merlin Press, London.

Macherey, Pierre (1978), *A Theory of Literary Production*, trans. Geoffrey Wall, Routledge & Kegan Paul, London.

Meisel, Perry (1981) (ed.), *Freud: a Collection of Critical Essays*, Prentice Hall.

Mitchell, Juliet and Rose, Jacqueline (1985) (eds), *Feminine Sexuality: Jacques Lacan and the école freudienne*, trans. Jacqueline Rose, Norton and Co., New York, Pantheon, New York and London.

Miller, J. Hillis (1982), *Fiction and Repetition: Seven English Novels*, Harvard University Press, Boston.

Montrelay, Michèle (1977), 'Recherches sur la féminité in *Critique*, vol. 278, July 1970.

Mulvey, Laura (1975), 'Visual Pleasure and Narrative Cinema' *Screen*, vol. 16, no. 3, autumn 1975.

Propp, Vladimir (1968), *Morphology of the Folktale*, trans. Lawrence Scott, University of Texas Press.

Propp, Vladimir (1984), *Theory and History of Folklore*, ed. Anatoly Liberman, trans. Ariadna Y. Martin and Richard P. Martin, University of Minnesota, Minneapolis.

Rice, Donald and Schofer, Peter (1983), *Rhetorical Poetics: Theory and Practice of Figural and Symbolic Reading in Modern French Literature*, University of Wisconsin, Madison.

Rose, Margaret (1979), *Parody/Metafiction*, Croom Helm, London.

de Rougemont, Denis (1962), *Passion and Society*, trans. Montgomery Belgion, Pantheon, New York.

Schafer, Roy (1981), 'Narration in the Psychoanalytic Dialogue' in (ed.) W. J. T. Mitchell, *On Narrative*, University of Chicago Press, pp. 25–49.

Schulze, Sydney (1982), *The Structure of Anna Karenina*, Ardis Press, Ann Arbor.

Shklovsky, Viktor (1963), *Lev Tolstoi*, Moscow.

Shklovsky, Viktor (1965), 'Sterne's Tristram Shandy: Stylistic Commentary' in Lee T. Lemon and Marion Reis (eds), *Russian Formalist Criticism: Four Essays*, University of Nebraska Press.

Showalter, Elaine (1985) (ed.), *The New Feminist Criticism: Essays on Women, Literature and Theory*, Pantheon Press, New York.

Shukman, Ann (1977), *Literature and Semiotics: a Study of the Writings of Yu. M. Lotman*, North Holland Publishing Company.

Skura, Meredith Anne (1981), *The Literary Use of the Psychoanalytic Process*, Yale University Press.

Stenbock-Fermor, Elisabeth (1975), *The Architecture of Anna Karenina*, Peter de Ridder, Lisse.

Tanner, Tony (1979), *Adultery in the Novel*, Johns Hopkins Press, Baltimore.

Todorov, Tsvetan (1984), *Mikhail Bakhtin: The Dialogical Principle*, trans. Wlad Godsich, University of Minnesota Press.

Tolstoy, Alexandra (1953), *Life of My Father*, Chekhov Press, New York.

Tolstoy, Sofia (1985), *Diaries*, trans. Cathy Porter, Jonathon Cape, London.

Torgovnick, Marianna (1981), *Closure in the Novel*, Princeton University Press.

Trilling, Lionel (1981), 'Freud and Literature', in Perry Meisel (ed.), *Freud: a Collection of Critical Essay*, Prentice Hall, pp. 73–94.

Troyat, Henri (1967), *Tolstoy*, Doubleday, New York.

Wasiolek, Edward (1978), *Tolstoy's Major Fiction*, University of Chicago Press.

White, Hayden (1973), *Metahistory: the Historical Imagination in Nineteenth-Century Europe*, Johns Hopkins University Press, Baltimore.

White, Hayden (1978), *Tropics of Discourse*, Johns Hopkins University Press, Baltimore.

White, Hayden (1979), 'The Problem of Style in Realistic Presentation: Marx and Flaubert' in Berel Lang (ed.), *The Concept of Style*, University of Pennsylvania Press.

Winnicott, D. W. (1971), *Playing and Reality*, Tavistock Publications, London.

Wolfenstein, Martha, *Psychoanalytic Study of the Child*, vol. 21, pp. 92–123; vol. 24, pp. 432–60; vol. 28, pp. 433–56.

# Index

199